Japanese

A ROUGH GUIDE
PHRASEBOOK

Compiled
by Lexus

Credits

Compiled by Lexus with T. Yahata Hyland and Kumi Liley

Lexus Series Editor:	Sally Davies
Rough Guides Phrasebook Editor:	Jonathan Buckley
Rough Guides Series Editor:	Mark Ellingham

This first edition published in 1998 by Rough Guides Ltd, 1 Mercer Street, London WC2H 9QJ.

Distributed by the Penguin Group.

Penguin Books Ltd, 27 Wrights Lane, London W8 5TZ
Penguin Books USA Inc., 375 Hudson Street, New York 10014, USA
Penguin Books Australia Ltd, 487 Maroondah Highway, PO Box 257, Ringwood, Victoria 3134, Australia
Penguin Books Canada Ltd, Alcorn Avenue, Toronto, Ontario, Canada M4V 1E4
Penguin Books (NZ) Ltd, 182–190 Wairau Road, Auckland 10, New Zealand

Typeset in Rough Serif and Rough Sans to an original design by Henry Iles. Printed by Cox & Wyman Ltd, Reading.

©Lexus Ltd 1998
272pp.

British Library Cataloguing in Publication Data
A catalogue for this book is available from the British Library.

ISBN 1-85828-303-5

CONTENTS

HELP US GET IT RIGHT

Lexus and Rough Guides have made great efforts to be accurate and
informative in this Rough Guide Japanese phrasebook. However, if you
feel we have overlooked a useful word or phrase, or have any other
comments to make about the book, please let us know. All
contributors will be acknowledged and the best letters will be
rewarded with a free Rough Guide phrasebook of your choice. Please
write to 'Japanese Phrasebook Update', at either Mercer Street
(London) or Hudson Street (New York) – for full address see opposite.
Alternatively you can email us at mail@roughguides.co.uk

Online information about Rough Guides can be found at our website
www.roughguides.com

INTRODUCTION

The Rough Guide Japanese phrasebook is a highly practical intro-
duction to the contemporary language. Laid out in clear A-Z style,
it uses key-word referencing to lead you straight to the words and
phrases you want – so if you need to book a room, just look up
'room'. The Rough Guide gets straight to the point in every situation, in bars and shops, on trains and buses, and in hotels and banks.

The first part of the Rough Guide is a section called **The Basics**, which
sets out the fundamental rules of the language and its pronunciation,
with plenty of practical examples. You'll also find here other essentials
like numbers, dates, telling the time and basic phrases.

Forming the heart of the guide, the **English-Japanese** section gives
easy-to-use transliterations of the Japanese words plus the text in
Japanese script, so that if the pronunciation proves too tricky, you
can simply indicate what you want to say. To get you involved
quickly in two-way communication, the Rough Guide also includes
dialogues featuring typical responses on key topics – such as rent-
ing a room and asking directions. Feature boxes fill you in on cul-
tural pitfalls as well as the simple mechanics of how to make a phone
call, what to do in an emergency, where to change money, and more.
Throughout this section, cross-references enable you to pinpoint
key facts and phrases, while asterisked words indicate where further information can be found in the Basics.

The **Japanese-English** section is in two parts: a dictionary, arranged phonetically, of all the words and phrases you're likely to
hear (starting with a section of slang and colloquialisms); then a
compilation, arranged by subject, of all the signs, labels, instruc-
tions and other basic words you might come across in print or in
public places.

Finally the Rough Guide rounds off with an extensive Menu Reader.
Consisting of food and drink sections arranged by subject (each
starting with a list of essential terms), it's indispensable whether
you're eating out, stopping for a quick drink, or browsing through
a local food market.

楽しいご旅行を！
tanoshī goryokō o!
have a good trip!

Traditionally, Japanese is written in vertical columns, starting at the top right and ending at the bottom left. However, many books and articles – especially technical ones – are also written in the Western way, from left to right, and from top to bottom. In newspapers, magazines and signs etc, you'll see a mixture of the two ways of writing.

Japanese is written in a combination of different writing systems: kanji (Chinese pictorial characters); hiragana, which has more rounded characters, and is normally used in conjunction with kanji; and katakana, which has squarer characters, and is used for writing the many loanwords from Western languages (especially English), for emphasis, or for other technical reasons.

The Basics

PRONUNCIATION

Throughout this book, Japanese words have been tran[slated]
into romanized form so that they can be read as though [in]
English, bearing in mind the notes on pronunciation give[n]

a	as in r**a**ther
e	as in b**e**d; **e** is always pronounced, even at the end [of a] word
i	like the **ee** in f**ee**t, but slightly shorter
o	as in n**o**t
u	as in p**u**t
ae	separate **a** followed by **e**, pronounced **ah-eh**
ai	as in Th**ai**
ei	as in w**ei**ght
ie	separate **ee** followed by **e**, pronounced **ee-eh**
ue	separate **u** followed by **e**, pronounced **oo-eh**
g	hard **g** as in **g**irl
s	always as in ma**ss** (never **z**)
y	as in **y**et

A bar over a vowel means that it is twice as long as a vowel without a bar.

A dot (·) between two letters indicates a slight pause.

Note that **ing** in Japanese is pronounced more strongly than in English.

In spoken Japanese certain sounds are shortened. For example, older methods of Japanese romanization will give **sofu** (grandfather) and **kip·pu** (ticket), but we have shortened these to **sof** and **kip·p** because this is how the words are actually pronounced.

Japanese is generally evenly stressed, with all syllables having the same emphasis.

ABBREVIATIONS

f	feminine	pol	polite
m	masculine	pl	plural
ob. part.	object particle	sing	singular
part.	particle	sub. part.	subject particle

The Japanese language has a number of characteristics which are very different from European languages, the most important of these being that there are no changes for case, number or gender and that verbs do not change according to the person or number. Also, pronouns, both personal and impersonal, are often omitted.

Another distinctive feature of Japanese is that small words known as postpositional particles are used after a noun or pronoun to indicate whether it is the subject, object or indirect object of a sentence. See pages 8–11.

ARTICLES

There is no equivalent in Japanese for either the definite article 'the' or the indefinite articles 'a' and 'an'. The exact meaning of a word or phrase will be clear from the context. Therefore, zas-shi (magazine) can mean 'a magazine' or 'the magazine'.

If you want to be more precise, you can use the demonstrative adjectives sono/ano (that) or kono (this) with the appropriate word (see page 17).

The number hitots (one) (see page 20) can also be used to translate 'a/an', but generally this is not necessary:

> bīru hitots, onegai shimas
> ['beer one please']
> a beer, please

NOUNS

Japanese nouns only have one form. Singular and plural forms of nouns are the same and there are no distinctions for gender (masculine/feminine/neuter). Therefore:

> hon can mean 'a book', 'the book', 'books', 'some books' or 'the books'
> bīru can mean: 'a beer', 'the beer', 'beers', 'some beers' or 'the beers'

Usually, what you mean will be perfectly clear from the context. Where necessary, you can be more specific by using numbers (see Counting page 20).

Although the form of the noun itself does not change, grammatical particles placed after the noun indicate whether it is the subject, object or indirect object of a sentence:

watashi no fak·ks wa
   todokimashta ka?
['I' + possessive part. 'fax' +
   sub. part. + 'arrived' +
   question part.]
has my fax arrived yet?

fak·ks o okurimashta ka?
['fax' + ob. part. + 'sent' +
   question part.]
did you send the fax?

Wa and o are are known as
postpositional particles (see
page 8).

One interesting aspect of
many nouns is that they can
be changed into verbs by just
adding suru (to do) or shimas
(polite form of 'to do'). Thus,
doksho is the Japanese word
for 'reading', and doksho suru
is the equivalent of 'to read'.

PRONOUNS

Generally, pronouns are
omitted in Japanese whenever
possible, but occasionally it
might be necessary to use
them for emphasis or to avoid
misunderstanding. It should
be remembered that, on the
whole, use of pronouns does
not show respect and should
be avoided, especially when
addressing one's superiors. If
it does become necessary to
use a personal pronoun, the
words listed in the sections
that follow can be used.

Personal Pronouns

watashi	I
bok	I (m, fam)
watakshi	I (pol)
anata	you (sing)
kimi	you (sing, fam, to a subordinate)
kare	he
kanojo	she
watashitachi	we
anatatachi	you (pl)
kimitachi	you (pl, fam, to subordinates)
karera	they (m)
kanojotachi	they (f)
sorera	they (inanimate objects)

watashi wa Igiris-jin des
['I' + sub. part. + 'English
   am']
I'm English

The subject of the sentence
above is followed by the
subject particle wa (see page
8).

Care should also be taken not
to address Japanese using
anata, the direct translation of
'you'. The best way to say, for
example, 'where are you
going?' in Japanese, is to use
the person's name plus -san,
instead of the word for 'you'.
Another acceptable way to
say this is to omit both 'you'
and the name in Japanese.

Eigo o hanasemas ka?
['English' + ob. part. + 'speak can' + question part.]
do you speak English?

Nakada-san wa Frans-go o hanasemas ka?
['surname Mr' + sub. part. + 'French' + ob. part. + 'speak' + question part.]
Mr Nakada, do you speak French?

See Addressing People page 32.

The form of the pronoun does not change, but there is a change in the postpositional particle that is placed after the pronoun; for direct object pronouns, use o instead of wa:

watashi o	me
bok o	me (m, fam)
watakshi o	me (pol)
anata o	you (sing)
kimi o	you (sing, fam, to a subordinate)
kare o	him
kanojo o	her
watashitachi o	us
anatatachi o	you (pl)
kimitachi o	you (pl, fam, to subordinates)
karera o	them (m)
kanojotachi o	them (f)
sorera o	them (inanimate objects)

kare o yonde kimashō
['he' + ob. part. + 'fetch']
I'll get him

'It'

Japanese has no word that is equivalent to the English pronoun 'it'; 'it' will be understood in phrases like the following:

doko des ka?
['where is' + question part.]
where is it?

tōi des ka?
['far is' + question part.]
is it far?

ame ga fut·te imas
['rain' + sub. part. + 'fall is']
it's raining

If you really need to emphasise 'it', you can use **sore**, but this is a demonstrative pronoun rather than a personal pronoun, and actually means 'that':

sore wa kare no kuruma des
['that' + sub. part. + 'he' + possessive part. + 'car is']
it's his car

Demonstrative Pronouns

kore this (one); these (ones)
sore that (one); those (ones) (nearby or just mentioned)
are that (one); those (ones) (further away)

kore wa watashi no des
['this' + sub. part. + 'I of am']
this is mine

sore dewa nak, kore des
['that as for not this is']
not that one, this one

are wa takai des
['that' + sub. part. +
  'expensive is']
that one is expensive

See Demonstrative
Adjectives, page 17.

POSSESSIVES

Possessive adjectives and
pronouns are the same in
Japanese. To form the
possessive, add the particle
no to the pronoun:

watashi no	my; mine
bok no	my; mine (m, fam)
watakshi no	my; mine (pol)
anata no	your; yours (sing)
kimi no	you (sing, fam, to a subordinate)
kare no	his
kanojo no	her; hers
watashitachi no	our; ours
anatatachi no	your; yours (pl)
kimitachi no	you (pl, fam, to subordinates)

karera no	their; theirs (m)
kanojotachi no	their; theirs (f)
sorera no	their; theirs (inanimate objects)

watashi no des
['I' + possessive part. + 'be']
it's mine

watashi no heya de
['I' + possessive part. + 'room in']
in my room

The possessive is generally
omitted if the meaning is
clear from the context:

handobag-g o nakshimashta
['handbag' + ob. part. + 'lost']
I've lost my handbag

In phrases like the one below,
it's more respectful to use the
possessive particle with the
person's name or job title:

shachō no kuruma
['director' + possessive part. +
  'car']
the director's car

rather than:

kare no kuruma
['he' + possessive part. + 'car']
his car

even if the English phrase
doesn't use the name or title.

POSTPOSITIONAL PARTICLES

Postpositional particles are small words that always follow the word they relate to. They have two main functions:

a) They indicate whether a noun or pronoun is the subject, object or indirect object of a sentence.

b) They are the equivalent of certain English grammatical elements, for example, prepositions (to, from, with etc), constructions such as 'and', 'because', 'also', and they are also used to indicate a question.

The following list shows the meanings of the various particles in brief; for further information and examples, see the text that follows this list.

ga	follows the subject of a sentence, emphasises the subject
wa	follows the subject of a sentence
o	follows the object of a sentence
ni	follows the indirect object of a sentence; or means on, in, to, at (referring to time and location)
e	to (indicates motion towards); towards; until
made	to; up to; until; as far as
kara	from; since
de	by, by means of; with; at; on; in (referring to location)
to	with, accompanied by; and, that
mo	too, also; even; both ... and; neither ... nor
no	of; possessive
ka?	question particle
ne?	question tag: isn't it?, haven't we?, haven't you? etc

Subject Particles

To indicate that a word is the subject of a sentence, the particles **ga** or **wa** are used:

> **onaka ga sukimashta ka?**
> ['stomach' + sub. part. + 'empty' + question part.]
> are you hungry?

The particle **ga** can indicate that the subject of the sentence is more important than the text that follows. In English this distinction can be achieved by tone of voice:

watashi ga ikimas
['I' + sub. part. + 'will go']
I will go, it's me who's
going (not anyone else)

watashi ga haraimas
['I' + sub. part. + 'pay']
I'll pay (nobody else has to
pay)

If wa is used instead of ga,
this gives less emphasis to the
subject and more to the rest
of the text:

watashi wa Amerika-jin des
['I' + sub. part. + 'American
am']
I'm American

watashi wa gaksei des
['I' + sub. part. + 'student am']
I'm a student

Ga is often used if the verb is
arimas or imas:

kyō wa sumō ga arimas
['today' + sub. part. + 'sumo'
+ sub. part. + 'is']
there's a sumo match today

and wa is often used when the
verb is des or a negative:

sore wa totemo omoshiroi
des
['that' + sub. part. + 'very
interesting is']
that's very interesting

watashi wa Igiris-jin des
['I' + sub. part. + 'English am']
I'm English

watashi wa ikimasen
['I' + sub. part. + 'go' +
negative]
I'm not going

kono hon wa omoshirok nai
des
['this book' + sub. part. +
'interesting not is']
this book is not interesting

Object Particle

The object particle o is placed
after the object of the verb:

yoyak o shite arimas
['reservation' + ob. part. +
'made']
I have a reservation

Eigo o hanasemas ka?
['English' + ob. part. + 'speak
can' + question part.]
can you speak English?

Indirect Object Particle

The particle ni is used to
indicate an indirect object:

sensei ni wain o agemashta
['teacher' + ind. ob. part. +
'wine' + ob. part. + 'gave']
I gave the teacher a bottle
of wine

Other Particles

The particle e indicates
motion towards something:

Kōbe e ikimas
['Kobe to go']
I'm going to Kobe

The particle made means 'to', 'up to', 'until' or 'as far as':

> **kūkō made, onegai shimas**
> ['airport to please']
> to the airport, please

> **... made nan-kiro arimas ka?**
> ['... to how many kilometres is' + question part.]
> how many kilometres is it to ...?

> **Doyōbi made**
> ['Saturday until']
> until Saturday

The particle kara means 'from' or 'since':

> **Rondon kara Tōkyō made**
> ['London from Tokyo to']
> from London to Tokyo

> **senshū kara**
> ['last week since']
> since last week

The particle ni (as well as being the indirect object particle) means 'on', 'in', 'to' or 'at', referring to time or location:

> **Doyōbi ni**
> ['Saturday on']
> on Saturday

> **Hiruton hoteru ni tomat-te imas**
> ['Hilton Hotel at staying']
> I'm staying at the Hilton Hotel

> **Tōkyō ni oba ga sunde imas**
> ['Tokyo in aunt' + sub. part. + 'lives']
> my aunt lives in Tokyo

The particle de can mean 'by', 'by means of' or 'with':

> **kuruma de**
> ['car by']
> by car

> **bas de**
> ['bus by']
> by bus

> **kurejit-to-kādo de haraemas ka?**
> ['credit card by can pay' + question part.]
> can I pay by credit card?

de can also mean 'at', 'on' or 'in', referring to location:

> **bā de suwat-te imashta**
> ['bar at was sitting']
> he was sitting at the bar

> **depāto no naka de aimashō**
> ['department store of inside in meet let's']
> I'll see you in the department store

The particle to means 'with', 'accompanying':

> **haha to kaimono shimas**
> ['mother with shopping do']
> I go shopping with my mother

See page 19 for when to use to meaning 'and'.

The particle mo can mean 'too', 'also' or 'even':

kimi mo heya ni itano ka?
['you too room in were' +
    question part.]
were you in the room too?

watashi mo
me too

mo can also be used to
translate 'both ... and' (in a
positive statement) and
'neither ... nor' (with a
negative verb, see page 14):

bīru mo sake mo nomimashta
['beer both sake and drank']
I drank both beer and sake

bīru mo sake mo nomimasen
    deshta
['beer both sake and not drank']
I drank neither beer nor
sake

The particle no means 'of' or
corresponds to the 's or the
possessive in English:

ane no hon
['sister of book']
my sister's book

kurab no membā
['club of member']
a member of the club

watashi no kuruma
['I of car']
my car

The particle ka is added to the
end of a statement to change
it into a question:

kip·p wa takai des
['ticket' + sub. part. +
    'expensive']
the tickets are expensive

kip·p wa takai des ka?
['ticket' + sub. part. +
    'expensive' + question part.]
are the tickets expensive?

The particle ne is the
equivalent of English tag
questions like 'isn't it?',
'haven't we?' and so on:

Keiko-san, kore wa anata no
    des ne?
['Keiko' + polite form + 'this'
    + sub. part. + 'you of is' +
    question tag]
it's yours, Keiko, isn't it?

koko ni kita koto ga arimas
    ne?
['here in that came' + sub. part.
    'be' + question tag]
we've been here, haven't
we?

VERBS

Unlike English verbs,
Japanese verbs do not change
their form according to first,
second, or third person
subjects, singular or plural.
Therefore, ikimas means:

to go	he/she/it goes
I go	we go
you go	they go

However, Japanese verbs do change their form according to various other criteria, for example, the degree of politeness required, the tense, or whether the verb indicates 'wanting' or 'necessity'.

Polite Verb Forms

The form of Japanese verbs is changed to indicate different levels of politeness. As a general rule, longer verb forms denote courtesy:

yomimas to read
shimbun yom ka? (basic form)
shimbun yomimas ka? (polite)
shimbun yomaremas ka? (very polite)
do you read the paper?

It is more straightforward for beginners in Japanese to stick to the second form given above (**yomimas**). This is the verb form we have generally given in the English-Japanese section of this book and it is polite enough for most situations.

Present Tense

To express the simple present, use the basic form of the verb ending in -mas:

ikimas to go
I go
you go
he/she/it goes
we go
they go

swarimas to sit down
I sit down
you sit down
he/she/it sits down
we sit down
they sit down

To express a continuing action in the present ('he is going', 'I am walking' etc), the -mas ending is removed from the verb and replaced with -te or -de and imas is placed after the verb:

nani o yonde imas ka?
['what' + ob. part. + 'reading' + question part.]
what are you reading?

karera wa tabete imas
['they' + sub. part. + 'eating']
they are eating

kare wa tabako o sut·te imas
['he' + sub. part. + 'cigarette' + ob. part. + 'inhale']
he is smoking

Past Tense

The ending -mashta indicates the past tense. Replace the -mas ending of the verb with -mashta:

ikimas to go		mimas to see; to watch	
ikimashta	I went	mimashta	I've seen
	you went		you've seen
	he/she/it went		he/she/it has seen
	we went		we have seen
	they went		they have seen

tskimas to arrive	tabemas to eat
kyō tskimashta	watashitachi wa mō tabemashta
['today arrived']	['we' + sub. part. + 'already have eaten']
we arrived today	we've already eaten

Future Tense

There is no real future tense in Japanese; instead the present tense is used to express the future:

mata ashita kimas
['again tomorrow come']
I'll come back tomorrow

rainen Kyōto ni ikimas
['next year Kyoto to go']
I'm going to Kyoto next year

Asking Permission

Asking permission to do something is indicated by the verb ending -te followed by ... ī des ka? (literally: is it allowed?):

anata ni tegami o kaite ī des ka?
['you to letter' + ob. part. + 'write is is allowed' + question part.]
can I write to you?

Indicating Necessity

Necessity is indicated by the verb ending -nakereba narimasen:

ikimas to go
mō ikanakereba narimasen
['already go must']
I have to go now

kakimas to write
tegami o kakanakereba narimasen
['letter' + ob. part. + 'write must']
I have to write a letter

GRAMMAR

Indicating Wanting

Wanting to do something is indicated by the verb ending -tai:

okurimas to send
kore o Igiris ni okuritai no des ga
['this' + ob. part. + 'England to send want request please']
I want to send this to England

karimas to rent
kuruma o karitai no des ga
['car' + ob. part. + 'buy want request please']
I'd like to rent a car

Negatives

There is no simple equivalent to 'not' in Japanese. Instead the form of the verb changes to indicate the negative. The -mas ending changes to -masen and the -tai (wanting) ending changes to -tak nai:

kono gak·kō e ikimas
['this school to go']
I go to this school

kono gak·kō e wa ikimasen
['this school to' + sub. part. + 'go' negative]
I don't go to this school

Igiris ni ikitai des
['England to want go' + polite ending]
I want to go to England

Igiris ni ikitak nai des
['England to want go' + negative + polite ending]
I don't want to go to England

Japanese has no words like 'nobody', 'no-one', 'never', 'none', 'neither', 'nor', '(not) any'; these must be expressed in Japanese by a negative verb construction:

dare mo kimasen deshta
['somebody even come' + negative]
nobody came

dare mo hakbutskan e ikitagarimasen
['somebody even museum to want to go' + negative]
nobody wants to visit the museum

Kōbe niwa ichido mo it·ta koto ga arimasen
['Kobe to' + sub. part. + 'not once even that' + sub. part. + negative]
I've never been to Kobe

mō hitots mo arimasen
['already one even exist' + negative]
there's none left

hoshik arimasen
['want' + negative]
I don't want any

ADJECTIVES

Japanese 'adjectives' are a special category of words, many of which behave in a way quite unlike their English counterparts. Many, indeed, are more like verbs since they have separate forms for present and past tenses and for positive and negative use. For example, the adjective for 'red' **akai** really means 'is red'.

There are two types of adjectives in Japanese. The first type end in -ai, -ī, -oi or -ui:

akai	is red
oishī	is delicious
omoshiroi	is interesting
warui	is bad

The final -i or -ī indicates the present positive form of the adjective, which is the basic form given in the English-Japanese section of this book; to make the past positive form, remove the -i or -ī to obtain the stem and add -kat·ta:

present positive	past positive
akai (is red)	akakat·ta (was red)
oishī (is delicious)	oishkat·ta (was delicious)
omoshiroi (is interesting)	omoshirokat·ta (was interesting)
warui (is bad)	warukat·ta (was bad)

These are all plain forms which generally would not be used by themselves; to make them polite forms, add des:

nimots wa omokat·ta des
['luggage' + sub. part. + 'was heavy' + polite ending]
the luggage was heavy

To form the present negative, remove -i or -ī, and add -k nai; for the past negative add -k nakat·ta to the stem:

present negative	past negative
akak nai (is not red)	akak nakat·ta (was not red)
oishik nai (is not delicious)	oishik nakat·ta (was not delicious)
omoshirok nai (is not interesting)	omoshirok nakat·ta (was not interesting)
waruk nai (is not bad)	waruk nakat·ta (was not bad)

To make the above polite forms (as used in speech), change -k nai to -k arimasen:

kono suika wa amak arimasen
['this watermelon' + sub. part. + 'sweet' + negative]
this watermelon is not sweet

Adjectival Nouns

The second type of Japanese adjective is more like an English adjective in that it does not change its ending and is not a form of verb. This type of adjective does not end in -ai, -ī, -oi or -ui, but consists of a noun followed by **na**:

shizuka (na)
quiet

Adjectival nouns are used with the following to form the present and past tenses (positive and negative):

	positive	
present	past
des	deshta

	negative	
present	past
dewa arimasen	dewa arimasen deshta

If the adjectival noun is followed by **des**, **na** can be omitted:

hoteru wa shizka des
['hotel' + sub. part. + 'quiet is']
the hotel is quiet

kono hon wa tekitō dewa arimasen
['this book' + sub. part. + 'suitable' + negative]
this book is not suitable

chit·toma shimpai dewa arimasen deshta
['not at all worried' + negative]
I wasn't worried at all

Comparatives and Superlatives

To form the comparative, put mot·to (more) in front of the adjective:

mot·to hayak
faster

mot·to omoshiroi
more interesting

To form the superlative, put ichi·ban (literally: number one) or mot·tomo (most) in front of the adjective:

ichi·ban omoshiroi toshi
['most is interesting city']
the most interesting city

mot·tomo takai hoteru
['most is expensive hotel']
the most expensive hotel

To express 'more ... than ...', '...-er than', use **yori** (than):

kono hoteru wa ryokan yori
takai des
['this hotel' + sub. part. +
'Japanese inn than expensive']
this hotel is more
expensive than a
Japanese inn

densha wa bas yori hayai des
['train' + sub. part. + 'bus than
fast is']
the train is faster than the
bus

To express 'as ... as ...' use to
onaji kurai (about the same
as):

Rondon wa Nagano to onaji
kurai samui des
['London' + sub. part. +
'Nagano as cold as is']
London is as cold as
Nagano

To express 'not as ... as ...',
use hodo ... nai:

Nippon wa Amerika hodo ōkik
nai des
['Japan' + sub. part. +
'America not as big as is']
Japan is not as big as
America

Demonstrative Adjectives

There are three demonstrative adjectives: kono, sono and ano:

kono	this; these
sono	that; those (nearby or just mentioned)
ano	that; those (further away)

kono densha	this train
sono tomodachi	that friend (of yours, that you mentioned)
ano bas	that bus (over there)

ADVERBS

To form an adverb from the first type of adjective (ending in
-ai, -ī, -oi or -ui), change the final -i to -k:

hayai	quick	hayak	quickly
osoi	slow	osok	slowly
yasashī	easy	yasashik	easily
warui	bad	waruk	badly
yasui	cheap	yask	cheaply

To form the adverb from the second type of adjective (shown
with (na) in the English-Japanese section), change na to ni:

shizka na heya
['quiet room']
a quiet room

Keiko-san wa shizka ni hanashimas
['Keiko' + polite form + sub. part. + 'quietly speaks']
Keiko speaks quietly

WORD ORDER

The normal word order in Japanese sentences is:

subject – object – verb

ane wa sushi o suki des ga, watashi wa suki dewa arimasen
['sister' + sub. part. + 'sushi' + ob. part. + 'like but I' + sub. part. + 'like not']
my sister likes sushi but I don't

Adjectives usually precede the noun they modify while particles and conjunctions follow the noun they refer to.

'YES' AND 'NO'

The words for 'yes' and 'no' are **hai** (or sometimes **ē**) and **īe** (or **ie**):

hai, onegai shimas
yes, please

īe kek·kō des
no thanks

yomimashta ka?
have you read the paper?

hai, yomimashta
yes, I have

In general, however, it is possible to omit **hai** and **īe** and answer simply by using the verb.

When the question is a negative one, however, **hai** and **īe** are used in quite a different way to English. This is because **hai** is used to confirm the statement, whether the answer is affirmative or negative:

anata wa Amerika-jin dewa arimasen ka?
['you' + sub. part. + 'American' + negative + question part.]
aren't you American?

hai, Igiris-jin des
['yes (I am not) English']
no, I'm English

This kind of negative question (as in English) implies the speaker may be slightly surprised or incredulous or wants to confirm something that they are almost sure of. If a positive question were asked, with no prior assumptions, the answer would be **īe**.

In the same way, when the

question is a negative one, iē is used to deny the sentence whether the answer is affirmative or negative:

> **soba o tabemasen deshta ka?**
> ['noodles' + ob. part. + 'eat did not' + question part.]
> didn't you eat the noodles? (implying you should have)

> **īe, tabemashta**
> ['no, did eat']
> yes, I did eat them

'AND'

There are different words for 'and' in Japanese. **To** is used with nouns and pronouns:

> **shio to koshō**
> salt and pepper

> **kōhī to satō o kaimashta**
> ['coffee and sugar' + ob. part. + 'bought']
> I bought coffee and sugar

> **Tōkyō to Rondon**
> Tokyo and London

Soshite also means 'and'; it is used with verbs, adjectives and adverbs:

> **watashitachi wa onsen ni hairi soshite shokji o shimashta**
> ['we' + sub. part. + 'hot spring in go and meal did']
> we had a bath in the hot spring and had a meal

> **kare wa hayak, soshite utskushik, ji o kakimas**
> ['he' + sub. part. + 'fast and neatly characters' + ob. part. + 'writes']
> he writes both fast and neatly

Sorekara means 'and then':

> **terebi o mite, sorekara benkyō shimas**
> ['television' + ob. part. + 'watched and then study']
> I'll watch television and then I'll study

FEMININE FORMS OF SPEECH

In the past, there were many different levels of courtesy in Japanese speech and special words and phrases were used, for example, to praise one's superiors, and to deprecate oneself. As well as this, women's speech was traditionally more polite than men's. Although the differences between male and female speech patterns are now less pronounced than they used to be, there are still many ways of speaking that are exclusively used by either men or women. Men speak with a more even tone of voice, whereas women speak in a more lilting manner. Men and women use different pronouns and interjections. Also, in informal speech, men tend to use yo or zo at the end of sentences for emphasis, whereas women will use wa, for example:

> bok wa Eigo ga hanaseru yo/zo! (said by a man)
> ['I' + sub. part. + 'English' + ob. part. + 'speak can emphasis']
> I can speak English!

> watashi wa okoto ga hikeru wa! (said by a woman)
> ['I' + sub. part. + polite prefix + 'Japanese harp' + ob. part. + 'play can' + emphasis]
> I can play the Japanese harp!

Women make more use of the polite prefix o- or go-, as in:

> denwa/odenwa
> (said by a man/woman)
> (your) telephone

> gokazok wa ogenki des ka?
> [polite prefix + 'family' + sub. part. + polite prefix + 'well' + question part.]
> are your family all well?

Women also tend to use emotional interjections more than men, such as 'kawaī' (cute!) or 'steki!' (marvellous!). To express surprise when meeting

somebody unexpectedly, women tend to say 'māl' or 'ara!', which are never used by men, who tend to say 'yāl' or 'ō!'.

COUNTING

Japanese has two sets of numbers from one to ten:

	set 1	set 2
1	ichi	hitots
2	ni	hutats
3	san	mit·ts
4	yon/shi*	yot·ts
5	go	itsuts
6	rok	mut·ts
7	nana/shichi*	nanats
8	hachi	yat·ts
9	kyū/ku*	kokonots
10	jū	tō

The first set is used when referring to expressions of time, quantities and measurements. They are used with the classifiers on the opposite page or with count words such as 'minute', 'yen' etc:

> go-fun
> five minutes

> ichijikan mae
> an hour ago

> gozen shichiji ni
> at 7am

> jū-en
> 10 yen

* The alternative numerals in the first set opposite must be used in the following time expressions:

yoji	four o'clock
shichiji	seven o'clock
kuji	nine o'clock

The second set of numbers is used for counting any other things not mentioned above. The number is placed after the object and is used without a count word (like 'minute') or a classifier:

> bīru futats, onegai shimas
> two beers, please

If you use the two sets of numbers in the way described above, this will be acceptable, but a further method of counting, using a counting word known as a classifier, is more commonly used. Classifiers equate roughly to English words like 'glassful', 'cupful', 'bottle of', 'sheets of' etc. Nouns or groups of nouns in Japanese have specific classifiers which are used when they are counted or quantified.

The most common classifiers are:

-dai	machines, cars, bikes, stereos
-hai	glassfuls, cupfuls
-hiki	animals
-hon	pens, cigarettes, other cylindrical objects
-ko	fruit, cakes, eggs and small chunky objects
-mai	pieces of paper, tickets, other things that are thin and flat
-nin	people
-sats	books
-tsū	letters

> kuruma ni-dai
> ['car two' + classifier]
> two cars

> kip·p o sam-mai, kudasai
> ['ticket' + ob. part. + 'three' + classifier + 'please']
> three tickets, please

> Nihon·go no hon o go-sats kaimashta
> ['Japanese of book' + ob. part. + 'five' + classifier + 'bought']
> I bought five Japanese books

> mājan wa yo-nin de shimas
> ['mahjong' + sub. part. + 'four' + classifier + 'by do']
> mahjong is played by four people

There is only one set of numbers above ten. See pages 24–25.

DATES

The word order for dates is:

year – month – day

There are two common ways of counting years in Japanese. The Western system is used thus:

sen-kyū-hyak-kyū-jū-hachi-
 nen
[thousand-nine-hundreds-nine-
 tens-eight-year]
1998

There is also a traditional system of counting from the first year of the current emperor's reign. The Heisei period (of Emperor Akihito) began in 1989:

Heisei ni-nen
[Heisei two year]
second year of Heisei
 (1990)

Heisei jū-nen
[Heisei ten year]
tenth year of Heisei (1998)

Kugats tsuitachi
[nine-month (September) first]
the first of September

Jūnigats futska
[twelve-month (December)
 second]
the second of December

sen-kyū-hyak-kyū-jū-hachi-
 nen Gogats san-jū-nichi
[thousand-nine-hundreds-nine-
 tens-eight-year five-month
 (May) thirtieth]
the thirtieth of May 1998

Heisei jū-nen Rokgats ni-jū
 san-ichi
[Heise-ten-year six-month
 (June) twenty-third]
the twenty-third of June
 1998

Dates are formed using the versions of the ordinal numbers below:

1st	tsuitachi	一日
2nd	futska	二日
3rd	mik·ka	三日
4th	yok·ka	四日
5th	itska	五日
6th	muika	六日
7th	nanoka	七日
8th	yōka	八日
9th	kokonoka	九日
10th	tōka	十日
11th	jū-ichi-nichi	十一日
12th	jū-ni-nichi	十二日
13th	jū-san-nichi	十三日
14th	jū-yok·ka	十四日
15th	jū-go-nichi	十五日
16th	jū-rok-nichi	十六日
17th	jū-shichi-nichi	十七日
18th	jū-hachi-nichi	十八日
19th	jū-ku-nichi	十九日
20th	hatska	二十日

21st	ni-jū-ichi nichi 二十一日
22nd	ni-jū-ni-nichi 二十二日
23rd	ni-jū-san-nichi 二十三日
24th	ni-jū-yok·ka 二十四日
25th	ni-jū-go-nichi 二十五日
26th	ni-jū-rok-nichi 二十六日
27th	ni-jū-shichi-nichi 二十七日
28th	ni-jū-hachi-nichi 二十八日
29th	ni-jū-ku-nichi 二十九日
30th	san-jū-nichi 三十日
31st	san-jū-ichi-nichi 三十一日

Japanese ordinals are written using the Chinese characters (kanji) above if writing vertically; otherwise, when writing left to right, Arabic numbers can be used instead.

DAYS

Monday Getsyōbi 月曜日
Tuesday Kayōbi 火曜日
Wednesday Suiyōbi 水曜日
Thursday Mok·yōbi 木曜日
Friday Kin·yōbi 金曜日
Saturday Doyōbi 土曜日
Sunday Nichiyōbi 日曜日

MONTHS

January Ichigats 一月
February Nigats 二月
March San·gats 三月
April Shigats 四月
May Gogats 五月
June Rokgats 六月
July Shichigats 七月
August Hachigats 八月
September Kugats 九月
October Jūgats 十月
November Jūichigats 十一月
December Jūnigats 十二月

TIME

what time is it? ima nanji des ka? 今何時ですか？
it's one o'clock ichiji 一時です。
it's two o'clock niji 二時です。
at one o'clock ichiji ni 一時に
at two o'clock niji ni 二時に
five past one ichiji go-fun 一時五分
ten past one ichiji jup·pun 一時十分
quarter past one ichiji jū-go-fun 一時十五分

quarter past two   niji jū-go-
fun   二時十五分

half past one   ichiji-han
一時半

half past two   niji-han
二時半

quarter to one   ichiji jū-go-fun
mae   一時十五分前

quarter to two   niji jū-go-fun
mae   二時十五分前

twenty to one   ichiji
nijup·pun mae
一時二十分前

ten to two   niji jup·pun mae
二時十分前

am   gozen   午前

pm   gogo   午後

at 1am   gozen ichiji ni
午前一時に

at 1pm   gogo ichiji ni
午後一時に

13.00   jū-sanji   十三時

14.00   jū-yoji   十四時

18.30   jū-hachiji sanjup·pun
十八時三十分

noon   shōgo   正午

midnight   mayonaka
真夜中

hour   jikan   時間

minute   fun   分

one minute   ip·pun   一分

two minutes   ni-fun   二分

second   byō   秒

quarter of an hour   jū-go-fun
十五分

half an hour   san-jup·pun
三十分

three quarters of an hour   yon-
jū-go-fun   四十五分

Minutes are expressed by
adding -fun (minute) to the
numbers below. This
sometimes changes to -pun
depending on the preceding
sound:

ni-fun
two minutes

go-fun   jup·pun
five minutes   ten minutes

NUMBERS

See Counting pages 20–21.

0	zero	ゼロ
1	ichi	一
2	ni	二
3	san	三
4	shi	四
5	go	五
6	rok	六
7	shichi	七
8	hachi	八
9	kyū	九
10	jū	十
11	jū-ichi	十一
12	jū-ni	十二
13	jū-san	十三
14	jū-shi	十四
15	jū-go	十五
16	jū-rok	十六
17	jū-shichi	十七
18	jū-hachi	十八

19	jū-kyū	十九
20	ni-jū	二十
21	ni-jū-ichi	二十一
22	ni-jū-ni	二十二
30	san-jū	三十
31	san-jū-ichi	三十一
32	san-jū-ni	三十二
40	yon-jū	四十
50	go-jū	五十
60	rok-jū	六十
70	shichi-jū	七十
80	hachi-jū	八十
90	kyū-jū	九十
100	hyak	百
101	hyak-ichi	百一
102	hyak-ni	百二
200	ni-hyak	二百
1,000	sen	千
2,000	ni-sen	二千
3,000	san-zen	三千
4,000	yon-sen	四千
5,000	go-sen	五千
10,000*	ichi-man	一万
20,000	ni-man	二万
1,000,000		
	hyak-man	百万
10,000,000		
	is·sem·man	一千万
100,000,000		
	ichi-ok	一億

*For 10,000 and above, use **man** instead of **sen**.

Japanese numbers are written using the Chinese characters (kanji) above if writing vertically; otherwise, when writing left to right, Arabic numbers can be used instead.

Ordinals

In Japanese, the words used for the dates (1st of March etc) and the ordinals in English sense (for example, 'third chair from the window') are different. The English ordinals can usually be translated by adding -bam·me to numbers.

1st   ichi-bam·me
一番目

2nd   ni-bam·me
二番目

3rd   san-bam-me
三番目

4th   yon-bam·me
四番目

5th   go-bam·me
五番目

6th   rok-bam·me
六番目

7th   nana-bam·me
七番目

8th   hachi-bam·me
八番目

9th   kyū-bam·me
九番目

10th   jyū-bam·me
十番目

See page 22 for the set of ordinals used to form dates.

BASIC PHRASES

yes
hai
はい

no
īe
いいえ

OK
ōkē
オーケー

hello
kon·nichi wa
こんにちは

(on phone)
moshi-moshi
もしもし

good morning
ohayō gozaimas
おはようございます

good evening
komban wa
こんばんは

good night (when leaving)
osaki ni
お先に

(when going to bed)
oyasuminasai
おやすみなさい

goodbye/see you (formal)
sayōnara
さようなら

(informal)
dewa mata
ではまた

(between friends)
jā ne
じゃあね

see you later!
ja, mata!
じゃ、また！

please (requesting something)
onegai shimas
お願いします

yes, please
hai, onegai shimas
はい、お願いします

could you please ...?
... -te kuremasen ka?
…ーてくれませんか？

thank you
arigatō
ありがとう

thank you very much
hontō ni arigatō gozaimas
ほんとうにありがと
うございます

no, thank you
īe kek·kō des
いいえ、けっこうです

don't mention it
dō itashimashte
どういたしまして

how do you do?
hajimemashte
はじめまして

how are you?
ogenki des ka?
お元気ですか？

I'm fine, thanks
okagesama de
おかげさまで

nice to meet you
hajimemashte
はじめまして

excuse me (to get past)
shitsurei shimas
失礼します

excuse me! (to get attention)
chot·to sumimasen!
ちょっとすみ
ません！

excuse me/sorry
gomen·nasai
ごめんなさい

sorry?/pardon me?
nante īmashta ka?
何て言いましたか？

I see/I understand
naruhodo
なるほど

I don't understand
wakarimasen
わかりません

do you speak English?
Eigo o hanasemas ka?
英語を話せますか？

I don't speak Japanese
nihon·go wa hanasemasen
日本語は話せません

could you speak more slowly?
mot·to yuk·kuri hanashite
  kuremasen ka?
もっとゆっくり話して
  くれませんか？

could you repeat that?
mō ichido it·te kuremasen ka?
もう一度言ってくれ
  ませんか？

CONVERSION TABLES

| 1 centimetre = 0.39 inches | 1 inch = 2.54 cm |

1 metre = 39.37 inches = 1.09 yards

1 foot = 30.48 cm

1 yard = 0.91 m

1 kilometre = 0.62 miles = 5/8 mile

1 mile = 1.61 km

km	1	2	3	4	5	10	20	30	40	50	100
miles	0.6	1.2	1.9	2.5	3.1	6.2	12.4	18.6	24.8	31.0	62.1

miles	1	2	3	4	5	10	20	30	40	50	100
km	1.6	3.2	4.8	6.4	8.0	16.1	32.2	48.3	64.4	80.5	161

1 gram = 0.035 ounces

1 kilo = 1000 g = 2.2 pounds

g	100	250	500
oz	3.5	8.75	17.5

1 oz = 28.35 g

1 lb = 0.45 kg

kg	0.5	1	2	3	4	5	6	7	8	9	10
lb	1.1	2.2	4.4	6.6	8.8	11.0	13.2	15.4	17.6	19.8	22.0

kg	20	30	40	50	60	70	80	90	100
lb	44	66	88	110	132	154	176	198	220

lb	0.5	1	2	3	4	5	6	7	8	9	10	20
kg	0.2	0.5	0.9	1.4	1.8	2.3	2.7	3.2	3.6	4.1	4.5	9.0

1 litre = 1.75 UK pints / 2.13 US pints

1 UK pint = 0.57 l

1 US pint = 0.47 l

1 UK gallon = 4.55 l

1 US gallon = 3.79 l

centigrade / Celsius

$C = (F - 32) \times 5/9$

C	-5	0	5	10	15	18	20	25	30	36.8	38
F	23	32	41	50	59	65	68	77	86	98.4	100.4

Fahrenheit

$F = (C \times 9/5) + 32$

F	23	32	40	50	60	65	70	80	85	98.4	101
C	-5	0	4	10	16	18	21	27	29	36.8	38.3

English-Japanese

A

a, an* hitots (no)
ひとつ（の）
about: about 20 ni-jū kurai
20くらい
it's about 5 o'clock goji goro
5時ごろ
a film about Japan Nihon ni
tsuite no eiga
日本についての映画
above ... no ue ni
…の上に
abroad gaikok de
外国で
absorbent cotton das·shimen
脱脂綿
accelerator akseru
アクセル
accept (present) uketorimas
受け取ります
(credit card etc) uketskemas
受け付けます
accident jiko
事故
there's been an accident jiko
ga arimashta
事故がありました
accommodation heya
部屋
see **room** and **hotel**
account kōza
口座
accurate seikak (na)
正確（な）

ache itami
痛み
my back aches koshi ga itai
des
腰が痛いです
across: across the road michi
no mukōgawa
道の向う側
adapter adaptā
アダプター
address jūsho
住所
what's your address? gojūsho
wa?
ご住所は？

Addresses are written as follows:

160-0022 (postcode)
Tokyo-to (city)
Shinjuku-ku (ward)
Shinjuku (area)
1-chōme (section)
2-34 (sub-division of chōme
 and house number)
NAKADA Hiroshi-sama (sur-
 name, given name, Mr/Mrs/
 Ms/Miss)

Addresses begin with the postcode (in most cases, a seven-
figure number), then the **ken**
(prefecture). The exceptions to
this are Tokyo-**to**, Osaka-**fu** and
Kyoto-**fu** (cities) and Hokkai**do**,
which all stand on their own
→

as administrative areas. Next comes the **shi** (the town or city), or in the country, **gun** (county) or **mura** (village).

The next line of the address indicates an area name known as a **chō** or **machi** – although these words do not always appear as part of the address. In larger cities, **ku** (ward) appears after the **shi** (city) with the exception of Tokyo, for which ku directly follows Tokyo-**to**. The number of the **chōme** (an area of a few square blocks) is written on the next line. The number of the chōme may sometimes be given by itself, without the word chōme. For example: **Shinjuku-ku, Shinjuku 1-2-34**. This final string of numbers can also be expressed as **2-34 Shinjuku, 1-chōme** (Shinju area, section 1). Although the 2 and 34 give a precise location within the chōme, finding this can be frustrating since numbers are not in sequential order, having usually been assigned when the building was first erected. Outside of the big cities, streets rarely have names – and even when they do – it will only be the main ones. After the chōme comes the →

house number and then the surname, given name and -**sama** (for Mr/Mrs/Ms/Miss).

If you're trying to locate an address, make sure you have it written down – preferably in Japanese – on a piece of paper you can show to people. Local police boxes (**kōban**) have detailed maps of their own areas. Have the phone number of your destination at hand too. If you get lost, don't be afraid to call: often someone will come to meet you and guide you to your destination.

It is acceptable to write addresses in Roman letters (called **rōma-ji**), either in the above order, or in the Western order. Care should be taken to print all letters clearly, since post office workers may have trouble deciphering Westerners' handwriting.

address book jūshorok
住所録

addressing people
There are several ways of addressing Japanese people. The most common is -**san**, which is roughly equivalent to 'Mr', 'Mrs' →

or 'Miss' and is added as a suffix to either someone's given name or family name. The more polite version of -san is **-sama**, which is always used in postal addresses.

In Japan, it's common practice to use the surname, particularly in business and when speaking to people of a higher rank. The given name is used almost exclusively with friends or family. The Japanese always write the family name before the given name.

In the workplace, senior staff are almost always addressed by their job title (rather than their name). The job title with the polite suffix -san is used if they are being addressed by their subordinates or people who do not know them. For example, the **kachō** (section chief in a company) will be addressed either as **kachō** or **kachō-san**. Alternatively the surname, followed by the person's job title, is used, for example, **Nakada kachō** (Section Chief Nakada). The same applies to teachers, doctors, dentists or very senior persons who are addressed either as **sensei** (literally: →

teacher), or by using the surname followed by sensei.

People in certain occupations can be addressed by their occupation (or the name of their shop) plus -san. For example: **o-mawari-san** (Mr Policeman/Officer) and **denki-ya-san** (Mr Electrical Goods Store).

Children up to about ten years of age can be addressed by their given name, often abbreviated, with the suffix **-chan** (a diminutive of -san). As they grow older, people will tend to address them using their surname and -san; this form of address becomes standard after they leave high school and enter work or embark on further study; the suffix **-kun** is sometimes preferred if a senior person is speaking to a junior.

admission charge nyūjōryō
入場料

adult otona
大人

advance: in advance mae·mot·te
前もって

aeroplane hikōki
飛行機

after ... no ato de
…の後で

after you dōzo osaki ni
どうぞお先に

after lunch chūshok-go ni
昼食後に

after all kek·kyok
結局

afternoon gogo
午後

in the afternoon gogo ni
午後に

this afternoon kyō no gogo ni
今日の午後に

aftershave aftā-shēb
アフターシェイブ

aftersun cream aftāsan-
rōshon
アフターサンロー
ション

afterwards ato de
後で

again mata
また

against (opposed to) ... to hantai
(no)
…と反対（の）

(position) ... ni tatekakete
…に立てかけて

age toshi
年

agent dairinin
代理人

ago mae
前

a week ago is·shūkan-mae
一週間前

an hour ago ichijikan-mae
一時間前

agree: I agree dōkan des
同感です

agreement kyōtei
協定

AIDS eizu
エイズ

air kūki
空気

by air (travel) hikōki de
飛行機で

(send) kōkūbin de
航空便で

air-conditioning eya-kon
エアコン

airmail: by airmail kōkūbin de
航空便で

airmail envelope kōkūbin-yō
fūtō
航空便用ふうとう

airplane hikōki
飛行機

airport kūkō
空港

to the airport, please kūkō
made, onegai shimas
空港までお願いしま
す

airport bus rimujin-bas
リムジンバス

aisle seat tsūrogawa no seki
通路側の席

alarm clock mezamashi-dokei
目覚まし時計

alcohol arukōru
アルコール

Alcohol is freely available in Japan, even from vending machines. Lunchtime drinking is hardly ever seen, but in the evening, drinking is regarded as an acceptable way to relax, as well as a major part of social life. Drunkenness among men is condoned in Japan, as long as it occurs in the right places (bars) and at the right time (in the evening, after work). These days more and more women drink, but the majority still think it's wise for women not to show the effects in public.

alcoholic drink osake
お酒
all: all the ... ... wa min·na
…はみんな
all of it sore zembu
それぜんぶ
all of them zembu
ぜんぶ
that's all, thanks sore dake des, dōmo arigatō
それだけです、どうもありがとう
allergic: I'm allergic to ... watashi wa ... arerugī des
私は…アレルギーです

allowed: is it allowed? ī des ka?
いいですか？
all right kek·kō des
けっこうです
(I agree) dōkan des
同感です
I'm all right daijōb des
大丈夫です
are you all right? daijōb des ka?
大丈夫ですか？
almost hotondo
ほとんど
alone hitori
ひとり
already mō
もう
also ... mo
…も
although ... keredomo
けれども
although it's expensive takai keredomo
高いけれども
altogether zembu de
ぜんぶで
always itsmo
いつも
am*: I am watashi wa ... des
私は…です
am: at 7am gozen shichiji ni
午前7時に
at 1am gozen ichiji ni
午後1時に
amazing (surprising) odorok-

beki
驚くべき
(very good) subarashī
すばらしい

ambulance kyūkyūsha
救急車

call an ambulance!
kyūkyūsha o yonde kudasai!
救急車を呼んでくだ
さい！

In Japan, the ambulance service is provided free of charge.
You can call this service free
from any payphone by dialling
119. As this number is for both
the ambulance service and the
fire brigade, you must specify
which is required.

America Amerika
アメリカ

American (adj) Amerika (no)
アメリカ（の）

I'm American watashi wa
Amerika-jin des
私はアメリカ人です

among ... no naka de
…のなかで

amount ryō
量

(of money) gak
額

amp: a 13-amp fuse

jūsan-ampeya no hyūz
13アンペアのヒュー
ズ

and* soshite
そして

(with nouns) to
と

(at beginning of sentence)
sorekara
それから

angry okot·ta
怒った

animal dōbuts
動物

ankle ashikubi
足首

anniversary (wedding) kek·kon-
kinen-bi
結婚記念日

annoy: this man's annoying me
kono hito wa watashi o
komarasete imas
このひとは私を困ら
せています

annoying iraira suru
いらいらする

another (different) bets no
別の

(one more) mō hitots
もうひとつ

can we have another room?
bets no heya wa arimas ka?
別の部屋はあります
か？

another beer, please bīru o

mō hitots onegai shimas
ビールをもうひとつ
お願いします

antibiotics kōsei-bus·shits
抗生物質

antihistamine kō-histamin-zai
坑ヒスタミン剤

antique: is it an antique? sore
wa kot·tōhin des ka?
それは骨董品です
か？

antique shop kot·tōhin-ten
骨董品店

antiseptic shōdok-zai
消毒剤

any: do you have any ...? ... o
mot·te imas ka?
…を持っています
か？

have you got any bread/
cherries? pan/sakuranbo wa
arimas ka?
パン／さくらんぼは
ありますか？

sorry, I don't have any
sumimasen, mot·te imasen
すみません、持って
いません

anybody dare ka
だれか

does anybody speak English?
dare ka Eigo ga hanasemas
ka?
だれか英語が話せま
すか？

there wasn't anybody there
soko niwa dare mo imasen
deshta
そこにはだれもいま
せんでした

anything nani ka
何か

• • • • • DIALOGUE • • • • •

anything else? hoka ni nani ka?

nothing else, thanks hoka niwa
nai des, arigatō

would you like anything to drink?
nani ka nomimas ka?

I don't want anything, thanks nani
mo hoshik arimasen, arigatō

apart from ... igai dewa
…以外では

apartment apāto
アパート

apartment block manshon
マンション

appetizer zensai
前菜

apple rin·go
りんご

appointment yoyak
予約

• • • • • DIALOGUE • • • • •

good morning, how can I help you?
ohayō gozaimas, ikaga
itashimashō?

I'd like to make an appointment
yoyak o shitai no des ga

what time would you like? nanji ga yoroshī des ka?

three o'clock sanji ga ī des

I'm afraid that's not possible, is four o'clock all right? mōshiwake arimasen ga sanji wa ip·pai des, yoji dewa ikaga des ka?

yes, that will be fine hai, ī des

the name was? onamae o itadakemas ka?

apricot anzu
あんず

April Shigats
四月

are* des
です

you are (sing) anata wa ... des
あなたは…です

they are (men/women) karera/kanojotachi wa ... des
彼ら／彼女たちは…です

area chīki
地域

area code shigai-kyokban
市外局番

arm ude
うで

arrange tehai shimas
手配します

will you arrange it for us? sore o tehai shite kuremas ka?

それを手配してくれますか？

arrival tōchak
到着

arrive tskimas
着きます

when do we arrive? itsu tskimas ka?
いつ着きますか？

has my fax arrived yet? watashi no fak·ks wa todokimashta ka?
私のファックスは届きましたか？

we arrived today kyō tskimashta
きょう着きました

art bijuts
美術

art gallery bijuts-kan
美術館

artist geijuts-ka
芸術家

as: as big as ... ... to onaji ōkisa no
…と同じ大きさの

as soon as possible dekiru dake hayak
できるだけ早く

ashtray haizara
灰皿

Asia Ajia
アジア

Asian (adj) Ajia (no)
アジア（の）

(noun) Ajia-jin
アジア人

ask tanomimas
頼みます

I didn't ask for this kore wa tanonde imasen
これは頼んでいません

could you ask him to ...? kare ni ... yō tanonde kuremasen ka?
彼に…よう頼んでくれませんか？

asleep: she's asleep kanojo wa nemut·te imas
彼女は眠っています

aspirin aspirin
アスピリン

asthma zensok
ぜんそく

astonishing odorok hodo (no)
驚くほど（の）

at: at the hotel hoteru de
ホテルで

at the station eki de
駅で

at six o'clock rokji ni
6時に

at Yukiko's Yukiko-san no tokoro de
ゆきこさんのところで

ATM genkin-jidō-shiharaiki
現金自動支払機

attractive miryok-teki (na)
魅力的（な）

August Hachigats
八月

aunt (one's own) oba
おば

(someone else's) oba-san
おばさん

Australia Ōstoraria
オーストラリア

Australian (adj) Ōstoraria (no)
オーストラリア（の）

I'm Australian watashi wa Ōstoraria-jin des
私はオーストラリア人です

automatic (adj) jidō (no)
自動（の）

(noun: car) ōtomatik·k
オートマティック

autumn aki
秋

in the autumn aki ni
秋に

avalanche nadare
なだれ

avenue ōdōri
大通り

average (not good) heikin-teki (na)
平均的（な）

on average heikin shite
平均して

awake: is he awake? kare wa

okite imas ka?

彼は起きていますか？

away: go away! at·chi e it·te!

あっちへいって！

is it far away? tōi des ka?

遠いですか？

awful hidoi

ひどい

B

baby akachan

赤ちゃん

baby food bebī-fūdo

ベビーフード

baby's bottle honyūbin

ほ乳びん

baby-sitter bebī-shit·tā

ベビーシッター

back (of body) senaka

背中

(back part) ura

裏

at the back ushiro ni

後ろに

can I have my money back?
okane o kaeshite kuremasen ka?

お金を返してくれませんか？

to come back modot·te kimas

戻ってきます

to go back modot·te ikimas

戻っていきます

backache koshi no itami

腰の痛み

bacon bēkon

ベーコン

bad warui

悪い

a bad headache hidoi zutsū

ひどい頭痛

not bad māmā des

まあまあです

badly hidok

ひどく

badminton badominton

バドミントン

bag kaban

かばん

(paper bag) fukuro

袋

(carrier bag) binīru-bukuro

ビニール袋

(handbag) handobag·g

ハンドバッグ

baggage nimots

荷物

baggage checkroom
tenimots-azkari-jo

手荷物預り所

baggage claim
tenimots-uketori-jo

手荷物受取所

baker's pan-ya

パン屋

balcony beranda
ベランダ
a room with a balcony
beranda-tski no heya
ベランダ付きの部屋
ball bōru
ボール
ballpoint pen bōru-pen
ボールペン
bamboo take
竹
bamboo shoots takenoko
たけのこ
banana banana
バナナ
band (musical) bando
バンド
bandage hōtai
包帯
Bandaid® bando-eido
バンドエイド
bank (money) ginkō
銀行

Banks open Mon–Fri 9am–
3pm, and 9am–noon on the first
and last Saturdays of the month.
In some banks, you have to take
a numbered ticket from a machine and wait your turn. If
changing money or traveller's
cheques, take along your passport for identification. In small
branches sterling may not always be accepted.   →

Cirrus, Plus and other networks
operate internationally through
cash machines/ATMs in urban
areas. Cash machines usually do
not operate 24 hours a day –
expect them to be shut from
8pm–5am and all day Sunday.
There are some exceptions in
city centres.

bank account ginkō-kōza
銀行口座
banker's draft kawase-
tegata
為替手形
bar bā
バー
a bar of chocolate chokorēto-
bā
チョコレートバー

Bars can be very expensive. Be-
ware of hostess bars, and places
serving you little titbits such as
rice crackers or peanuts, as
these can push up the price by
a huge amount. The safest bars,
usually with standard prices,
are the places run by large companies such as Suntory or Nikka
– you will see their signs outside. Other inexpensive places
are beer halls and **izaka-ya**
(the Japanese equivalent of the   →

British pub), where food is also available.
see **drinking** and **alcohol**

barber's toko-ya
床屋
baseball yakyū
野球
basket kago
かご
(in shop) basket·to
バスケット
basketball basket·to-borū
バスケットボール
bath ofuro
お風呂
can I have a bath? ofuro ni hait·te mo ī des ka?
お風呂にはいっても
いいですか？

---

bathing

Taking a bath in Japan comes with a clear set of rules – whether bathing at home, in public baths or **onsen** (hot spring). The main difference is that the bath tub is for soaking in, not for washing, which must be done outside of the bath. In homes and many smaller hotels and **ryokan** (traditional inns), the tub is often box-like and you will soak with the water lapping
→

---

up to your neck. Public baths and onsens have one large (sometimes several) pools which you share with fellow bathers. The temperatures in these pools can be very hot – the trick to dealing with it is not to move around once you're in. Western-style hotels usually offer a Western-style bathtub with a shower.

---

bathroom ofuro-ba
お風呂場
with a private bathroom
bas-tski no heya
バス付きの部屋
bath towel bas-taoru
バスタオル
bathtub yoksō
浴槽
battery (for radio etc) denchi
電池
(for car) bat·terī
バッテリー
bay wan
湾
be* des
です
beach hamabe
浜辺
on the beach hamabe de
浜辺で
bean curd tōf
豆腐

beans mame
豆
soya beans daizu
大豆
beard hige
ひげ
beautiful (object, painting)
subarashī
すばらしい
(person, view) kirei (na)
きれいな
(building) utsukushī
美しい
because nazenara
なぜなら
because of ... ... no tame ni
…のために
bed (Western-style) bed·do
ベッド
(Japanese-style) nedoko
寝床
I'm going to bed now
sorosoro nemas
そろそろ寝ます

Beds in Western-style hotels differ little from the ones you are used to at home. Japanese-style beds or **futon** consist of pliable mattresses or **shiki-buton** and thick quilts or **kake-buton** as well as pillows, **makura**. They are stored in cupboards during the day and spread out at night on the tatami-mat floor. If you →

stay in a **ryokan** (traditional inn), the maid will lay out your bed after you have had dinner in your room. But in a less expensive **minshuk** (guesthouse), bedding has to be laid out and put away by the guest.

bed and breakfast
chōshok-tski yado
朝食付き宿
see **hotel**
bedding (Japanese) futon
ふとん
bedroom shinshits
寝室
beef gyūnik
牛肉
beer bīru
ビール
two beers, please bīru futats,
onegai shimas
ビールふたつ、お願
いします

Beer has become very popular, and the Japanese brands, mostly modelled on German lager, are very good indeed. Beer is always served chilled. Some popular brands are Santory, Sapporo, Kirin and Asahi. If you prefer draught beer, you may find Yebisu beer more to your →

taste. Guinness is available in cans and is one of the well-known imported brands as are Budweiser and Heineken. Some pubs and bars offer a wide selection of foreign beers including German, French, Chinese, Brazilian and other Asian makes.

before ... mae ni
…前に

begin hajimarimas
始まります

when does it begin? itsu hajimarimas ka?
いつ始まりますか？

beginner shoshinsha
初心者

beginning: at the beginning hajime ni
始めに

behind ... no ushiro ni
…の後ろに

behind me watashi no ushiro ni
私の後ろに

below ... no shita ni
…の下に

belt beruto
ベルト

bend (in road) kāb
カーブ

berth (on ship) shindai
寝台

beside ... no soba ni
…のそばに

best saikō (no)
最高（の）

better mot·to ī
もっと良い

are you feeling better? kibun wa yok narimashta ka?
気分はよくなりましたか？

between ... no aida ni
…の間に

beyond ... no mukō ni
…の向こうに

bicycle jitensha
自転車

Bicycles are a method of transport which should be seriously considered as a means of making short journeys. In resorts and tourist areas, bikes can easily be hired, usually from just outside railway stations. Most railway stations have a huge number of bikes lined up outside and some even have two-storey or three-storey **jitensha-okiba** (bicycle parks) where you can 'park' your bike.

big ōkī
大きい

too big ōkīsugimas
大きすぎます

it's not big enough
chīsasugimas
小さすぎます

bikini bikini
ビキニ

bill seikyūsho
請求書

(in restaurant, bar etc) okanjō
お勘定

(US: banknote) shihei
紙幣

could I have the bill, please?
okanjō o onegai shimas
お勘定をお願いします

In Japan, paying a bill is treated discreetly. Generally, your Japanese host or business associate will tend to invite you out and then pick up the tab themselves since you are a guest in their country. You should therefore try to reciprocate when they visit your country or you can also extend a return invitation and take them to a Western-style restaurant in Japan.

Except among good friends or students it's unusual to go Dutch. However, during informal drinking the suggestion may be made: 'warikan de nomimashō ka?' in which case everyone pays separately. In such cases, the bill is usually split evenly, rather than calculating individual consumption. If you want to pay, say: 'watashi ga haraimas!' (I'll pay!). Bills and change are not scrutinized in reputable places: to do so would show lack of trust in the establishment.

bin gomibako
ごみ箱

bird tori
鳥

birthday tanjōbi
誕生日

happy birthday! otanjōbi omedetō gozaimas!
お誕生日おめでとうございます

biscuit bisket·to
ビスケット

bit: a little bit skoshi
すこし

a big bit ōkī bubun
大きい部分

a bit of … … o skoshi
…をすこし

a bit expensive chot·to takai des
ちょっと 高いです

bite (by insect) mushi-sasare
虫さされ

(by dog) inu no kamikizu
犬の噛み傷

bitter (taste etc) nigai
にがい

black kuroi
黒い

blanket mōf
毛布

blind me no fujiyū na
hito (no)
目の不自由な人
（の）

blinds buraindo
ブラインド

blocked (road, pipe)
fusagat·ta
ふさがった
(sink) tsmat·ta
つまった

blond (adj) kimpats (no)
金髪（の）

blood kets·eki
血液
high blood pressure
kōkets·ats
高血圧

blouse buraus
ブラウス

blow-dry burō-dorai
ブロードライ
I'd like a cut and blow-dry
kat·to to burō-dorai o
onegai shimas
カットとブロードラ
イをお願いします

blue aoi
青い

boarding pass tōjōken
搭乗券

boat bōto
ボート
(for passengers) fune
船

body karada
からだ

boiled egg yude-tamago
ゆでたまご

boiled rice gohan
ごはん

bone hone
ほね

bonnet (of car) bon·net·to
ボンネット

book (noun) hon
本
(verb) yoyak shimas
予約します
can I book a seat? seki o
yoyak dekimas ka?
席を予約できます
か？

•••••• DIALOGUE ••••••

I'd like to book a table for two
tēburu o futari-yō ni yoyak shitai
no des ga
what time would you like it booked
for? nanji ni otorishimashō ka?
half past seven shichiji-han ni
onegai shimas
that's fine o-uke-itashimas
and your name? dochirasama des
ka?

bookshop, bookstore hon-ya
本屋

boot (of footwear) būts
ブーツ

(of car) torank
トランク

border (of country) kok·kyō
国境

bored: I'm bored taikuts des
退屈です

boring taikuts (na)
退屈な

born: I was born in ... (place) ...
de umaremashta
…で生まれました

(year) ... ni umaremashta
に生まれました

borrow karimas
借ります

may I borrow ...? ... o
okarishite mo ī des ka?
…をお借りしてもい
いですか？

both ryōhō
両方

bother: sorry to bother you
otesū o okakeshite
sumimasen
お手数をおかけして
すみません

bottle bin
びん

a bottle of sake sake
ip·pon
酒一本

bottle-opener sen·nuki
栓抜き

bottom (of person) oshiri
お尻

at the bottom of the ... ... no
soko ni
…の底に

(hill, mountain) ... no fumoto
ni
…のふもとに

(road, street) ... no tskiatari ni
…のつきあたりに

---

bowing

It's customary to bow when
greeting someone. There are
various depths of bow depending on the degree of politeness
you wish to convey. The rules of
bowing need not concern foreign
visitors, from whom a slight nod
of the head is perfectly acceptable. Sometimes you'll be offered a handshake instead.

---

bowl (porcelain) chawan
茶碗

(wooden) owan
お椀

box hako
箱

(wooden) kibako
木箱

box office kip·p-uriba
切符売り場

boy otoko no ko
男の子

boyfriend bōi-frendo
ボーイフレンド

bra brajā
ブラジャー

bracelet buresuret·to
ブレスレット

brake (noun) burēki
ブレーキ

brandy burandē
ブランデー

bread pan
パン

white bread shiro-pan
白パン

brown bread kuro-pan
黒パン

wholemeal bread zenryūko
no pan
全粒粉のパン

break (verb) kowashimas
壊します

I've broken the ... ... o
kowashite shimai-
mashta
…を壊してしまい
ました

I think I've broken my wrist
dōmo tekubi o ot·ta yō des
どうも手首を折った
ようです

break down koshō shimas
故障します

I've broken down kuruma ga

enko shimashta
車がエンコしました

breakdown koshō
故障

breakdown service
rek·kā-sha
レッカー車

breakfast chōshok
朝食

These days between 6 and 8am
more than half of all Japanese
households have a Western-style
breakfast, especially in urban
areas. Japanese-style breakfast
consists of rice, miso soup
(made from soy beans), a raw
egg or Japanese-style omelette,
nori (seaweed), nat·to (sticky
beans) and tskemono (pickles). Most hotels offer you a
choice between a Japanese- or
Western-style breakfast; in a
ryokan (traditional inn) you are
more likely to be served a traditional breakfast.

break-in: I've had a break-in
dorobō ni hairaremashta
どろぼうにはいられ
ました

breast chibusa
乳房

bridge (over river) hashi
橋

brief mijikai
短い

briefcase burīf-kēs
ブリーフケース

bright (light etc) akarui
あかるい

(colour) azayaka (na)
あざやか（な）

brilliant subarashī
すばらしい

bring mot·te kimas
持ってきます

I'll bring it back later atode
kaeshi ni kimas
後で返しにきます

Britain Eikok
英国

British (adj) Eikok (no)
英国（の）

brochure panfret·to
パンフレット

broken kowareta
壊れた

(leg etc) hone ga oreta
骨が折れた

brooch burōchi
ブローチ

brother kyōdai
兄弟

(elder: one's own) ani
兄

(someone else's) onī-san
お兄さん

(younger: one's own) otōto
弟

(someone else's) otōto-san
弟さん

brother-in-law giri no kyōdai
義理の兄弟

(elder: one's own) giri no ani
義理の兄

(someone else's) giri no
onī-san
義理のお兄さん

(younger: one's own) giri no
otōto
義理の弟

(someone else's) giri no
otōto-san
義理の弟さん

brown cha-iro (no)
茶色

bruise dabok-shō
打撲傷

brush (for hair) burashi
ブラシ

(artist's) efude
絵筆

(for cleaning) hōki
ほうき

Buddha hotoke-sama
仏様

Buddhism Buk·kyō
仏教

Buddhist (adj) Buk·kyō (no)
仏教（の）

(noun) Buk·kyōto
仏教徒

buffet car shokdōsha
食堂車

buggy (for child) uba-guruma
乳母車
building biru
ビル
bullet train shinkansen
新幹線
bunk shindai
寝台
bureau de change ryōgae-jo
両替所
burglary oshikomi-gōtō
押し込み強盗
burn (noun) yakedo
やけど
(verb) yakedo shimas
やけどします
burnt: this is burnt (food) kore
wa kogete imas
これは焦げています
bus bas
バス
what number bus is it to ...?
...-iki no bas wa namban des
ka?
……—行きのバスは何
番ですか？
when is the next bus to ...?
tsgi no ...-iki no bas wa nanji
des ka?
次の……—行きのバス
は何時ですか？
what time is the last bus?
saishū bas wa nanji des ka?
最終バスは何時です
か？

In most cities and towns, the bus service is very efficient. In urban areas, buses often operate a flat-fare system and you board by the front door. However, it's more common for the fare to be based on the distance you travel, in which case, you take a ticket when you get on through the rear door; when you arrive at your stop, the amount of the fare is displayed under your number on a board at the front of the bus. Various reductions are available in the form of season tickets, multi-journey and day tickets. These tickets sometimes allow you to use tube or train services as well. You can also buy a **kaisūken** (book of 11 tickets for the price of 10), which can often be purchased on boarding the bus.

There are long distance-buses between major cities. These services, provided by Japan Rail, may not be very comfortable, but are inexpensive. You can also use a Japan Rail Pass if you have one. The terminals are often attached to major railway stations.

•••••• DIALOGUE ••••••

does this bus go to ...? kono bas wa ...-iki des ka?

no, you need a number ... ie, ... ban no bas des

business shigoto
仕事
(company) kaisha
会社
business card meishi
名刺

A business card is essential in Japanese business. Every town has services which can provide them within 24 hours. The Japanese exchange them at all meetings: they are offered with both hands and you should read them before slipping them into your pocket or to one side.

business hotel bijines-hoteru
ビジネスホテル
see hotel
businessman bijines-man
ビジネスマン
business trip shut·chō
出張
businesswoman kyaria-ūman
キャリアウーマン
bus station bas-tāminaru
バスターミナル
bus stop bas-tei
バス停

bust basto
バスト
busy (restaurant etc) konde iru
込んでいる
I'm busy tomorrow ashita wa isogashī des
あしたは忙しいです
but demo
でも
butcher's nik-ya
肉屋
butter batā
バター
button botan
ボタン
buy kaimas
買います
where can I buy ...? doko de ... ga kaemas ka?
どこで…が買えますか？
by: by car kuruma de
車で
by bus bas de
バスで
written by ... ... ga kaita
…が書いた
by the window mado no soba
窓のそば
by the sea umi no soba
海のそば
by Thursday Mok·yōbi made ni
木曜日までに

bye **dewa mata**
ではまた
(between friends) **jā ne**
じゃあね

C

cabin (on ship) **senshits**
船室
(in mountains) **yamagoya**
山小屋
cable car **kēburu-kā**
ケーブルカー
café **kis·saten**
喫茶店
see **restaurant**
cake **kēki**
ケーキ
cake shop **kēki-ya**
ケーキ屋
calendar **karendā**
カレンダー
lunar calendar **kyūreki**
旧暦
call (verb: to phone) **denwa shimas**
電話します
what's it called? **kore wa nan to īmas ka?**
これはなんと言いますか？
he/she is called ... **kare/kanojo wa ... to īmas**
彼／彼女は…と言います

please call the doctor **isha o yonde kudasai**
医者を呼んでください
please give me a call at 7.30am tomorrow **ashita no asa shichi-ji han ni denwa o kudasai**
あしたの朝７時半に電話をください
please ask him to call me **kare ni denwa o kureru yō tstaete kudasai**
彼に電話をくれるよう伝えてください
call back: I'll call back later **ato de mata ukagaimas**
後でまたうかがいます
(phone back) **ato de mata denwa shimas**
後でまた電話します
call round: I'll call round tomorrow **ashita ukagaimas**
あしたうかがいます
calligraphy **shodō**
書道
camcorder **bideo-kamera**
ビデオカメラ
camera **kamera**
カメラ
camera shop **kamera-ya**
カメラ屋
campsite **kyamp-jō**
キャンプ場

can kanzume
缶詰め

a can of beer kam-bīru
缶ビール

can*: can you …? …-koto ga dekimas ka?
…—ことができますか？

can I have …? … o morat·te mo ī des ka?
…をもらってもいいですか？

I can't … …-koto ga dekimasen
…—ことができません

Canada Kanada
カナダ

Canadian (adj) Kanada (no)
カナダ（の）

I'm Canadian watashi wa Kanada-jin des
私はカナダ人です

canal un·ga
運河

cancel torikeshimas
取り消します

candies kyandī
キャンディー

candle rōsok
ロウソク

canoe kanū
カヌー

canoeing kanūing
カヌーイング

can-opener kankiri
缶切り

cap (hat) bōshi
ぼうし

(of bottle) futa
ふた

car kuruma
車

by car kuruma de
車で

card (birthday etc) kādo
カード

New Year's card nen·gajō
年賀状

here's my (business) card watashi no meishi des
私の名刺です

cardphone kādo-denwa
カード電話

careful chūibukai
注意深い

be careful! ki o tskete!
気をつけて！

carp koi
こい

car park chūshajō
駐車場

carpet jūtan
じゅうたん

carp streamer koi-nobori
こいのぼり

car rental rentakā
レンタカー

carriage (of train) kyaksha
客車

carrier bag binīru-bukuro
ビニール袋

carrot ninjin
にんじん

carry mochimas
持ちます

carry-cot keitai-yō bebī-bed·do
携帯用ベビーベッド

carton pak·k
パック

cartoon (film) animēshon
アニメーション

cash (noun) genkin
現金

(verb) genkin ni kaemas
現金に換えます

will you cash this for me?
genkin ni kaete kuremasen ka?
現金に換えてくれませんか？

cash desk kaikei
会計

cash dispenser
genkin-jidō-shiharaiki
現金自動支払機

cassette kaset·to
カセット

cassette recorder
kaset·to-rekōdā
カセットレコーダー

castle shiro
城

casualty department

kyūkyūbyōtō
救急病棟

cat neko
ねこ

catch tskamaemas
捕まえます

where do we catch the bus
to ...? ...-iki no bas wa doko
kara dete imas ka?
……—行きのバスはどこから出ていますか？

Catholic (adj) Katorik·k (no)
カトリック（の）

cauliflower karifrawā
カリフラワー

cave hora-ana
洞穴

CD shī-dī
シーディー

ceiling tenjō
天井

cemetery bochi
墓地

centigrade ses·shi
摂氏

centimetre senchi-mētoru
センチメートル

central chūshin (no)
中心（の）

centre chūshin
中心

how do we get to the city
centre? hankagai niwa dō

ikimas ka?

繁華街にはどう行き
ますか？

cereal kōnfrēk

コーンフレーク

ceremony shikiten

式典

opening ceremony
kaikaishiki

開会式

tea ceremony chakai

茶会

certainly tashika ni

たしかに

certainly not! (that's wrong)
zet·tai chigaimas!

絶対違います！

(refusal) dame des!

だめです！

certificate shōmeisho

証明書

chair isu

いす

change (verb: replace)
torikaemas

取りかえます

(trains etc) norikaemas

乗り換えます

(money) kuzushimas

くずします

(noun: money) kozeni

小銭

can I change this for ..., please?
kore o ... to torikaete
kudasai

これを…と取りかえ

where do I change trains?
doko de norikaereba ī des
ka?

どこで乗り換えれば
いいですか？

I don't have any change
kozeni ga arimasen

小銭がありません

can you give me change for a
1,000-yen note? sen-en-sats
o kuzushite kuremasen ka?

千円札をくずして
くれませんか？

•••••• DIALOGUE ••••••

do we have to change (trains)?
norikae-nakte wa narimasen ka?

yes, change at Tokyo/no, it's a
direct train hai, Tokyo-eki de
norikae des/īe, choktsū des

changed: to get changed
kigaemas

着替えます

character (written) kanji

漢字

charge (noun) ryōkin

料金

(verb) seikyū shimas

請求します

charge card kurejit·to-kādo

クレジットカード

see credit card

cheap yasui

安い

do you have anything cheaper?

mō skoshi yasui no wa
arimas ka?

もう少し安いの
はありますか？

check (US: noun) kogit·te

小切手

(bill) seikyūsho

請求書

(in restaurant, bar etc) okanjō

お勘定

could I have the check, please?

okanjō o onegai shimas

お勘定をお願します

see bill

check (verb) shirabemas

調べます

could you check the ...? ... o
shirabete kuremasen ka?

…を調べてくれ
ませんか？

check-in chek·k·in

チェックイン

check in chek·k·in shimas

チェックインします

where do we have to check in?

doko de chek·k·in shinakte
wa narimasen ka?

どこでチェックイン
しなくてはなりませ
んか？

cheek (on face) hō

ほお

cheerio! bai-bai!

バイバイ！

cheers! (toast) kampai!

乾杯！

cheese chīz

チーズ

chemist's yak·kyok

薬局

cheque kogit·te

小切手

cherry sakurambo

さくらんぼ

cherry blossom sakura

桜

cherry tree sakura no ki

桜の木

chess (Western) ches

チェス

(Japanese) shōgi

将棋

chest mune

胸

chestnut kuri

くり

chewing gum chūin·gam

チューインガム

chicken (meat) torinik

鶏肉

chickenpox mizubōsō

水ぼうそう

child kodomo

子供

children kodomo-
tachi

子供たち

child minder komori

子守

children's pool kodomo-yō
pūru
子供用プール

children's portion okosama-yō
お子様用

chin ago
あご

china setomono
瀬戸もの

China Chūgok
中国

Chinese (adj) Chūgok (no)
中国 (の)

chips (French fries) french-
frai
フレンチフライ
(US) poteto-chip·p
ポテトチップ

chocolate chokorēto
チョコレート

milk chocolate
miruk-chokorēto
ミルクチョコレート

plain chocolate
burak·k-chokorēto
ブラックチョコレー
ト

a hot chocolate kokoa
ココア

choose erabimas
選びます

chopstick rest hashioki
はしおき

chopsticks hashi
はし

Christmas Kurismas
クリスマス

merry Christmas!
Merī-Kurismas!
メリークリスマス

As a non-Christian country, Christmas in Japan is a commercially oriented festival. It's not a national holiday, but most young people celebrate it in a way that resembles New Year celebrations in the West.

Christmas Eve Kurismas-Ibu
クリスマスイブ

church kyōkai
教会

cider rin·goshu
りんご酒

cigar hamaki
葉巻

cigarette tabako
タバコ

Cigarettes are one of the few things which are cheaper in Japan than in the UK and they can easily be bought from 24-hour vending machines.
The most popular brand is Japanese Mild Seven and its milder versions. Foreign brands also have a good share of the market. American cigarettes like →

Marlboro, Philip Morris and Camel are popular amongst young people.
Smoking is allowed in most public places, except for Japan Rail train stations and tube stations in Tokyo which have a no-smoking policy. Smoking is banned on urban trains and buses and there are non-smoking sections on all long-distance trains.

cigarette lighter raitā
ライター

cinema eiga
映画

circle en
円

(in theatre) barukonī-seki
バルコニー席

city toshi
都市

city centre hankagai
繁華街

clean (adj) kirei (na)
きれい（な）

(verb) kirei ni shimas
きれいにします

can you clean these for me?
kore o kirei ni shite
kuremasen ka?
これをきれいにして
くれませんか？

cleaning solution (for contact lenses) kontakto-renzu-yō kurīnā
コンタクトレンズ用
クリーナー

cleansing lotion
kurenjing-rōshon
クレンジングロー
ション

clear tōmei (na)
透明（な）

(obvious) akiraka (na)
明らか（な）

clever kashikoi
かしこい

client irainin
依頼人

cliff gake
崖

climbing tozan
登山

clinic shinryōjo
診療所

cloakroom kurōk
クローク

clock tokei
時計

close (verb) shimarimas
閉まります

•••••• DIALOGUE ••••••

what time do you close? nanji ni shimarimas ka?

we close at 8pm on weekdays, and 6pm on Saturdays heijits wa

hachiji, Doyōbi wa rokji ni
shimarimas

do you close for lunch?
hiruyasumi wa arimas ka?

yes, between 12 and 1pm hai,
jūniji kara ichiji des

closed (door) shimat·ta
閉まった
(shop) heiten (no)
閉店（の）

cloth (fabric) nunoji
布地
(for cleaning etc) zōkin
ぞうきん

clothes (Western) yōfuk
洋服
(Japanese) kimono
着物

cloudy kumori (no)
くもり（の）

clutch (in car) kurat·chi
クラッチ

coach (bus) chōkyori-bas
長距離バス
(on train) kyaksha
客車

coach station bas-tāminaru
バスターミナル

coach trip bas-ryokō
バス旅行

coast kaigan
海岸
on the coast engan ni
沿岸に

coat (long coat) kōto
コート
(jacket) jaket·to
ジャケット

coathanger han·gā
ハンガー

code (for phoning)
shigai-kyokban
市外局番
what's the (dialling) code for
Osaka? Osaka no
shigai-kyokban wa namban
des ka?
大阪の市外局番は
何番ですか？

coffee kōhī
コーヒー
two coffees, please
kōhī futats, onegai
shimas
コーヒーふたつ、
お願いします

coin kōka
硬貨

Coke® kōla
コーラ

cold tsmetai
冷たい
(weather, person) samui
寒い
I'm cold samui des
寒いです
I have a cold kaze o
hikimashta
風邪を引きました

collar eri
えり

collect atsmemas
集めます

I've come to collect ... ... o
tori ni kimashta
…を取りに来ました

collect call korekto-kōru
コレクトコール

college daigak
大学

colour iro
色

do you have this in other
colours? hoka no iro wa
arimas ka?
ほかの色はあります
か？

colour film karā-firum
カラーフィルム

comb kushi
くし

come kimas
来ます

• • • • • • DIALOGUE • • • • • •

where do you come from? doko
kara iras·shaimashta ka?
I come from Edinburgh Ejinbara
kara kimashta

come back modot·te kimas
戻ってきます

I'll come back tomorrow mata
ashita kimas
またあした来ます

come in hairimas
入ります

comfortable yut·tari shita
ゆったりした

comic book man·ga
漫画

compact disc kompakto-disk
コンパクトディスク

company (business) kaisha
会社

compare kurabemas
比べます

compartment (on train) koshits
個室

compass kompas
コンパス

complain kujō o īmas
苦情を言います

complaint kujō
苦情

I have a complaint kujō ga
arimas
苦情があります

completely kanzen ni
完全に

computer kompyūtā
コンピューター

concert konsāto
コンサート

conditioner (for hair) rins
リンス

condom kondōm
コンドーム

conference kaigi
会議

conference room kaigijō
会議場

confirm kaknin shimas
確認します

congratulations! omedetō!
おめでとう！

connecting flight setszokbin
接続便

connection (in travelling)
setszok
接続

constipation bempi
便秘

consulate ryōjikan
領事館

contact (verb) renrak shimas
連絡します

contact lenses kontakto-renzu
コンタクトレンズ

contract keiyak
契約

convenient (time) tsgō no ī
都合のいい

(location, object) benri (na)
便利（な）

that's not convenient sore wa
tsgō ga yok arimasen
それは都合がよくあ
りません

cook (verb) ryōri shimas
料理します

not cooked han·nama (na)
半なま（な）

cooker renji
レンジ

cookie bisket·to
ビスケット

cool suzushī
涼しい

cork koruk
コルク

corkscrew koruk-nuki
コルク抜き

corner: on the corner
machikado ni
街角に

in the corner sumi ni
隅に

cornflakes kōnfrēk
コーンフレーク

correct (right) tadashī
正しい

corridor rōka
廊下

cosmetics keshōhin
化粧品

cost (noun) hiyō
費用

(verb) hiyō ga
kakarimas
費用がかかります

how much does it cost? ikura
des ka?
いくらですか？

cot bebī-bed·do
ベビーベッド

cotton momen
木綿

cotton wool das·shimen
脱脂綿

couchette shindai
寝台

cough (noun) seki
せき

cough medicine
sekidome
せき止め

could: could you ...? ...-te
kuremasen ka?
…ーてくれません
か？

could I have ...? ... o
kuremasen ka?
…をくれませんか？

I couldn't ... ... koto wa
dekimasen deshta
…ことはできません
でした

country (nation) kuni
国

(countryside) inaka
いなか

countryside inaka
いなか

couple: a couple of ... ... futats
…ふたつ

courier gaido
ガイド

course kōs
コース

of course mochiron
もちろん

of course not mochiron
chigaimas
もちろん違います

cousin itoko
いとこ

crab kani
かに

cracker (biscuit) kurak·kā
クラッカー

craft shop min·geihin-ten
民芸品店

crash (noun) shōtots-jiko
衝突事故

I've had a crash shōtots-jiko
ni aimashta
衝突事故にあい
ました

crazy muchū (na)
夢中（な）

cream kurīm
クリーム

creche takji-sho
託児所

credit card kurejit·to-kādo
クレジットカード

do you take credit cards?
kurejit·to-kādo wa tskaemas
ka?
クレジットカードは
使えますか？

Credit cards are widely accepted
in Japan and can be used to
withdraw money from cash ma-
chines/ATMs.

can I pay by credit card?
kurejit·to-kādo de haraemas ka?

which card do you want to use?
doko no kādo des ka?

Mastercard/Visa mastā/biza des

yes, sir hai, oshiharai
itadakemas

what's the number? ban·gō o
itadakemas ka?

and the expiry date? yūkōkigen
wa itsu des ka?

crisps poteto-chip·p
ポテトチップ

crockery tōjiki
陶磁器

crossing (by sea) ōdan
横断

crossroads jūjiro
十字路

crowd hitogomi
ひと込み

crowded konda
込んだ

crown (dental) kuraun
クラウン

cruise kōkai
航海

crutches matsbazue
松葉杖

cry (verb) nakimas
泣きます

cucumber kyūri
きゅうり

cup kap·p
カップ

a cup of …, please … o hitots
kudasai
…をひとつください

cupboard oshīre
押し入れ

(with shelves) todana
戸棚

curly kārī-hea (no)
カーリーヘア
（の）

curtains kāten
カーテン

cushion kus·shon
クッション

floor cushion zabuton
ざぶとん

Often used as seating at a low dining table, **zabuton** (floor cushions) are spread on straw mats called **tatami**. The proper way to sit on them is with one's feet (with shoes or slippers removed) under the body, one big toe over the other. In practice, however, it doesn't matter if you can do this or not as nowadays a lot of Japanese, especially the younger generation, find it hard to do.

custom shūkan
習慣

customer **kyak**
客
Customs **zeikan**
税関
cut (noun) **kirikizu**
切り傷
(verb) **kirimas**
切ります
I've cut myself **kit·te
shimaimashta**
切ってしまいました
cutlery **naif-fōk-rui**
ナイフ・フォーク類
cycling **saikuring**
サイクリング
cyclist **saikuristo**
サイクリスト

D

daily **mainichi** (no)
毎日
damage (verb) **kowashimas**
壊します
damaged **kowareta**
壊れた
I'm sorry, I've damaged this
**sumimasen, kore o
kowashite shimaimashta**
すみません、これを
壊してしまいました
damn! **chikshō!**
ちくしょう！
damp **shimet·ta**
しめった

dance (noun) **dans**
ダンス
(verb) **odorimas**
おどります
would you like to dance?
odorimasen ka?
おどりませんか？
dangerous **abunai**
危ない
Danish (adj) **Dem·māk** (no)
デンマーク（の）
dark (adj: colour) **koi**
濃い
(hair) **kuroi**
黒い
it's getting dark **kurak nat·te
kimashta**
暗くなってきました
date*: what's the date today?
kyō wa nan·nichi des ka?
きょうは何日です
か？
let's make a date for next
Monday **raishū no Getsyōbi
ni shimashō**
来週の月曜日に
しましょう
daughter (one's own) **musume**
娘
(someone else's) **ojō-san**
お嬢さん
daughter-in-law (one's own) **giri
no musume**
義理の娘
(someone else's) **giri no**

musume-san
義理の娘さん

dawn yoake
夜明け

at dawn yoake ni
夜明けに

day hi
日

the day after sono
tsgi no hi
その次の日

the day after tomorrow
as·sat·te
あさって

the day before sono mae
no hi
その前の日

the day before yesterday
ototoi
おととい

every day mainichi
毎日

all day ichinichi-jū
一日中

in two days' time
futsuka-inai ni
二日以内に

have a nice day! gokigen·yō!
ごきげんよう！

day trip higaeri-ryokō
日帰り旅行

dead shinda
死んだ

deaf mimi ga kikoenai
耳がきこえない

deal (business) torihiki
取り引き

it's a deal sore de te o
uchimashō
それで手を打ちま
しょう

death shi
死

decaffeinated coffee kafein
nuki no kōhī
カフェイン抜きの
コーヒー

December Jūnigats
十二月

decide kimemas
決めます

we haven't decided yet mada
kimete imasen
まだ決めていません

decision ket·tei
決定

deck (on ship) dek·ki
デッキ

deckchair dek·ki-chea
デッキチェア

deep fukai
深い

definitely mat·tak sono tōri des
まったくそのとおり
です

definitely not mat·tak
chigaimas
まったく違います

degree do
度

(qualification) gakui
学位

delay (noun) okure
遅れ

deliberately waza to
わざと

delicatessen sōzai-ya
惣菜屋

delicious totemo oishī
とてもおいしい

deliver haitats shimas
配達します

delivery haitats
配達

Denmark Dem·māk
デンマーク

dental floss dentaru-fros
デンタルフロス

dentist haisha
歯医者

•••••• DIALOGUE ••••••

it's this one here koko no kore des
this one? kore des ka?
no that one īe, sore des
here? koko des ka?
yes hai

dentures ireba
入れ歯

deodorant deodoranto
デオドラント

department bumon
部門

department store depāto
デパート

departure shup·pats
出発

departure lounge
shup·pats-raunji
出発ラウンジ

depend: it depends bāi ni
yorimas
場合によります

it depends on ... ... ni
yorimas
…によります

deposit (for bike/boat hire)
hoshōkin
保証金

(as part payment) atamakin
頭金

description setsmei
説明

design dezain
デザイン

dessert dezāto
デザート

destination moktekichi
目的地

develop genzō shimas
現像します

•••••• DIALOGUE ••••••

could you develop these films?
kono firum o genzō shite
kuremasen ka?
yes, certainly hai, genzō des ne
when will they be ready? itsu
dekiagarimas ka?
tomorrow afternoon ashita no

gogo des

how much is the four-hour service?

yojikan no sābis wa ikura des ka?

diabetic (noun) tōnyōbyō-kanja
糖尿病患者

diabetic foods

tōnyōbyō-kanja-yō shokhin
糖尿病患者用食品

dial (verb) daiyaru shimas
ダイヤルします

dialling code shigai-kyokban
市外局番

There are three main international phone companies operating in Japan and this is why there are three international codes: 001, 0041, and 0061.

Country codes are:

UK 44
USA 1
Canada 1
Ireland 353
Australia 61
New Zealand 64

When dialling an international number, first dial the international code, then the country code, followed by the area code (without the first 0) and finally the number you wish to call. For operator services, dial (0051).

diamond daiyamondo
ダイアモンド

diaper omuts
おむつ

diarrhoea geri
下痢

do you have any medicine for diarrhoea? geridome wa arimas ka?
下痢止めはあります
か？

diary (business etc) techō
手帳

(for personal experiences) nik·ki
日記

dictionary jisho
辞書

didn't* ...-masen deshta
…－ませんでした
see **not**

die shinimas
死にます

diesel dīzeru-sha
ディーセル車

diet daiet·to
ダイエット

I'm on a diet daiet·to-chū des
ダイエット中です

I have to follow a special diet shokji-seigen ga arimas
食事制限があります

difference chigai
違い

what's the difference? chigai

wa nan des ka?
違いは何ですか？

different chigau
違う

this one is different kore wa chigaimas
これは違います

a different table chigau têburu
違うテーブル

difficult muzkashī
むずかしい

dining room shokdō
食堂

dinner (evening meal) yūshok
夕食

to have dinner shokji o shimas
食事をします

direct (adj) choksets (no)
直接（の）

is there a direct train? choktsū no densha wa arimas ka?
直通の電車はありますか？

direction hōkō
方向

which direction is it? dot·chi no hōkō des ka?
どっちの方向ですか？

is it in this direction? kono hōkō des ka?
この方向ですか？

director (section chief) kachō
課長

(of department) buchō
部長

(of company) shachō
社長

directory enquiries
denwa-ban·gō-an·nai
電話番号案内

> The number for directory enquiries within Japan is 104, but the operator may not speak English. You can call 0057 for international directory enquiries.

dirt yogore
汚れ

dirty kitanai
汚い

disabled: disabled person
shintai-shōgai-sha
身体障害者

is there access for the disabled? shintai-shōgai-sha mo riyō dekimas ka?
身体障害者も利用できますか？

disappear naknarimas
なくなります

it's disappeared naknarimashta
なくなりました

disappointed gak·kari shita
がっかりした

disappointing kitai hazure (no)
期待はずれ（の）

disaster saigai
災害

　this is a disaster kore wa
　hidoi des
　これはひどいです

disco disko
ディスコ

discount waribiki
割引

　is there a discount? waribiki
　ni narimas ka?
　割引になりますか？

disease byōki
病気

disgusting iya (na)
いや（な）

dish (meal) ryōri
料理

　(plate) sara
　皿

disk (for computer) disk
ディスク

disposable diapers/nappies
kami-omuts
紙おむつ

distance kyori
距離

　in the distance tōk ni
　遠くに

district chihō
地方

disturb jama shimas
じゃまします

do not disturb okosanaide
kudasai
起こさないで
ください

diversion (detour)
mawari-michi
回り道

divorced rikon shita
離婚した

dizzy: I feel dizzy memai ga
shimas
めまいがします

do (verb) shimas
します

　what shall we do? nani o
　shimashō ka?
　何をしましょうか？

　how do you do it? dōyat·te
　surundes ka?
　どうやってするん
　ですか？

　will you do it for me? sōshite
　kuremasen ka?
　そうしてくれません
　か？

• • • • • • DIALOGUE • • • • • •

how do you do? hajimemashite,
dōzo yoroshik

nice to meet you o-aidekite
ureshīdes

what do you do? (work) oshigoto
wa nan des ka?

I'm a teacher, and you? watashi
wa kyōshi des ga anata wa?

I'm a student watashi wa gaksei des

what are you doing tonight? komban wa nani o shite imas ka?

we're going out for a drink, do you want to join us? watashitachi wa nomi ni ikimas ga, is·sho ni kimasen ka?

do you want tea? ocha wa ikaga des ka?

I do, but she doesn't watashi wa itadakimas ga, kanojo niwa kek·kō des

doctor isha

医者

we need a doctor isha ga hitsyō des

医者が必要です

please call a doctor isha o yonde kudasai

医者を呼んで
ください

•••••• DIALOGUE ••••••

where does it hurt? doko ga itai des ka?

right here koko des

does that hurt now? kore wa itai des ka?

yes hai

take this to the chemist kore o mot·te ksuri-ya ni ikinasai

document shorui

書類

dog inu

犬

doll nin·gyō

人形

domestic flight koknaisen

国内線

don't!* dame!

だめ！

don't do that! yoshinasai!

よしなさい！

see not

door doa

ドア

(of house: Japanese-style) to

戸

sliding door (wooden lattice and paper) shōji

障子

(patterned) fusma

ふすま

doorman doaman

ドアマン

doorway genkan

玄関

double nibai (no)

二倍

double whisky daburu

ダブル

double bed daburu-bed·do

ダブルベッド

double room daburu

ダブル

doughnut dōnat·ts
ドーナッツ

down: down here kono shita
des
この下です

put it down over there soko
ni oite kudasai
そこに置いて
ください

it's down there on the right
soko o it·te migi des
そこを行って右です

it's further down the road
mot·to saki des
もっと先です

downmarket (restaurant etc)
yasup·poi
安っぽい

downstairs shita
下

dozen ichi-dās (no)
1ダース

half a dozen han-dās (no)
半ダース

draught beer nama-bīru
生ビール

draughty: it's draughty
sukima-kaze ga
hairimas
すきま風がはいり
ます

drawer hikidashi
引出し

drawing e
絵

dreadful hidoi
ひどい

dream (noun) yume
夢

dress (noun) dores
ドレス

dressed: to get dressed fuk o
kimas
服を着ます

dressing gown gaun
ガウン

drink (noun) nomimono
飲物

(alcoholic) osake
お酒

(non-alcoholic) seiryō-inryō
清涼飲料

(verb) nomimas
飲みます

a cold drink tsmetai
nomimono
冷たい飲物

can I get you a drink?
nomimono wa ikaga des ka?
飲物はいかがです
か？

what would you like (to drink)?
nani o nomimas ka?
何を飲みますか？

no thanks, I don't drink
arigatō, demo arukōru wa
nomimasen
ありがとう、でもア
ルコールは飲み
ません

72

I'll just have a drink of water
mizu o kudasai
水をください
see **bar**

---

drinking

If out drinking with Japanese,
remember to pour your
colleagues' drinks before your
own; in return they take care of
your glass. In fact, you'll find
your glass being topped up after every couple of sips, making
it difficult to judge how much
you're drinking. Toasts are
made by saying '**kampai!**'
(cheers!). In recent years beer
has become the most popular
drink, but whisky is also popular. Whisky is drunk with lots of
water and ice: this combination
is called **mizuwari**.

---

drinking water inryōsui
飲料水
is this drinking water? kore
wa inryōsui des ka?
これは飲料水です
か？
drive (verb) unten shimas
運転します
we drove here kuruma de
kimashta
車で来ました
I'll drive you home okut·te

ikimas
送って行きます

---

driving

To drive in Japan you need an
international driver's licence.
The Japanese drive on the left
side of the road. Main roads
have signs both in Japanese and
in English script. You need to
have a detailed road map since,
in large cities, big intersections
can be tricky and one-way systems are infamous. In cities,
roads are extremely congested
and it's advisable to use public
transport whenever you can. Although driving costs a lot due to
the high price of petrol and ex-
orbitant motorway tolls, it's often the best means to explore
rural Japan.

---

driver untenshu
運転手
driving licence
untem-menkyo-shō
運転免許証
drop: just a drop, please (of
drink) hon no skoshi dake
kudasai
ほんの少しだけ
ください
drug (medicine) ksuri
薬

drugs (narcotics) mayak
麻薬

drunk (adj) yop·parat·ta
酔っぱらった

dry (adj) kawaita
乾いた

(wine) karakuchi (no)
辛口（の）

dry-cleaner's kurīning-ya
クリーニング屋

due: he was due to arrive
yesterday kare wa kinō
tōchak suru hazu deshta
彼はきのう到着する
はずでした

when is the train due?
densha wa itsu kuru hazu
des ka?
電車はいつ来るはず
ですか？

dull (pain) zuki-zuki
ずきずき

(weather) kumori (no)
くもり（の）

(uninteresting) tsmaranai
つまらない

dummy (baby's) oshaburi
おしゃぶり

during ... no aida ni
…の間に

dust hokori
ほこり

dustbin gomibako
ごみ箱

dusty hokorip·poi
ほこりっぽい

Dutch (adj) Oranda (no)
オランダ

duty-free (goods) menzei(hin)
免税（品）

duty-free shop menzeihin-ten
免税品店

duvet kakebuton
かけぶとん

E

each (every) sorezore (no)
それぞれ（の）

how much are they each?
hitots ikura des ka?
ひとついくらです
か？

ear mimi
耳

earache: I have earache mimi
ga itai des
耳が痛いです

early hayai
早い

early in the morning asa
hayak
朝早く

I called by earlier
sakihodo mo
ukagaimashta
先程もうかがい
ました

earrings iyaring
イヤリング

earthquake jishin

地震

east higashi

東

in the east higashi ni

東に

Easter Fuk·kats·sai

復活祭

Eastern (oriental) tōyō (no)

東洋（の）

easy yasashī

やさしい

eat tabemas

食べます

we've already eaten

watashitachi wa mō

tabemashta

私たちはもう食べ
ました

eating

Before you start to eat in most restaurants you may be handed a damp, folded white hand towel (**oshibori**) to cleanse your hands. On starting, everyone bows slightly and says 'itadakimas', the equivalent of the French 'bon appetit'.

If using chopsticks, there are a few rules to follow: don't stick them in your rice bowl when not in use; don't pass pieces of food between chopsticks; try not to cross the chopsticks when you →

put them on the table; and never use them to point at things.

If eating soupy noodles, it's considered good form to slurp noisily. If drinking soup, it's fine to bring the bowl to your lips and drink directly from it.

If you enjoyed your meal, it's polite to say '**gochisō sama deshita**' to the chef or waiters on leaving. There's no need to leave a tip.

see **breakfast and lunch**

eau de toilette ō-do-toware

オードトワレ

economy class ekonomī-kuras

エコノミークラス

eel unagi

うなぎ

egg tamago

たまご

either: either ... or ... ... ka ... ka

…か…か

either of them dochiraka

どちらか

elbow hiji

ひじ

electric denki (no)

電気（の）

electrical appliances denki-kig

電気器具

electrician denki-ya

電気屋

electricity denki
電気

elevator erebētā
エレベーター

else: something else nani ka
hoka no mono
何かほかのもの

somewhere else doko ka
hoka no tokoro
どこかほかのところ

•••••• DIALOGUE ••••••

would you like anything else?
hoka ni nani ka irimas ka?
no, nothing else, thanks īe, hoka
niwa nani mo irimasen, arigato

email ī-meiru
イーメール

embassy taishikan
大使館

emergency kinkyū
緊急

this is an emergency! kinkyū
des!
緊急です

emergency exit hijōguchi
非常口

Emperor of Japan Ten·nō-
Heika
天皇陛下

Empress of Japan Kōgō-Heika
皇后陛下

empty kara (no)
から（の）

end (noun) owari
終わり

at the end of the street sono
michi no tskiatari ni
その道の突き当たり
に

when does it end? itsu owari
mas ka?
いつ終わりますか？

engaged (toilet) shiyō-chū
使用中

(phone) hanashi-chū
話し中

(to be married) kon·yak shita
婚約した

engine (car) enjin
エンジン

England Igiris
イギリス

English (adj) Igiris (no)
イギリス（の）

(language) Eigo
英語

I'm English watashi wa
Igiris-jin des
私はイギリス人です

do you speak English? Eigo
ga hanasemas ka?
英語が話せますか？

enjoy: to enjoy oneself
tanoshimimas
楽しみます

•••••• DIALOGUE ••••••

how did you like the film? eiga wa
dō deshta ka?
I enjoyed it very much, did you
enjoy it? totemo tanoshikat·ta
des, anata wa dō deshta ka?

enlargement (of photo)
hiki-nobashi
引き伸ばし

enormous totemo ōkī
とても大きい

enough jūbun
十分

there's not enough
tarimasen
たりません

it's not big enough
chīsasugimas
小さすぎます

that's enough sore de jūbun
des
それで十分です

entrance iriguchi
入り口

(of house) genkan
玄関

envelope fūtō
ふうとう

epileptic tenkan-kanja
てんかん患者

equipment setsbi
設備

(for climbing etc) sōbi
装備

error machigai
まちがい

especially tok ni
とくに

essential hitsyō (na)
必要（な）

it is essential that ... ...-koto
wa hitsyō des
……ーことは必要です

Europe Yōrop·pa
ヨーロッパ

European (adj) Yōrop·pa (no)
ヨーロッパ（の）

even: even the ... ... demo
…でも

even if ... moshi ... demo
もし…でも

evening yūgata
夕方

this evening komban
今晩

in the evening yoru ni
夜に

evening meal yūshok
夕食

eventually tsui ni
ついに

ever: I hardly ever ... hotondo
...-masen
ほとんど…ーません

have you ever been to Hiroshima?
Hiroshima ni it·ta koto ga
arimas ka?
yes, I was there two years ago
hai, ni-nen mae ni ikimashta

every subete no
すべての
every day mainichi
毎日
everyone mina-san
皆さん
everything subete
すべて
everywhere doko demo
どこでも
exactly! sono tōri des!
そのとおりです！
exam shiken
試験
example rei
例
for example tatoeba
たとえば
excellent subarashī
すばらしい
(food) totemo oishī
とてもおいしい
(hotel) ichiryū (no)
一流（の）
excellent! subarashī!
すばらしい！
except ... igai wa
…以外は

excess baggage
chōka-tenimots
超過手荷物
exchange rate ryōgae-rēto
両替レート
exciting omoshiroi
おもしろい
excuse me (to get past) shitsurei
shimas
失礼します
(to say sorry) gomen·nasai
ごめんなさい
(to get attention) chot·to
sumimasen!
ちょっとすみません
executive kanrishok
管理職
exhaust (pipe) haikikan
排気管
exhibition tenrankai
展覧会
exit deguchi
出口
where's the nearest exit?
ichiban chikai deguchi wa
doko des ka?
いちばん近い出口は
どこですか？
expensive takai
高い
experienced keiken no aru
経験のある
explain setsmei shimas
説明します
can you explain that? setsmei

shite kuremasen ka?

説明してくれませんか？

express (mail) soktats

速達

(train) tok·kyū

特急

extension (telephone) naisen

内線

extension ..., please naisen no ..., onegai shimas

内線の…、お願いします

extension lead encho-kōdo

延長コード

extra: can we have an extra one? mō hitots moraemasen ka?

もうひとつもらえませんか？

do you charge extra for that? sore wa bets-ryōkin des ka?

それは別料金ですか？

extraordinary mezurashī

めずらしい

extremely totemo

とても

eye me

目

will you keep an eye on my suitcase for me? chot·to sūtskēs o mite ite kuremasen ka?

ちょっとスーッケー

スを見ていてくれませんか？

---

eye contact

In formal situations Japanese make less eye contact than Westerners. It's considered impolite to stare. However, a moderate level of eye contact is accepted, especially when you are engaged in a conversation.

---

eyeglasses (US: spectacles) megane

めがね

eyeliner ai-rainā

アイライナー

eye make-up remover ai-mēk-otoshi

アイメーク落し

eye shadow ai-shadō

アイシャドウ

F

face kao

かお

---

loss of face

Traditionally, for Japanese, losing face is something shameful, and they avoid it by various means. They don't express strong emotions and vagueness and understatement character-

→

ize their speech. Another approach they adopt is to follow other people's behaviour so that they don't stand out.

This reserve may cause great frustration to Westerners, especially when no decisions seem to be being made. In formal or business situations, the only thing you can do is not to show that you are annoyed. In a more informal, friendly setting, you can suggest what you would like to do, but do this in a modest way showing great care for the feelings of the other person. They will not find this offensive, especially when they know that you are from a different culture.

face mask (for colds) mask
マスク
factory kōjō
工場
Fahrenheit kashi
華氏
faint (verb) ki o ushinaimas
気を失います
she's fainted kanojo wa ki o ushinaimashta
彼女は気を失いました
I feel faint fura-fura shimas
ふらふらします

fair (funfair) yūenchi
遊園地
(trade fair) mihon-ichi
見本市
(impartial) kōhei (na)
公平（な）
(amount) kanari (no)
かなり（の）
fairly (quite) kanari
かなり
fake (adj) nise (no)
にせ（の）
fall (US: season) aki
秋
in the fall aki ni
秋に
fall (verb) korobimas
ころびます
she's had a fall kanojo wa korobimashta
彼女はころびました
false (not true) machigat-ta
まちがった
family kazok
家族
famous yūmei (na)
有名（な）
fan (electrical) sempūki
扇風機
(handheld) sensu
せんす
(sports) fan
ファン
fantastic subarashī
すばらしい

far tōi
遠い

• • • • • DIALOGUE • • • • •

is it far from here? koko kara tōi
des ka?

no, not very far īe, amari tōk nai
des

well how far? dono kurai des ka?

it's about 20 kilometres ni-
juk·kiro kurai des

fare ryōkin
料金

fare box (on buses) ryōkinbako
料金箱

farm nōjō
農場

fashionable oshare (na)
おしゃれ（な）

fast hayai
速い

fat (person) futot·ta
太った

(on meat) aburami
あぶらみ

father (one's own) chichi
父

(someone else's) otō-san
お父さん

father-in-law (one's own) giri no
chichi
義理の父

(someone else's) giri no

otō-san
義理のお父さん

faucet jaguchi
じゃ口

fault: sorry, it was my fault
gomen·nasai, watashi no sei
deshta
ごめんなさい、私の
せいでした

it's not my fault watashi no
sei dewa arimasen
私のせいではあり
ません

faulty chōshi ga okashī
調子がおかしい

favourite oki ni iri (no)
お気に入り（の）

fax (noun) fak·ks
ファックス

(verb) fak·ks o okurimas
ファックスを送り
ます

February Nigats
二月

feel kanjimas
感じます

I feel hot atsui des
暑いです

I feel unwell kibun ga yok
nai des
気分がよくないです

I feel like going for a walk
sampo ni ikitai des
散歩にいきたいです

how are you feeling? ikaga

des ka?
いかがですか？
I'm feeling better zut·to ī des
ずっといいです

fence (noun) hei
塀

fencing fensing
フェンシング
Japanese fencing kendō
剣道

ferry ferī
フェリー

> There are ferry services to most of Japan's islands. You can purchase tickets in advance from travel agencies or just before boarding. Ferries are slow but inexpensive compared to flights. The journey, however, might be unpleasant and the service unreliable in the rainy or typhoon seasons.

festival omatsuri
お祭り

fetch (person) tsurete kimas
連れてきます
(object) tot·te kimas
取ってきます
I'll fetch him kare o yonde kimashō
彼を呼んできましょう
will you come and fetch me
later? atode mukae ni kite kuremasen ka?
後でむかえに来てくれませんか？

feverish netsup·poi
熱っぽい

few: a few skoshi no
少しの
a few days ni-san nichi
二三日

fiancé(e) kon·yaksha
婚約者

field hatake
畑

fight (noun) kenka
けんか

fill in kinyū shimas
記入します
do I have to fill this in?
kinyū shinakte wa narimasen ka?
記入しなくてはなりませんか？

fill up ip·pai ni shimas
いっぱいにします
fill it up, please ip·pai ni shite kudasai
いっぱいにしてください

filling (in cake, sandwich) nakami
なかみ
(in tooth) ha no tsmemono
歯の詰めもの

film (movie) eiga
映画

(for camera) firum
フィルム

••••• DIALOGUE •••••

do you have this kind of film?
kon·na firum wa arimas ka?

yes, how many exposures? hai,
nam·mai dori des ka?

36 san-jū-rok-mai des

film processing genzō
現像

final (adj) saigo (no)
最後（の）

find (verb) mitskemas
見つけます

I can't find it mitskarimasen
見つかりません

I've found it mitskemashta
見つけました

find out shirabemas
調べます

could you find out for me?
shirabete kuremasen ka?
調べてくれません
か？

fine (weather) hareta
晴れた

(punishment) bak·kin
罰金

••••• DIALOGUE •••••

how are you? ogenki des ka?

I'm fine, thanks okagesama de

is that OK? sore de ī des ka?

that's fine, thanks ē, kek·kō des

finger yubi
指

finish (verb) owarimas
終わります

I haven't finished yet mada
owat·te imasen
まだ終わっていませ
ん

when does it finish? itsu
owarimas ka?
いつ終わりますか？

fire (in hearth) hi
火

(blaze) kaji
火事

fire! kaji da!
火事だ！

can we light a fire here? koko
de hi o taite mo ī des ka?
ここで火をたいても
いいですか？

it's on fire kaji des
火事です

fire alarm kasai-hōchiki
火災報知機

fire brigade shōbōtai
消防隊

The number for the fire brigade
is 119. Since this number is also
the same as for the ambulance
service, you must specify the
service you wish.

fire escape hijōguchi
非常口

fire extinguisher shōkaki
消火器

fireworks hanabi
花火

first saisho (no)
最初（の）

I was first watashi ga saki
deshta
私が先でした

at first saisho ni
最初に

the first time hajimete
はじめて

first on the left hidarigawa no
saisho
左がわの最初

first aid ōkyū-te-ate
応急手当

first-aid kit kyūkyūbako
救急箱

first class (train) gurīnsha
グリーン車
   (plane) fāsto-kuras
ファーストクラス

first-class ticket (train)
gurīnsha jōshaken
グリーン車乗車券
   (plane) fāsto-kuras
chiket·to
ファーストクラスチ
ケット

first floor ni-kai
二階
   (US) ik·kai
一階

first name namae
名前

fish (noun) sakana
さかな

fishmonger's sakana-ya
魚屋

fit (attack) hos·sa
発作

fit: it doesn't fit me sore wa
watashi ni aimasen
それは私に合い
ません

fitting room shichak-shits
試着室

fix (verb: arrange) tehai shimas
手配します

can you fix this? (repair)
naosemas ka?
なおせますか？

fizzy tansan (no)
炭酸（の）

fizzy orange tansan-iri orenji
jūs
炭酸入りオレンジジ
ュース

flag hata
はた

flannel taoru
タオル

flash (for camera) frash
フラッシュ

flat (noun: apartment) apāto
アパート
   (adj) taira (na)
たいら（な）

I've got a flat tyre taiya ga pank shimashta
タイヤがパンクしました

flavour fūmi
風味

flea nomi
のみ

flight hikō
飛行

flight number bim·mei
便名

flood kōzui
洪水

floor (of room) yuka
床

(storey) kai
階

on the floor yuka ni
床に

florist's hana-ya
花屋

flower hana
花

flower arranging ikebana
生け花

flu infruenza
インフルエンザ

fluent: he speaks fluent Japanese kare wa ryūchō na Nihon-go o hanashimas
彼は流暢な日本語を話します

fly (noun) hae
ハエ

(verb) tobimas
飛びます

can we fly there? hikōki de ikemas ka?
飛行機で行けますか？

fog kiri
霧

foggy: it's foggy kiri ga dete imas
霧が出ています

food (in general) tabemono
食べ物

(in shop) shokryōhin
食料品

(in restaurant) ryōri
料理

food poisoning shokchūdok
食中毒

food shop/store shokryōhin-ten
食料品店

foot (of person) ashi
足

on foot aruite
歩いて

football (game) sak·kā
サッカー

(ball) sak·kā-bōru
サッカーボール

footwarmer kotats
こたつ

for: do you have something for ...? (headache/diarrhoea etc)

... ni kik ksuri wa arimas ka?
…に効く薬はありま
すか？

•••••• DIALOGUES ••••••

who's the tempura for? tempura
wa dochira des ka?
that's for me watashi des
and this one? kore wa dochira
des ka?
that's for her kanojo des

where do I get the bus for
Shinjuku? Shinjuku-iki no bas wa
doko de noremas ka?
the bus for Shinjuku leaves from
Tokyo station Shinjuku-iki no bas
wa Tōkyō eki kara dete imas
how long have you been here?
koko niwa mō dono kurai ni
narimas ka?

I've been here for two days, how about
you? futska des ga, anata wa?
I've been here for a week
is·shūkan ni narimas

forehead odeko
おでこ
foreign gaikok (no)
外国
foreigner gaijin
外人
forest mori
森
forget wasuremas
忘れます

I forget, I've forgotten
wasurete shimaimashta
忘れてしまいました
fork fōk
フォーク
(in road) bunkiten
分岐点
form (document) yōshi
用紙
formal seishiki (na)
正式（な）
(dress) aratamat·ta
あらたまった
fortnight nishūkan
二週間
fortunately un·yok
運よく
forward: could you forward my
mail? tegami o tensō shite
kuremasen ka?
手紙を転送して
くれませんか？
forwarding address tensō saki
転送先
foundation (make-up)
fandēshon
ファンデーション
fountain (ornamental) funsui
噴水
(for drinking) kyūsuiki
給水器
foyer robī
ロビー
fracture (noun) kos·sets
骨折

France Frans
フランス

free (no charge) tada, muryō
ただ、無料

is it free (of charge)? muryō
des ka?
無料ですか？

freeway kōsokdōro
高速道路

freezer reitōko
冷凍庫

French (adj) Frans (no)
フランス（の）

(language) Frans-go
フランス語

French fries french-frai
フレンチフライ

frequent tabitabi (no)
たびたび（の）

how frequent is the bus to
Kobe? Kōbe-iki no bas wa
nambon kurai dete imas ka?
神戸行きのバスは何
本くらいでています
か？

fresh (food) shinsen (na)
新鮮（な）

Friday Kin·yōbi
金曜日

fridge reizōko
冷蔵庫

fried itameta
いためた

fried egg medamayaki
めだまやき

fried rice chāhan
チャーハン

friend tomodachi
友達

friendly shinsets (na)
親切（な）

from kara
から

when does the next train from
Hakata arrive? tsgi no Hakata
hats no res·sha wa itsu
tskimas ka?
次の博多発の列車は
いつ着きますか？

from Monday to Friday
Getsyōbi kara Kin·yōbi
月曜日から金曜日

from next Thursday tsgi no
Mok·yōbi kara
次の木曜日から

••••• DIALOGUE •••••

where are you from? doko kara
kimashta ka?

I'm from Manchester Manchestā
kara des

front mae
前

in front mae ni
前に

in front of the hotel hoteru no
mae ni
ホテルの前に

at the front mae de
前で

frost shimo
霜

frozen reitō shita
冷凍した

fruit kudamono
くだもの

fruit juice frūts-jūs
フルーツジュース

full ip·pai
いっぱい

it's full of ... ... de ip·pai des
…でいっぱいです

I'm full onaka ga ip·pai des
おなかがいっぱい
です

full board san-shok-tski
三食付き

fun: it was fun omoshirokat·ta
des
おもしろかったです

funeral osōshiki
お葬式

funny (strange) okashī
おかしい

(amusing) omoshiroi
おもしろい

furniture kag
家具

further mot·to tōk
もっと遠く

it's further down the road
sono michi no mot·to saki
des
その道のもっと先
です

how much further is it to Kinkakuji?
Kinkakuji ewa dono kurai
arimas ka?

about 5 kilometres go-kiro kurai
des

fuse (noun) hyūz
ヒューズ

future shōrai
将来

in future kore kara
これから

G

gallon galon
ガロン

game (cards etc) gēm
ゲーム

(match) shiai
試合

garage (for fuel) gasorin-stando
ガソリンスタンド

(for repairs) shūrikōjō
修理工場

(for parking) shako
車庫

garden niwa
庭

garlic nin·nik
ニンニク

gas gas
ガス

(US) gasorin
ガソリン

gas permeable lenses
sanso-tōka-sei kontakto-renzu
酸素透過性コンタクトレンズ

gas station (US) gasorin-stando
ガソリンスタンド

gate mon
門

(at airport) gēto
ゲート

gay homo (no)
ホモ

gay bar gei-bā
ゲイバー

gears (in car) giya
ギア

general (adj) ip·pan-teki (na)
一般的（な）

gents' toilet dansei-yō toire
男性用トイレ

genuine (antique etc) hom·mono (no)
本物（の）

German (adj) Doits (no)
ドイツ（の）

Germany Doits
ドイツ

---

gestures

Some gestures can be readily understood by Westerners; for example, an invitation to a drinking party by miming the →

holding of a sake cup and performing a slight 'throw-away' motion with the wrist.

However, misunderstandings can occur with certain gestures. Making a circle with the index finger and thumb traditionally refers to **okane** (money) in Japan, while in the West this is a sign for 'OK'. Calling somebody towards oneself is achieved by extending the arm slightly, palm turned downwards, and fluttering the fingers. From a distance this can be interpreted by Westerners as waving goodbye, exactly the opposite of the effect intended.

The hand waved limply in front of the face, with the thumb nearest to it, indicates somebody's desire to pass closely in front of another person. It is accompanied by one or several slight bows.

You should avoid touching people: for example, don't slap them on the back or grab them by the arm when the discussion gets animated as this could cause offence. It's considered rude to point at a person with one's finger. Neither should you point to objects with your foot.

get (fetch) te ni iremas
手に入れます

could you get me another one, please? mō hitots moraemas ka?
もうひとつもらえ
ますか？

how do I get to …? … ewa dō ikeba ī des ka?
…へはどう行けばい
いですか？

do you know where I can get them? sore wa dokode te ni hairimas ka?
それはどこで手に入
りますか？

• • • • • • DIALOGUE • • • • •

can I get you a drink? nomimono wa ikaga des ka?

no, I'll get this one, what would you like? ie, kore wa watashi mochi des, nani ga ī des ka?

a beer, please bīru kudasai

get back (return)
modorimas
戻ります

get in (arrive) tōchak shimas
到着します

get off orimas
降ります

where do I get off? doko de orireba ī des ka?
どこで降りればいい
ですか？

get on (to train etc) norimas
乗ります

get out (of car etc) orimas
降ります

(take out) toridashimas
取り出します

get up (in the morning) okimas
起きます

gift okurimono
贈り物

An invitation to someone's home is a rare honour. If you receive one you should take a gift of food, drink, or flowers. Japanese have a social custom of exchanging gifts around New Year and in summer. Gifts should always be wrapped, but most shops and all department stores do this for you.
When offering a gift, make a polite but modest presentation expressing your hope that the person will like it; when receiving a gift, you should show your gratitude for their consideration as well as for the gift itself. Most importantly, never refuse a gift offered to you.

gift shop gifto-shop·p
ギフトショップ

gin jin
ジン

a gin and tonic, please
jin-tonik·k o onegai
shimas
ジントニックをお願
いします

girl on·na no ko
女の子

girlfriend gāru-frendo
ガールフレンド

give agemas
あげます

can you give me some
change? kore o kuzushite
kuremasen ka?
これをくずしてくれ
ませんか？

I gave it to him sore wa kare
ni watashimashta
それは彼にわたし
ました

will you give this to ...? kore o
... ni watashite kuremasen
ka?
これを…にわたして
くれませんか？

give back kaeshimas
返します

glad ureshī
うれしい

glass (material) garas
ガラス

(for drinking) kop·p
コップ

a glass of wine wain o ip·pai
ワインを一杯

glasses (spectacles) megane
めがね

gloves tebukuro
手袋

glue (noun) set·chak-zai
接着剤

go ikimas
行きます

we'd like to go to Tokyo
Disneyland
Tōkyō-Dizunīrando ni it·te
mitai des
東京ディズニーラン
ドに行ってみたい
です

where are you going? doko e
ikundes ka?
どこへ行くんです
か？

where does this bus go?
kono bas wa doko e ikimas
ka?
このバスはどこへ行
きますか？

let's go! ikimashō!
行きましょう！

hamburger to go hanbāgā o
teik-auto de
ハンバーガーをテイ
クアウトで

she's gone (left) kanojo wa
it·te shimaimashta
彼女は行ってしまい
ました

where has he gone? kare wa

doko e ikimashta ka?

彼はどこへ行き
ましたか？

I went there last week senshū

soko e ikimashta

先週そこへ行き
ました

go away dekakemas

出かけます

go away! at·chi e it·te!

あっちへいって！

go back (return) kaerimas

帰ります

go down (the stairs etc) shita e
ikimas

下へ行きます

go in naka e hairimas

なかへ入ります

go out (in the evening) gaishuts
shimas

外出します

do you want to go out tonight?
komban dekaketai des ka?

今晩出かけたいです
か？

go through tōrinukemas

通り抜けます

go up (the stairs etc) ue e ikimas

上へ行きます

God kami-sama

神様

goggles gōguru

ゴーグル

gold kin

金

goldfish kin·gyo

金魚

golf goruf

ゴルフ

golf course goruf-jō

ゴルフ場

good ī

よい

good! yokat·ta!

よかった！

it's no good sore wa dame
des

それはだめ
です

goodbye (formal) sayōnara

さようなら

(informal) dewa mata

ではまた

(between friends) jā ne

じゃあね

> The word 'sayōnara' is usually
> only used when you won't be
> seeing someone again for a long
> time; to say goodbye you could
> say: 'oyasuminasai' (good
> night) or 'dewa mata' (see you
> again). To close friends you
> can use the familiar 'jā ne'
> (cheerio).

good evening komban wa

こんばんは

Good Friday Sei-Kin·yōbi

聖金曜日

good morning ohayō gozaimas
おはようございます

good night (when leaving) osaki
ni
お先に
(when going to bed)
oyasuminasai
おやすみなさい

got: we've got to leave mō
ikanakereba narimasen
もう行かなければな
りません

have you got any …? … o
mot·te imas ka?
を持っていますか？

government seif
政府

gradually dandan
だんだん

gram(me) guram
グラム

granddaughter (one's own)
magomusme
孫娘
(someone else's) omago-san
お孫さん

grandfather (one's own) sof
祖父
(someone else's) ojī-san
おじいさん

grandmother (one's own) sobo
祖母
(someone else's) obā-san
おばあさん

grandson (one's own)

magomusko
孫息子
(someone else's) omago-san
お孫さん

grapefruit gurēp-frūts
グレープフルーツ

grapes budō
ぶどう

grass ksa
草

grateful ureshī
うれしい

gravy gurēbī-sōs
グレービーソース

great (excellent) subarashī
すばらしい
that's great! sore wa sugoi!
それはすごい！
a great success daiseikō
大成功

Great Britain Eikok
英国

greedy yokbari (na)
よくばり（な）
(for food) kuishimbō (no)
くいしんぼうの

green midori (no)
みどり（の）

green card (car insurance)
jidōsha-hoken
自動車保険

greengrocer's yao-ya
八百屋

greeting people
To greet people before noon, you should say **'ohayō gozaimas!'** (good morning) and then up to around 5pm, use **'kon·nichi wa'** (literally: good day). After 5pm, use **'komban wa'** (good evening).

Minshuk are similar to bed and breakfast accommodation found in the West. Prices are very reasonable although service is minimal. Meals are provided and you can usually expect traditional home cooking. As with all types of accommodation in Japan, reservations are recommended.

grey hai-iro (no)
灰色（の）
grilled guriru de yaita
グリルで焼いた
grocer's shokryōhin-ten
食料品店
ground jimen
地面
on the ground jimen ni
地面に
ground floor ik·kai
一階
group gurūp
グループ
guarantee (noun) hoshō
保証
is it guaranteed? hoshō-tski des ka?
保証付きですか？
guest okyak-sama
お客さま
guesthouse minshuk
民宿

guide (person) gaido
ガイド
guidebook gaido-buk·k
ガイドブック
guided tour gaido-tski tuā
ガイド付きツアー
gum (in mouth) haguki
歯ぐき
gun (rifle) jū
銃
(pistol) pistoru
ピストル
gym jim
ジム

H

hair kami
髪
hairbrush burashi
ブラシ
haircut (man's) sampats
散髪

(woman's) heya-kat·to
ヘアカット

hairdresser's (men's) toko-ya
床屋

(women's) biyōin
美容院

hairdryer doraiyā
ドライヤー

hair gel jeru
ジェル

hairgrips heya-pin
ヘヤピン

hair spray heya-suprē
ヘヤスプレー

half hambun
半分

half an hour han-jikan
半時間

half a litre han-rit·toru
半リットル

about half that sono hambun kurai
その半分くらい

half board asayū-nishok-tski
朝夕二食付き

half-bottle hāf-botoru
ハーフボトル

half fare hangak
半額

half-price hangak (no)
半額（の）

ham ham
ハム

hamburger hambāgā
ハンバーガー

hand te
手

holding hands

Although excessive displays of emotion in public are considered inappropriate, the Japanese attitude towards expressions of affection is becoming more relaxed. In cities, you see a lot of young couples openly holding hands in the street, but it's less acceptable to display affection in rural areas.

handbag handobag·g
ハンドバッグ

handbrake handoburēki
ハンドブレーキ

handkerchief hankachi
ハンカチ

While sniffling is accepted, loud blowing of one's nose in a handkerchief is not. Should you have a cold, try to wipe your nose silently and discreetly with tissues. You often see people wearing a gauze mask over the mouth and nose when they have a cold.

handle (on door) tot·te
取っ手

(on suitcase) mochite
持ち手

hand luggage tenimots
手荷物

hang-gliding hanguraiding
ハングライディング

hangover futskayoi
ふつか酔い

I've got a hangover futskayoi
des
ふつか酔いです

happen okorimas
起ります

what's happening? dō nat·te
imas ka?
どうなっています
か？

(what's on?) nani o yat·te imas
ka?
何をやっています
か？

(what's wrong?) dō shitandes
ka?
どうしたんですか？

what has happened? nani ga
at·tandes ka?
何があったんです
か？

happy ureshī
うれしい

I'm not happy about this
sore niwa nat·tok
dekimasen
それには納得でき
ません

harbour minato
港

hard katai
かたい

(difficult) muzkashī
むずかしい

hard-boiled egg
katayude-tamago
かたゆでたまご

hard lenses hādo-kontakto
ハードコンタクト

hardly: I hardly ever ... hotondo
...-masen
ほとんど…―ません

I hardly ever go met·ta ni
ikimasen
めったに行きません

I hardly know him kare no
koto wa hotondo shirimasen
彼のことはほとんど
知りません

hardware shop kanamono-ya
金物屋

hat bōshi
ぼうし

hate (verb) kirai des
きらいです

have mochimas
持ちます

can I have a ...? ... o morat·te
mo ī des ka?
…をもらってもいい
ですか？

can we have some ...? ... o
ikutska moraemas ka?
…をいくつかもらえ
ますか？

do you have …? … o mot·te imas ka?
…を持っていますか？

what'll you have (to drink)? nani ni shimas ka?
何にしますか？

I have to … …-nakte wa narimasen
…―なくてはなりません

I have to leave now mō ikanakte wa narimasen
もう行かなくてはなりません

do I have to …? …-nakte wa narimasen ka?
…―なくてはなりませんか？

hayfever kafun-shō
花粉症

he* kare
彼

head atama
あたま

headache zutsū
頭痛

headlights hed·do-raito
ヘッドライト

headphones hed·do-hon
ヘッドホン

healthy (person) kenkō (na)
健康（な）

(food) karada ni ī
からだにいい

hear kikoemas
きこえます

• • • • • DIALOGUE • • • • •

can you hear me? kikoemas ka?
I can't hear you, could you repeat that? kikoemasen, mō ichido it·te kuremasen ka?

hearing aid hochōki
補聴器

heart shinzō
心臓

heart attack shinzōmahi
心臓麻痺

heat atsusa
暑さ

heater (in room) dambō
暖房

(in car) hītā
ヒーター

heating dambō
暖房

heavy omoi
おもい

heel (of foot) kakato
かかと

(of shoe) hīru
ヒール

could you heel these? hīru o naoshite kuremasen ka?
ヒールをなおしてくれませんか？

height (of person) shincho
身長

(of object) takasa
高さ

helicopter herikoptā
ヘリコプター

hello kon·nichi wa
こんにちは

(on phone) moshi-moshi
もしもし

helmet (for motorcycle)
herumet·to
ヘルメット

help (noun) kyōryok
協力

(verb) tetsdaimas
手伝います

help! taskete!
たすけて！

can you help me? tetsdat·te
kuremasen ka?
手伝ってくれません
か？

thank you very much for your
help tetsdat·te kurete dōmo
arigatō
手伝ってくれてどう
もありがとう

helpful yak ni tats
役に立つ

hepatitis kan-en
肝炎

her* kanojo (o)
彼女（を）

to her kanojo ni
彼女に

with her kanojo to
彼女と

for her kanojo no tame ni
彼女のために

that's her kanojo des
彼女です

I haven't seen her kanojo
niwa at·te imasen
彼女には会って
いません

her ... kanojo no ...
彼女の…

it's her car sore wa kanojo
no kuruma des
それは彼女の車です

herbal tea hāb-tī
ハーブティー

herbs (for cooking) hāb
ハーブ

(medicinal) yaksō
薬草

here koko
ここ

here is/are ... ... wa koko des
…はここです

here you are (offering) hai,
dōzo
はい、どうぞ

hers* kanojo no
彼女の

that's hers sore wa kanojo
no des
それは彼女のです

hey! chot·to!
ちょっと！

hi! (hello) dōmo!
どうも！

high takai
高い

highchair bebī-chea
ベビーチェア

highway kōsokdōro
高速道路

hill oka
丘

him* kare (o)
彼（を）

to him kare ni
彼に

with him kare to
彼と

for him kare no tame ni
彼のために

that's him kare des
彼です

I haven't seen him kare niwa at·te imasen
彼には会っていません

hip oshiri
おしり

hire karimas
借ります

for hire rentaru (no)
レンタル（の）

where can I hire a bike? doko de jitensha ga kariraremas ka?
どこで自転車が借りられますか？

see rent

his* kare no
彼の

it's his car sore wa kare no kuruma des
それは彼の車です

that's his sore wa kare no des
それは彼のです

hitch-hike hit·chi-haik
ヒッチハイク

hobby shumi
趣味

hold (verb) mochimas
持ちます

hole ana
あな

holiday yasumi
休み

on holiday yasumi de
休みで

Holland Oranda
オランダ

home uchi
うち

at home (in my house) uchi de
うちで

(in my country) watashi no kuni de
私の国で

we go home tomorrow watashitachi wa ashita kikok shimas
私たちはあした帰国します

honey hachimits
はちみつ

honeymoon shinkon-ryokō
新婚旅行

hood (US: of car) bon·net·to
ボンネット

hope kibō
希望

I hope so sō da to ī des ne
そうだといいですね

I hope not sō de nai to ī des ne
そうでないといいですね

hopefully dekireba
できれば

horrible osoroshī
おそろしい

horse uma
馬

horse riding jōba
乗馬

hospital byōin
病院

hospitality omotenashi
おもてなし

thank you for your hospitality omotenashi dōmo arigatō gozaimashta
おもてなしどうもありがとうございました

hot atsui
暑い

(spicy) karai
からい

I'm hot atsui des
暑いです

it's hot today kyō wa atsui des
きょうは暑いです

hotel hoteru
ホテル

(Japanese-style) ryokan
旅館

In Japan accommodation tends to be very expensive. Japanese-style traditional inns are called **ryokan** and are completely different from Western-style hotels. The rooms have tatami mats and sliding paper doors and they are decorated with scrolls and Japanese flower arrangements. Bathrooms are generally communal. Meals are beautifully laid out in the room by a maid and usually include a wide range of local specialities. After you have finished, the maid will clear the table and lay out the futons for sleeping. Breakfast is included and will be Japanese-style: rice, fish, pickles, miso soup and green tea. Although they are fairly →

expensive, ryokan are worth every penny for the level of service and comfort they provide. Welcome extras in your hotel room may include slippers, facilities for brewing Japanese tea, as well as a neatly folded **yukata** and **obi** (thin cotton gown with belt) which is used for nightwear. Take care to fold the left part of the (buttonless) yukata over the right before girding yourself with the obi – the opposite way, right over left, is used for the corpse at a funeral. Many ryokan are built on the site of an **onsen** (hot spring). For something equivalent to Western tastes, try a business hotel. These have fewer frills than international hotels (for example, they do not have room service), but are considerably cheaper. Rooms (usually Western-style) are small, but clean and functional with an en-suite bathroom/toilet. Usually they are located near railway stations. You might have trouble making yourself understood in English.

hotel room hoteru no heya
ホテルの部屋

hot spring onsen
温泉
hour jikan
時間
house ie
家
hovercraft hobā-kurafto
ホバークラフト
how dō
どう
how many? ikuts?
いくつ？
how do you do?
hajimemashte
はじめまして

• • • • • DIALOGUE • • • • •

how are you? ogenki des ka?
fine, thanks, and you? e, okagesama de, sochira wa dō des ka?

how much is it? ikura des ka?
520 yen go-hyaku-ni-jū-en des
I'll take it ja, sore o kudasai

humid mushi-atsui
蒸し暑い
hungry onaka ga suita
おなかがすいた
are you hungry? onaka ga sukimashta ka?
おなかがすきました
か？
hurry (verb) isogimas
急ぎます

I'm in a hurry isoide imas
急いでいます

there's no hurry isog koto wa
arimasen
急ぐことはあり
ません

hurry up! isoide kudasai!
急いでください！

hurt (verb) itamimas
痛みます

it really hurts totemo
itamimas
とても痛みます

husband (one's own) shujin
主人

(someone else's) goshujin
御主人

my husband uchi no shujin
うちの主人

hydrofoil suichū-yoksen
水中翼船

I

I watashi
私

ice kōri
氷

with ice kōri-iri
氷入り

no ice, thanks kōri
wa ī des
氷はいいです

ice cream ais-kurīm
アイスクリーム

ice-cream cone ais-kurīm no
kōn
アイスクリームの
コーン

ice lolly ais-kyandī
アイスキャンディー

idea kan·gae
考え

idiot hakchi
白痴

if moshi
もし

ill byōki (no)
病気（の）

I feel ill kibun ga warui des
気分が悪いです

illness byōki
病気

imitation (leather etc) mozōhin
模造品

immediately sug
すぐ

important taisets (na)
大切（な）

it's very important totemo
taisets des
とても大切です

it's not important dō demo ī
koto des
どうでもいいこと
です

impossible fukanō (na)
不可能（な）

impressive inshō-teki (na)
印象的（な）

improve: I want to improve my Japanese Nihon-go ga umak naritai des

日本語がうまくなりたいです

in: it's in the centre sore wa hankagai ni arimas

それは繁華街にあります

in my car watashi no kuruma no naka

私の車のなか

in Sapporo Sapporo ni

札幌に

in May Gogats ni

五月に

in English Eigo de

英語で

in Japanese Nihon-go de

日本語で

in two days from now ima kara futska de

いまから二日で

in five minutes go-fun de

五分で

is he in? kare wa imas ka?

彼はいますか？

incense okō

お香

inch inchi

インチ

include fukmimas

含みます

does that include meals?

shokji wa komi des ka?

食事は込みですか？

is that included? sore mo ryōkin ni fukmarete imas ka?

それも料金に含まれていますか？

inconvenient fuben (na)

不便（な）

incredible shinjirarenai

信じられない

Indian (adj) Indo (no)

インド（の）

indicator winkā

ウィンカー

indigestion shōkafuryō

消化不良

indoor pool okunai-pūru

屋内プール

indoors okunai

屋内

inexpensive tegoro (na)

手ごろ（な）

infection kansenshō

感染症

infectious densensei (no)

伝染性（の）

inflammation enshō

炎症

informal kudaketa

くだけた

information jōhō

情報

do you have any information about ...? ... ni tsuite no jōhō

ga arimas ka?
…についての情報が
ありますか？

information desk an·naisho
案内所

injection chūsha
注射

injured kega o shita
けがをした
she's been injured kanojo wa
kega o shimashta
彼女はけがをし
ました

inn (Japanese-style) ryokan
旅館

inner tube (for tyre) chūb
チューブ

insect mushi
虫

insect bite mushi-sasare
虫さされ
do you have anything for
insect bites? mushi-
sasare no ksuri wa arimas
ka?
虫さされの薬はあり
ますか？

insect repellent mushiyoke
虫よけ

inside: inside the hotel hoteru
no naka
ホテルのなか
let's sit inside naka ni
suwarimashō
なかに座りましょう

insist īharimas
言いはります
I insist dōka zehi
どうかぜひ
if you insist dō shitemo to
iunara
どうしてもと
いうなら

instant coffee instanto-kōhī
インスタント
コーヒー

instead: give me that one
instead kawari ni sot·chi o
kudasai
かわりにそっちを
ください
instead of … … no kawari ni
…のかわりに

insulin inshurin
インシュリン

insurance hoken
保険

intelligent atama ga ī
あたまがいい

interested: I'm interested in … …
ni kyōmi ga arimas
…に興味があります

interesting omoshiroi
おもしろい
that's very interesting sore wa
totemo omoshiroi des
それはとてもおもし
ろいです

international koksai-teki (na)
国際的（な）

internet intānet·to
インターネット

interpreter tsūyak
通訳

intersection kōsaten
交差点

interval (at theatre) kyūkei-jikan
休憩時間

into … ni
…に

I'm not into … … wa suki dewa arimasen
…は好きではあり
ません

introduce shōkai shimas
紹介します

may I introduce …? (formal)
… o goshōkai itashimas
…をご紹介いたし
ます

(informal) … o shōkai shimas
…を紹介します

invitation shōtai
招待

invite shōtai shimas
招待します

invoice seikyūsho
請求書

Ireland Airurando
アイルランド

Irish Airurando (no)
アイルランド
（の）

I'm Irish watashi wa

Airurando-jin des
私はアイルランド人
です

iron (for ironing) airon
アイロン

can you iron these for me?
kore ni airon o kakete kuremasen ka?
これにアイロンをか
けてくれませんか？

is* … des
…です

island shima
島

it sore
それ

it is … sore wa … des
それは…です

is it …? … des ka?
…ですか？

where is it? doko des ka?
どこですか？

it's him kare des
彼です

it was … … deshta
…でした

Italian (adj) Itaria (no)
イタリア（の）

Italy Itaria
イタリア

itch: it itches kayui des
かゆいです

ivory zōge
ぞうげ

J

jacket jaket·to
ジャケット

jam (preserve) jam
ジャム

jammed: it's jammed tsmat·te imas
つまっています

January Ichigats
一月

Japan Nihon
日本

Japanese (adj) Nihon (no)
日本（の）
(noun) Nihon-jin
日本人
(language) Nihon-go
日本語
the Japanese Nihon-jin
日本人

Japanese food washok
和食

Japanese-style wafū
和風

Japan Sea Nihon-kai
日本海

jar (noun) bin
びん

jaw ago
あご

jazz jazu
ジャズ

jeans jīnzu
ジーンズ

jellyfish kurage
くらげ

jersey sētā
セーター

jetty sambashi
さんばし

jeweller's hōseki-ten
宝石店

jewellery hōseki
宝石

Jewish Yudaya (no)
ユダヤ（の）

job shigoto
仕事

jogging joging
ジョギング

joke jōdan
冗談

joss stick osenko
お線香

journey ryokō
旅行
have a good journey! sore dewa tanoshī ryokō o!
それでは楽しい旅行を！

judo jūdō
柔道

jug mizusashi
水さし
a jug of water mizusashi ip·pai no mizu
水さし一杯の水

juice fres·sh·jūs
フレッシュジュース

July Shichigats
七月

jump (verb) jamp shimas
ジャンプします

junction (in road) kōsaten
交差点

(on motorway) intāchenji
インターチェンジ

June Rokgats
六月

just (only) ... dake
…だけ

just two futats dake
ふたつだけ

just for me watashi ni dake
私にだけ

just here chōdo koko de
ちょうどここで

not just now ima wa dame des
いまはだめです

we've just arrived ima tsuita tokoro des
いま着いたところ
です

K

keep (verb) tot·te okimas
取っておきます

keep the change otsuri wa kek·kō des
おつりはけっこう
です

can I keep it? morat·te mo ī des ka?
もらってもいいです
か？

please keep it dōzo omochi kudasai
どうぞお持ち
ください

ketchup kechap·p
ケチャップ

kettle yakan
やかん

key kagi
かぎ

the key for room 201, please ni-maru-ichi-gō no kagi o onegai shimas
201号のかぎをお願い
します

keyring kīhorudā
キーホルダー

kidneys jinzō
腎臓

kilo kiro
キロ

kilometre kiromētoru
キロメートル

how many kilometres is it to ...? ... made nan-kiro arimas ka?
…まで何キロあり
ますか？

kind (generous) shinsets
親切

that's very kind sore wa

goshinsets ni
それはご親切に

• • • • • DIALOGUE • • • • •

which kind do you want? dochira
ga ī des ka?

I want this/that kind kono/sono
shurui ga hoshī des

kiosk kiosk
キオスク

kiss (noun) kis
キス

(verb) kis shimas
キスします

---

kissing

Kissing in public is rarely seen
except in large cities, and is not
yet widely accepted. Kissing has
far stronger erotic connotations
than in the West. Social kissing,
for example, of one's children,
relatives or friends, is unknown
in Japan.

---

kitchen daidokoro
台所

kite tako
たこ

kite-flying tako-age
たこあげ

Kleenex® tis·sh-pēpā
ティッシュペーパー

knee hiza
ひざ

knickers shōts
ショーツ

knife naif
ナイフ

knock (verb) nok·k shimas
ノックします

knock over (object) hik·kuri
kaeshimas
ひっくり返します

(pedestrian) hanemas
はねます

he's been knocked over kare
wa kuruma ni
hanerareмashta
彼は車にはねられ
ました

know shit·te imas
知っています

I don't know shirimasen
知りません

I didn't know that sore wa
shirimasen deshta
それは知りません
でした

do you know where I can
find ...? doko de ... ga te ni
hairimas ka?
どこで…が手に入り
ますか？

Korean (adj) Kankok (no)
韓国（の）

L

label raberu
ラベル

lacquerware shik·ki
漆器

ladies' room, ladies' toilets
keshōshits
化粧室

ladies' wear fujinfuku-uriba
婦人服売り場

lady josei
女性

lager ragā-bīru
ラガービール
see beer

lake mizūmi
湖

lamb (meat) kohitsuji
仔羊

lamp stando
スタンド

lane (motorway) shasen
車線
(small road) roji
路地

language kotoba
言葉
(foreign language)
gaikok-go
外国語

language course gogak-kōs
語学コース

large ōkī
大きい

last (final) saigo (no)
最後（の）

last week senshū
先週

last Friday senshū no
Kin·yōbi
先週の金曜日

last night yūbe
ゆうべ

what time is the last train to
Yokohama? Yokohama-iki no
saishū-densha wa nanji des
ka?
横浜行きの最終電車
は何時ですか？

late osoi
遅い

sorry I'm late okurete
sumimasen
遅れてすみません

the train was late densha ga
okuremashta
電車が遅れました

we must go – we'll be late
ikanaito chikok shite
shimaimas
行かないと遅刻して
しまいます

it's getting late zuibun osok
narimashta
ずいぶん遅くなり
ました

later ato de
あとで

I'll come back later ato de

modot·te kimas
あとで戻ってきます

see you later sore jā mata
それじゃあまた

later on ato de
あとで

latest (most recent) saishin (no)
最新（の）

by Wednesday at the latest
osok-tomo Suiyōbi made ni
遅くとも水曜日まで
に

laugh (verb) waraimas
笑います

launderette, laundromat
koin-randorī
コインランドリー

laundry (clothes) sentak-mono
せんたくもの

(place) sentak-ya
せんたく屋

lavatory toire
トイレ

law hōrits
法律

lawn shibaf
しばふ

lawyer ben·goshi
弁護士

laxative gezai
下剤

lazy namake-mono
なまけもの

lead (electrical) kōdo
コード

lead (verb) tsūjite imas
通じています

where does this road lead?
kono michi wa doko ni
tsūjite imas ka?
この道はどこに
通じていますか？

leaf hap·pa
葉っぱ

leaflet chirashi
ちらし

leak (noun) more
もれ

the roof leaks amamori ga
shimas
雨もりがします

learn naraimas
習います

least: not in the least zenzen
ぜんぜん

at least skunak-tomo
すくなくとも

leather kawa
革

leave (verb: depart) shup·pats
shimas
出発します

(put somewhere) okimas
置きます

(forget) okiwasuremas
置き忘れます

I am leaving tomorrow ashita
shup·pats shimas
あした出発します

he left yesterday kare wa

kinō tachimashta

彼はきのう立ち
ました

when does the bus for
Kanazawa leave? Kanazawa-
iki no bas wa itsu shup·pats
shimas ka?

金沢行きのバスはい
つ出発しますか？

may I leave this here? koko ni
oite mo ī des ka?

ここに置いてもいい
ですか？

I left my coat in the bar bā ni
kōto o okiwasuremashta

バーにコートを置き
忘れました

left hidari

左

on the left hidari ni

左に

to the left hidari e

左へ

turn left hidari e magat·te
kudasai

左へ曲がって
ください

there's none left mō
arimasen

もうありません

left-handed hidari-kiki (no)

左きき

left luggage (office)

tenimots-azkari-jo

手荷物預り所

leg ashi

足

lemon remon

レモン

lemonade remonēdo

レモネード

lend kashimas

貸します

will you lend me your ...?
... o kashite kuremasen
ka?

…を貸してくれ
ませんか？

lens (of camera) renzu

レンズ

lesbian rezubian

レズビアン

less mot·to skunak

もっとすくなく

less than ... ika

…以下

less expensive sore hodo
takak nai

それほど高くない

lesson jugyō

授業

let: will you let me know?
shirasete kuremasen
ka?

知らせてくれません
か？

I'll let you know oshirase
shimas

お知らせします

let's go for something to eat

nani ka tabe ni ikimashō

何か食べに行き
ましょう

let off oroshimas

降ろします

will you let me off at …? … de oroshite kuremasen ka?

…で降ろしてくれ
ませんか？

letter tegami

手紙

do you have any letters for me? watashi-ate no tegami wa arimas ka?

私宛ての手紙はあり
ますか？

letterbox posto

ポスト

Letterboxes are red and square-shaped with two slots: one for domestic mail and the other for international and express mail. See **Signs and Notices** page 229.

lettuce retas

レタス

library toshokan

図書館

licence menkyo

免許

lid futa

ふた

lie (verb: tell untruth) uso o tskimas

うそをつきます

lie down yoko ni narimas

横になります

lifebelt kyūmeitai

救命帯

lifeguard raif-gādo

ライフガード

life jacket kyūmei-dōi

救命胴衣

lift (elevator) erebētā

エレベーター

could you give me a lift? nosete kuremasen ka?

乗せてくれません
か？

would you like a lift? nosete agemashō ka?

乗せてあげましょう
か？

light (noun) hikari

ひかり

(electric) denki

電気

(adj: not heavy) karui

かるい

do you have a light? (for cigarette) hi o mot·te imas ka?

火を持っています
か？

light green usu-midori (no)

うすみどり（の）

light bulb denkyū

電球

I need a new light bulb atarashī denkyū ga hitsyō des

新しい電球が必要です

lighter (cigarette) raitā

ライター

lightning inabikari

いなびかり

like (verb) suki des

好きです

I like it suki des

好きです

I like going for walks sampo ni ikuno ga suki des

散歩にいくのが好きです

I like you anata ga suki des

あなたが好きです

I don't like it suki ja arimasen

好きじゃありません

do you like ...? ... ga suki des ka?

…が好きですか？

I'd like a beer bīru ga hoshī des

ビールが欲しいです

I'd like to go swimming oyogi ni ikitai des

泳ぎにいきたいです

would you like a drink? nomimono wa ikaga des ka?

飲み物はいかがですか？

would you like to go for a walk? sampo ni ikitak arimasen ka?

散歩にいきたくありませんか？

what's it like? dō yū kanji des ka?

どういう感じですか？

I want one like this kon·na no ga hoshī des

こんなのが欲しいです

lime raim

ライム

line sen

線

could you give me an outside line? gaisen ni tsunaide kudasai

外線につないでください

lips kuchibiru

くちびる

lipstick kuchibeni

口紅

liqueur rikyūru

リキュール

listen kikimas

聞きます

litre rit·toru

リットル

little skoshi

すこし

just a little, thanks arigatō,

hon no skoshi

ありがとう、ほんの
すこし

a little milk miruk o hon no
skoshi

ミルクをほんの
すこし

a little bit more mō skoshi

もうすこし

live (verb) sunde imas

住んでいます

we live together is·sho ni
sunde imas

一緒に住んでいます

• • • • • DIALOGUE • • • • •

where do you live? doko ni sunde
imas ka?

I live in London Rondon ni sunde
imas

lively iki-iki shita

いきいきした

liver (in body) kanzō

肝臓

(food) rebā

レバー

lobby (in hotel) robī

ロビー

lobster ise-ebi

いせえび

local jimoto no

地元の

lock (noun) kagi

かぎ

it's locked kagi ga kakat·te

imas

かぎがかかって
います

lock in tojikomemas

閉じ込めます

lock out shimedashimas

締め出します

I've locked myself out of my
room kagi o naka ni
wasuremashta

かぎを中に忘れ
ました

locker (for luggage etc) rok·kā

ロッカー

lollipop kyandī

キャンディー

London Rondon

ロンドン

long nagai

長い

how long will it take to fix it?
naosu no ni dono kurai
kakarimas ka?

なおすのにどのくら
いかかりますか？

how long does it take? dono
kurai kakarimas ka?

どのくらいかかり
ますか？

a long time nagai aida

長い間

long-distance call

chōkyori-denwa

長距離電話

look: I'm just looking, thanks

Lo

miteru dake des, arigatō
見てるだけです、
ありがとう

you don't look well guai ga
yok nasasō des ne
具合いがよくなさそ
うですね

look out! ki o tskete!
気をつけて！

can I have a look? chot·to
misete kuremasen ka?
ちょっと見せてくれ
ませんか？

look after sewa o shimas
世話をします

look at mimas
見ます

look for sagashimas
さがします

I'm looking for ... ... o
sagashite imas
…をさがしています

look forward to tanoshimi ni
shimas
楽しみにします

I'm looking forward to it
tanoshimi ni shite imas
楽しみにしています

loose (handle etc) yurui
ゆるい

lorry torak·k
トラック

lose nakshimas
なくします

I've lost my way michi ni

mayot·te shimaimashta
道に迷ってしまい
ました

I'm lost, I want to get to ...
... e ikitai no des ga,
mayot·te shimaimashta
…へ行きたいのです
が、迷ってしまい
ました

I've lost my bag bag·g o
nakshimashta
バッグをなくし
ました

lost property (office) ishitsbuts-
toriatskai-jo
遺失物取扱所

lot: a lot, lots taksan
たくさん

not a lot an-mari ōk nak
あんまり多くなく

a lot of people taksan no
hito
たくさんのひと

a lot bigger zut·to ōkī
ずっとおおきい

I like it a lot totemo suki des
とても好きです

lotion rōshon
ローション

loud sawagashī
騒がしい

lounge raunji
ラウンジ

love (noun) ai
愛

(verb) daisuki des
大好きです
I love Japan Nihon ga daisuki des
日本が大好きです
lovely steki (na)
すてき（な）
low (prices) yasui
安い
(bridge) hikui
低い
luck un
運
good luck! umak ikimas yōni!
うまくいきます
ように！
luggage nimots
荷物
luggage trolley nimots-yō kāto
荷物用カート
lunch chūshok
昼食
boxed lunch obentō
おべんとう

Since the main meal in Japan is the evening meal, lunch tends to be relatively light. Many restaurants, noodle bars and cafés have set lunch menus which are usually good value for money. An alternative is a boxed lunch (obentō). These are available →

from shops and diners to take away and can be eaten either cold or hot.

lungs hai
肺
luxurious zeitak (na)
ぜいたく（な）

M

machine kikai
機械
magazine zas·shi
雑誌
maid (in hotel) kyakshits-gakari
客室係
(in Japanese inn, restaurant) nakai-san
仲居さん
maiden name kyūsei
旧姓
mail (noun) yūbin
郵便
(verb) yūsō shimas
郵送します
is there any mail for me? nani ka yūbin ga kite imas ka?
何か郵便がきて
いますか？
see post office
mailbox posto
ポスト
main omo (na)
主（な）

main course mein-kōs
メインコース

main post office yūbinkyok no honkyok
郵便局の本局

main road ōdōri
大通り

mains switch dengen
電源

make (brand name) shurui
種類

(verb) tskurimas
つくります

I make it 500 yen tat·ta go-hyak-en des
たった五百円です

what is it made of? nani de dekite imas ka?
何で出来ています か？

make-up keshō
化粧

Malaysia Marēshia
マレーシア

Malaysian (adj) Marēshia (no)
マレーシア（の）

man otoko no hito
男の人

manager (in restaurant, hotel) shihainin
支配人

(in shop) tenchō
店長

(in business) keieisha
経営者

can I see the manager?
shihainin ni awasete kuremasen ka?
支配人に会わせて くれませんか？

managing director shachō
社長

manual (car with manual gears) manyuaru (no)
マニュアル（の）

many taksan (no)
たくさん（の）

not many amari ōk nai
あまり多くない

map chizu
地図

network map rosenzu
路線図

March San·gats
三月

margarine māgarin
マーガリン

market ichiba
市場

(in business) shijō
市場

marmalade māmarēdo
マーマレード

married: I'm married kek·kon shite imas
結婚しています

are you married? kek·kon shite imas ka?
結婚していますか？

martial arts budō
武道

mascara maskara
マスカラ

massage (noun) mas·sāji
マッサージ

mat (Japanese) tatami
たたみ

match (football etc) shiai
試合

matches mat·chi
マッチ

material (fabric) kiji
生地

matter: it doesn't matter nan
demo ī des
なんでもいいです

what's the matter? dō
shimashta ka?
どうしましたか？

mattress futon
ふとん

May Gogats
五月

may: may I have another one?
mō hitots morat·te mo ī des
ka?
もうひとつもらって
もいいですか？

may I come in? hait·te mo ī
des ka?
入ってもいいです
か？

may I see it? mite mo ī des ka?
見てもいいですか？

may I sit here? koko ni
suwat·te mo ī des ka?
ここに座ってもいい
ですか？

maybe tabun
たぶん

mayonnaise mayonēz
マヨネーズ

me* watashi (o)
私（を）

that's for me sore wa watashi
no des
それは私のです

send it to me okut·te
kudasai
送ってください

me too watashi mo
私も

meal gohan, shokji
ごはん、食事

•••••• DIALOGUE ••••••

did you enjoy your meal? oshokji
no hō wa ikaga deshta ka?

it was excellent, thank you arigatō
gozaimas, totemo oishikat·ta des

mean: what do you mean? dō
iu koto des ka?
どういうことです
か？

•••••• DIALOGUE ••••••

what does this word mean? kono
kotoba wa dō iu imi des ka?

it means ... in English Eigo de ...
to iu imi des

measles hashika
はしか
German measles fūshin
風疹
meat nik
肉
mechanic shūrikō
修理工
medicine ksuri
薬
medium (adj) chū kurai (no)
中くらい（の）
(clothes) em-saiz
エムサイズ
medium-dry chū kurai no karasa (no)
中くらいの辛さ（の）
medium-rare midiam-reya (no)
ミディアム・レア（の）
medium-sized chū kurai (no)
中くらい（の）
meet aimas
会います
nice to meet you hajimemashite
はじめまして
where shall I meet you? doko de aimashō ka?
どこで会いましょうか？
meeting shūkai
集会

(business) kaigi
会議
meeting place machi-awase-basho
待ち合わせ場所
men dansei
男性
mend naoshimas
なおします
could you mend this for me? kore o naoshite kuremasen ka?
これをなおしてくれませんか？
men's room dansei-yō toire
男性用トイレ
menswear shinshifuk-uriba
紳士服売り場
mention: don't mention it dō itashimashte
どういたしまして
menu menyū
メニュー
may I see the menu, please? menyū o onegai shimas
メニューをお願いします
see menu reader page 249
message dengon
伝言
are there any messages for me? dengon ga nani ka arimasen deshta ka?
伝言が何かありませんでしたか？

I want to leave a message
for ... ...-san ni dengon o
onegai shimas
…一さんに伝言をお
願いします

metal kinzok
金属

metre mētoru
メートル

microwave (oven) denshi-renji
電子レンジ

midday shōgo
正午

at midday shōgo ni
正午に

middle: in the middle
man·naka ni
真ん中に

in the middle of the night
mayonaka ni
真夜中に

the middle one man·naka no
真ん中の

midnight mayonaka
真夜中

at midnight mayonaka ni
真夜中に

might: I might go iku kamo
shiremasen
行くかもしれません

I might not go ikanai kamo
shiremasen
行かないかもしれ
ません

I might want to stay another

day mō ip·pak suru kamo
shiremasen
もう一泊する
かもしれません

migraine henzutsū
偏頭痛

mild (taste) usuaji (no)
うすあじ（の）

(weather) atatakai
あたたかい

mile mairu
マイル

milk miruk
ミルク

milkshake miruk-sēki
ミルクセーキ

millimetre mirimētoru
ミリメートル

mind: never mind ki ni
shinaide kudasai
気にしないで
ください

I've changed my mind ki ga
kawarimashta
気が変わりました

•••••• DIALOGUE ••••••

do you mind if I open the window?
mado o akete mo ī desho ka?
no, I don't mind ē, dōzo

mine*: it's mine watashi no
des
私のです

mineral water mineraru-uōtā
ミネラルウォーター

mints minto
ミント

minute fun
分

in a minute sug ni
すぐに

just a minute chot·to mat·te kudasai
ちょっと待って
ください

mirror kagami
かがみ

Miss ... ...-san
…—さん

miss: I missed the bus bas ni noriokuremashta
バスに乗り遅れ
ました

missing: one of my ... is missing
... ga hitots miatarimasen
…がひとつ見あたり
ません

there's a suitcase missing
sūtskēs ga miatarimasen
スーツケースが見あ
たりません

mist kiri
霧

mistake (noun) machigai
まちがい

I think there's a mistake
dōmo machigai ga aru yō nan des ga
どうもまちがいがあ
るようなんですが

sorry, I've made a mistake
sumimasen, machigaemashta
すみません、まちが
えました

mix-up: sorry, there's been a mix-up sumimasen, techigai deshta
すみません、手違い
でした

mobile phone keitaidenwa
携帯電話

modern modan (na)
モダン（な）

moisturizer nyūeki
乳液

moment: I won't be a moment
sug modorimas
すぐ戻ります

monastery sōin
僧院

Monday Getsyōbi
月曜日

money okane
お金

Japanese currency is the yen. Bank notes come in denominations of 1,000 (sen-en), 5,000 (go-sen-en) and 10,000 (ichi-man-en) yen; coins are as follows: 1, 5, 10, 50 100 and 500 yen. Most bills are settled in cash, although the use of credit cards has become widespread. Personal cheques are not used.

month (this, last, next etc) gets
月
(one, two, three etc) kagets
ヶ月
monument kinenhi
記念碑
moon tski
月
moped tansha
単車
more* mot·to
もっと
can I have some more water,
please? omizu o mō skoshi
moraemas ka?
お水をもうすこし
もらえますか？
more expensive/interesting
mot·to takai/omoshiroi
もっと高い／おも
しろい
more than 50 go-jū ijō
50以上
more than that sore ijō
それ以上
a lot more mot·to taksan
もっとたくさん

•••••• DIALOGUE ••••••

would you like some more? mō
skoshi ikaga des ka?
no, no more for me, thanks īe, mō
kek·ko des
how about you? sochira wa dō
des ka?

I don't want any more, thanks mō
kek·ko des

morning asa
朝
this morning kesa
けさ
in the morning asa ni
朝に
mosquito ka
蚊
mosquito repellent
kayoke-supurē
蚊よけスプレー
most: I like this one most of all
kore ga ichiban suki des
これがいちばん好き
です
most of the time taitei
たいてい
most tourists taitei no
ryokōkyak
たいていの旅行客
mostly taitei
たいてい
mother (one's own) haha
母
(someone else's) okā-san
お母さん
mother-in-law (one's own) giri no
haha
義理の母
(someone else's) giri no okā-
san
義理のお母さん

motorbike ōtobai
オートバイ

motorboat mōtābōto
モーターボート

motorway kōsokdōro
高速道路

> In Japan, you must pay to use
> the motorway/highway and it's
> not cheap. You are given a ticket
> when you go onto the motorway
> and pay when you get off. If you
> do not have the exact fare,
> choose a toll booth with an at-
> tendant.

mountain yama
山

up in the mountains yama ni
山に

mountaineering tozan
登山

mouse nezumi
ねずみ

moustache kuchihige
くちひげ

mouth kuchi
口

move (verb) ugokashimas
動かします

he's moved to another room
kare wa hik·koshimashta
彼は引っ越しました

could you move your car?
kuruma o ugokashite

kuremasen ka?
車を動かしてくれま
せんか？

could you move up a little?
skoshi tsmete kuremasen
ka?
すこしつめてくれま
せんか？

movie eiga
映画

movie theater eigakan
映画館

Mr ...-san
…－さん

Mrs ...-san
…－さん

Ms ...-san
…－さん

much taksan (no)
たくさん（の）

much better zut·to ī des
ずっといいです

much worse nao warui
des
なお悪いです

much hotter zut·to atsui
ずっと暑い

not much skoshi
すこし

not very much amari
あまり

I don't want very much amari
hoshik nai des
あまり欲しくない
です

mud doro
どろ

mug (for drinking) magkap·p
マグカップ

I've been mugged gōtō ni
osowaremashta
強盗におそわれ
ました

mum mama
ママ

mumps otafuk-kaze
おたふくかぜ

museum hakbutskan
博物館

Museums run by the government or local councils open Tues–Sun, 9am–4pm. Private museums and galleries usually have a variety of different opening times. Some private museums and galleries are open in the evening on one day of the week.

mushrooms kinoko
きのこ

music on·gak
音楽

musician on·gak-ka
音楽家

Muslim (adj) Isuramkyo (no)
イスラム教

mussels mūrugai
ムール貝

must: I must … …-nakereba
narimasen
…ーなければなりま
せん

I mustn't drink alcohol
watashi wa arukōru o nonde
wa ikenain des
私はアルコールを飲
んではいけないん
です

mustard mastādo
マスタード

(Japanese) karashi
からし

my* watashi no
私の

myself: I'll do it myself jibun de
shimas
自分でします

by myself jibun de
自分で

N

nail (finger) tsme
つめ

(metal) kugi
くぎ

nailbrush tsme-burashi
つめブラシ

nail varnish manikyua
マニキュア

name namae
名前

my name's John watashi no

namae wa John des

私の名前はジョン
です

what's your name? shitsurei
des ga, onamae wa?

失礼ですがお名前
は？

what is the name of this
street? kono tōri no namae
wa nan des ka?

この通りの名前は何
ですか？

see **addressing people**

napkin napkin

ナプキン

nappy omuts

おむつ

narrow (street) semai

せまい

nasty (person) iya (na)

いや（な）

(weather, accident etc) hidoi

ひどい

national kokrits (no)

国立（の）

nationality kokseki

国籍

natural shizen (na)

自然（な）

nausea hakike

吐き気

navy (blue) kon-iro (no)

紺色（の）

near ... no soba

…のそば

is it near the city centre?
hankagai kara chikai des ka?

繁華街から近いです
か？

do you go near the Osaka-jo?
Osaka-jo no chikak e ikimas
ka?

大阪城の近くへ行き
ますか？

where is the nearest ...?
ichiban chikai ... wa doko
des ka?

いちばん近い…はど
こですか？

nearby chikai

近い

nearly hotondo

ほとんど

necessary hitsyō (na)

必要（な）

neck kubi

くび

necklace nek·kures

ネックレス

necktie nektai

ネクタイ

need: I need ... ... ga hitsyō
des

…が必要です

do I need to pay? okane wa
haraun deshō ka?

お金は払うん
でしょうか？

needle hari

針

negative (film) nega
ネガ

neither: neither (one) of them
dochira demo nai
どちらでもない

neither ... nor ... ... demo ...
demo nai
…でも…でもない

nephew (one's own) oi
甥

(someone else's) oigo-san
甥御さん

net (in sport) net·to
ネット

net price seika
正価

never* kes·shite ...-masen
けっして…－ません

I never go there soko e wa
kes·shite ikimasen
そこへはけっして
行きません

(never been/done) ... koto ga
arimasen
…ことがありません

•••••• DIALOGUE ••••••

have you ever been to Tokyo?
Tōkyō ni it·ta koto wa arimas
ka?

no, I've never been there īe,
ichido mo it·ta koto ga
arimasen

new atarashī
新しい

news (radio, TV etc) nyūs
ニュース

newsagent's shimbun-ya
新聞屋

newspaper shimbun
新聞

New Year oshōgats
お正月

Happy New Year! akemashte
omedetō gozaimas!
明けましておめでと
うございます！

New Year in Japan is celebrated as a season of renewal and is full of related rituals. At midnight on New Year's Eve, people visit the local shrine to pray for good luck in the coming year. The bell tolls 108 times to signal the passing of the old year. Families celebrate New Year with special feasts and a drink called **otoso** (sweet type of sake). For up to three days most shops are closed, but the public transport system operates as usual. It's traditional to send greeting cards during the first week of January.

New Year's Day gantan
元旦

New Year's Eve ōmisoka
大晦日

New Zealand Nyū-Jīrando
ニュージーランド

New Zealander: I'm a New
Zealander watashi wa Nyū-
Jīrando-jin des
私はニュージーラン
ド人です

next tsgi (no)
次（の）

the next turning/street on the
left tsgi no hidari no
magarikado/michi
次の左の曲り角／道

at the next stop tsgi no
teiryū-jo de
次の停留所で

next week raishū
来週

next to ... no tonari
…のとなり

nice (food) oishī
おいしい

(looks, view etc) kirei (na)
きれい（な）

(person) shinsets (na)
親切（な）

niece (one's own) mei
姪

(someone else's) meigo-san
姪御さん

night yoru
夜

at night yoru ni
夜に

good night oyasuminasai
おやすみなさい

• • • • • • DIALOGUE • • • • • •

do you have a single room for one
night? ip·pak des ga shinguru wa
aite imas ka?

yes, madam hai, gozaimas

how much is it per night? ip·pak
ikura des ka?

5,000 yen ip·pak go-sen-en ni
narimas

thank you, I'll take it ja, onegai
shimas

nightclub naitokurab
ナイトクラブ

nightdress naitodores
ナイトドレス

night porter yakan no fronto-
gakari
夜間のフロント係

no* (answer) īe
いいえ

no ... ... ga arimasen
…がありません

I've no change kozeni ga
arimasen
小銭がありません

there's no ... left ... ga mō
arimasen
…がもうありません

no way! tondemo nai!
とんでもない！

oh no! (upset) masaka!
まさか！

Generally, Japanese people try not to express opinions and often avoid saying 'no' so as not to cause offence, which can be confusing for straight-talking Westerners. Directness is often seen as pushy and impolite amongst Japanese; however, frank speech by a Westerner is more likely to cause bewilderment, but would not be seen as offensive.

---

nobody* dare mo ...-masen
だれも…ーません
there's nobody there soko niwa dare mo imasen
そこにはだれもいません
noise sō-on
騒音
noisy urusai
うるさい
non-alcoholic arukōru-nuki (no)
アルコール抜き（の）
none* (people) dare mo ...-masen
だれも…ーません
(things) dore mo ...-masen
どれも…ーません
nonsmoking compartment kin·en·koshits
禁煙個室

noodles menrui
めん類
noon shōgo
正午
at noon shōgo ni
正午に
no-one* dare mo ...-masen
だれも…ーません
nor: nor do I watashi mo sō des
私もそうです
normal futsū (no)
ふつう（の）
north kita
北
in the north kita ni
北に
to the north kita e
北へ
north of Kanazawa Kanazawa no kita
金沢の北
northeast hoktō
北東
Northern Ireland Kita-Airurando
北アイルランド
North Korea Kita-Chōsen
北朝鮮
northwest hoksei
北西
Norway Noruē
ノルウェー
Norwegian (adj) Noruē (no)
ノルウェー（の）

nose hana
鼻
not* ...-masen
…—ません
no, I'm not hungry īe, onaka ga suite imasen
いいえ、おなかが
すいていません
I don't want any, thank you arigatō, demo watashi wa kek·kō des
ありがとう、でも私はけっこうです
it's not necessary hitsyō nai des
必要ないです
I didn't know that sore wa shirimasen deshita
それは知りませんでした
not that one sore ja arimasen
それじゃありません
not that one, this one sore ja nakte, kore des
それじゃなくてこれです
note (banknote) shihei
紙幣
notebook techō
手帳
nothing nani mo
…-masen
何も…—ません
nothing for me, thanks nani

mo irimasen
何もいりません
novel shōsets
小説
November Jūichigats
十一月
now ima
いま
number ban·gō
番号
(figure) sūji
数字
I've got the wrong number ban·go o machigaemashta
番号をまちがえました
what is your phone number? denwaban·go wa nam-ban des ka?
電話番号は何番ですか？
number plate nambā-purēto
ナンバープレート
nurse (man) kan·goshi
看護士
(woman) kan·gof
看護婦
nuts nat·ts
ナッツ

0

Occidental seiyō (no)
西洋（の）
occupied (phone)

hanashi-chū
話し中
(toilet) shiyō-chū
使用中
October Jūgats
十月
o'clock ji
時
odd (strange) kawat·ta
変わった
of* ... no
…の
off (lights) kiete iru
消えている
it's just off ... sore wa ... kara
sug des
それは…からすぐ
です
we're off tomorrow ashita
tachimas
あした立ちます
office (place of work) jimusho
事務所
officer (said to policeman)
omawari-san
おまわりさん
often yok
よく
not often met·ta ni
めったに
how often are the buses? bas
wa nam-bon kurai arimas
ka?
バスは何本くらいあ
りますか？

oil (for car) oiru
オイル
(for cooking) abura
あぶら
(for salad) sarada-oiru
サラダオイル
ointment nankō
軟膏
OK ōkē
オーケー
are you OK? daijōb des ka?
大丈夫ですか？
is that OK with you? sore de ī
des ka?
それでいいですか？
is it OK to ...? ... shite mo ī
des ka?
…してもいいです
か？
that's OK, thanks sore de
kamaimasen, arigatō
それでかまいませ
ん、ありがとう
I'm OK (nothing for me) watashi
wa kek·ko des
私はけっこうです
(I feel OK) daijōb des
大丈夫です
is this train OK for ...? kono
densha wa ... e ikimas
ka?
この電車は…へ行き
ますか？
old (person) toshi o tot·ta
年をとった

(thing) furui
古い

• • • • • DIALOGUE • • • • •

how old are you? oikuts des ka?
I'm 25 ni-jū-go des
and you? anata wa?

old-fashioned mukashi-fū
(no)
昔風（の）
old town (old part of town)
kyūshigai
旧市街
in the old town kyūshigai ni
旧市街に
omelette omurets
オムレツ
on ... no ue
…の上
on the street tōri de
通りで
is it on this road? sore wa
kono michizoi des ka?
それはこの道沿い
ですか？
on the plane hikōki de
飛行機で
on Saturday Doyōbi ni
土曜日に
on television terebi de
テレビで
I haven't got it on me ima
mot·te imasen
いま持っていません
this one's on me (drink) kore

wa watashi mochi des
これは私持ちです
the light wasn't on denki ga
tsuite imasen deshta
電気がついてい
ませんでした
what's on tonight? komban
wa nani o yat·te imas ka?
今晩は何をやって
いますか？
once (on one occasion) ik·kai
一回
(formerly) mae ni
前に
(as soon as) it·tan ...-tara
いったん…―たら
at once (immediately) sug
すぐ
one* hitots
ひとつ
the white one shiroi no
しろいの
one-way ticket katamichi-kip·p
片道切符
a one-way ticket to ...
... made katamichi-kip·p o
ichi-mai
…までの片道切符を
一枚
onion tamanegi
たまねぎ
only ... dake
…だけ
only one hitots dake
ひとつだけ

it's only 6 o'clock mada rokji
des
まだ6時です

I've only just got here mada
tsuita bakari des
まだ着いたばかり
です

on/off switch suit·chi
スイッチ

open (adj) hiraita
開いた

(verb: door) akemas
開けます

(of shop) eigyō-chū
営業中

when do you open? koko wa
itsu akimas ka?
ここはいつ開きます
か？

I can't get it open
akimasen
開きません

in the open air kogai de
戸外で

opening times eigyōjikan
営業時間

open ticket ōpun-chiket·to
オープンチケット

opera opera
オペラ

operation (medical) shujuts
手術

operator (telephone) operētā
オペレーター

opposite: the opposite direction

hantaihōkō
反対方向

the bar opposite mukai no bā
向かいのバー

opposite my hotel hoteru no
mukaigawa ni
ホテルの向かい側に

optician megane-ya
めがね屋

or mata wa
または

orange (fruit) orenji
オレンジ

(colour) orenji-iro (no)
オレンジ色（の）

orange juice orenji-jūs
オレンジジュース

orchestra ōkestora
オーケストラ

order (noun) chūmon
注文

(verb) chūmon shimas
注文します

can we order now? (in
restaurant) chūmon shite mo ī
des ka?
注文してもいいです
か？

I've already ordered mō
chūmon shimashta
もう注文しました

I didn't order this kore wa
chūmon shimasen deshta
これは注文しません
でした

out of order kowarete imas
こわれています

ordinary futsū (no)
ふつう（の）

other hoka no
ほか（の）

the other one mō katahō no
もう片方の

the other day sūjits mae
数日前

I'm waiting for the others hoka
no hitotachi o mat·te imas
ほかのひとたちを待
っています

do you have any others? hoka
nimo arimas ka?
ほかにもあります
か？

otherwise samonaito
さもないと

Oriental tōyō (no)
東洋（の）

our(s)* watashitachi no
私たちの

out: he's out kare wa
gaishuts-chū des
彼は外出中です

three kilometres out of town
machi kara san-kiro
町から3キロ

outdoor pool okugai-pūru
屋外プール

outside ... no soto ni
…の外に

can we sit outside? soto ni

suwaremas ka?
外に座れますか？

oven ōbun
オーブン

over: over here koko ni
ここに

over there asoko ni
あそこに

over 500 go-hyak ijō
500以上

it's over owarimashta
終わりました

overcharge: you've overcharged
me kore wa torisugi des
これは取りすぎです

overcoat ōbā
オーバー

overland mail sarubin
サル便

overnight (travel) ip·pak (no)
一泊（の）

overtake oikoshimas
追い越します

owe: how much do I owe you?
ikura haraeba ī des ka?
いくら払えばいい
ですか？

own: my own ... watashi-jishin
no ...
私自身の…

are you on your own? ohitori
des ka?
おひとりですか？

I'm on my own hitori des
ひとりです

owner mochinushi
持ち主

oyster kaki
かき

P

Pacific Ocean Taiheiyō
太平洋

pack (verb) nimots o tsmemas
荷物をつめます

　a pack of … … hito-pak·k
　ひとパック

package (parcel) kozutsmi
小包

package holiday pak·k-ryokō
パック旅行

packed lunch obentō
お弁当

packet: a packet of cigarettes
tabako hito-hako
たばこ1箱

paddy field tambo
たんぼ

page (of book) pēji
ページ

　could you page Mr …? …-san
　o yobidashite kuremasen
　ka?
　…ーさんを呼び出
　しでくれませんか？

pagoda tō
塔

pain itami
痛み

I have a pain here koko ga
itai des
ここが痛いです

painful itai
痛い

painkillers itamidome
痛み止め

painting e
絵

pair: a pair of … hito-kumi
no …
一組の…

palace kyūden
宮殿

pale (colour) usu-…
うすー…

　pale blue usu-aoi
　うすあおい

pan fraipan
フライパン

panties (women's underwear) shōts
ショーツ

pants (underwear: men's) pants
パンツ

　(women's) shōts
　ショーツ

　(US: trousers) zubon
　ズボン

pantyhose pantī-stok·king
パンティーストッキ
ング

paper kami
紙

　(Japanese) washi
　和紙

(newspaper) shimbun

新聞

a piece of paper kami
ichi-mai

紙一枚

paper folding origami

折り紙

paper handkerchiefs tis·sh-
pēpā

ティッシュペーパー

parcel kozutsmi

小包

pardon (me)? (didn't understand/
hear) nante īmashta ka?

なんて言いました
か？

parents (one's own) ryōshin

両親

(someone else's) goryōshin

御両親

park (noun) kōen

公園

(verb) chūshajo

駐車場

can I park here? koko ni
chūsha shite mo ī des ka?

ここに駐車しても
いいですか？

parking lot chūshajō

駐車場

part (noun) bubun

部分

partner (boyfriend, girlfriend etc)
pātonā

パートナー

(in business) kyōdo-keiei-sha

共同経営者

party (group) dantai

団体

(celebration) pātī

パーティー

passenger jōkyak

乗客

passport paspōto

パスポート

past*: in the past mae ni

まえに

just past the information office
an·naijo o koete sug

案内所を越えてすぐ

path komichi

小道

pattern moyō

もよう

pavement hodō

歩道

on the pavement hodō de

歩道で

pavilion tenjikan

展示館

pay (verb) shiharaimas

支払います

can I pay, please? okanjō o
onegai shimas

お勘定をお願い
します

it's already paid for mō
harat·te arimas

もう払ってあります

• • • • • • DIALOGUE • • • • • •

who's paying? dare ga haraimas ka?

I'll pay watashi ga haraimas

no, you paid last time, I'll pay īe, konomae harat·te moraimashta, watashi ga haraimas

payment shiharai
支払い

payphone kōshŭdenwa
公衆電話

peaceful shizka (na)
しずか（な）

peach momo
もも

peanuts pīnat·ts
ピーナッツ

pear nashi
なし

pearl shinju
真珠

peculiar (strange) kawat·ta
変わった

pedestrian crossing ōdanhodō
横断歩道

pedestrian zone hokōsha-ten·gok
歩行者天国

peg (for washing) sentak-basami
せんたくばさみ
(for tent) peg
ペグ

pen pen
ペン

pencil empits
えんぴつ

penfriend pemparu
ペンパル

penicillin penishirin
ペニシリン

penknife poket·to-naif
ポケットナイフ

pensioner nenkin-seikats·sha
年金生活者

people hito
ひと
the other people in the hotel
hoteru no hoka no tomarikyak
ホテルのほかの泊り客
too many people hito ga ōsugi
ひとが多すぎ

pepper (spice) koshō
こしょう

per: per night hito-ban ni tski
一晩につき
how much per day? ichinichi ikura des ka?
一日いくらですか？
per cent pāsento
パーセント

perfect kampeki (na)
完璧（な）

perfume kōsui
香水

perhaps tabun
たぶん

perhaps not tabun chigau deshō
たぶん違うでしょう

period (of time) kikan
期間

(menstruation) seiri
生理

permit (noun) kyoka
許可

person hito
ひと

personal stereo uōkman
ウォークマン

petrol gasorin
ガソリン

There are three types of petrol: yūen (4-star); and two types of muen gasorin (unleaded petrol): regyurā (regular unleaded) and hai-ok (higher performance unleaded). You can also buy keiyu for a diesel car at petrol stations. There are staff to refuel your car and all you have to do is to tell them which type and how much you want and hand over the key.

petrol can sekiyukan
石油缶

petrol station gasorin-stando
ガソリンスタンド

pharmacy yak·kyok, ksuri-ya
薬局、薬屋

Philippines Firipin
フィリピン

phone (noun) denwa
電話

(verb) denwa shimas
電話します

There are several different types of payphone in Japan. The most common type is a green phone with a silver (domestic use only) or gold plate on the front. These both take coins, phonecards and credit cards. Terehon-kādo (phonecards) are widely available from shops and vending machines in the phone boxes. Restaurants and pubs may have pink payphones which are coin-operated and for domestic use only.

phone book denwachō
電話帳

phone box kōshūdenwa
公衆電話

phonecard terefōn-kādo
テレホンカード

phone number denwaban·gō
電話番号

photo shashin
写真

excuse me, could you take a photo of us? chot·to sumimasen, shashin tot·te

kuremasen ka?
ちょっとすみ
ません、写真とって
くれませんか？

phrasebook kaiwa-hyōgen-
shū
会話表現集

piano piano
ピアノ

pickpocket suri
スリ

pick up: will you be there to pick
me up? soko made mukae ni
kite kuremasen ka?
そこまでむかえに来
てくれませんか？

picnic (noun) piknik·k
ピクニック

picture (painting) e
絵
(photo) shashin
写真

piece hitots
ひとつ
a piece of ... hito-kire no ...
ひときれの…

pill piru
ピル
I'm on the pill piru o nonde
imas
ピルを飲んでいます

pillow makura
まくら

pillow case makura-kabā
まくらカバー

pin (noun) pin
ピン

pinball pachinko
パチンコ

pine mats
松

pineapple painap·puru
パイナップル

pink pink-iro (no)
ピンク色（の）

pipe (for smoking) paip
パイプ
(for water) suidōkan
水道管

pity: it's a pity zan·nen des
残念です

pizza piza
ピザ

place (noun) tokoro
ところ
at your place anata no
tokoro de
あなたのところで
at his place kare no tokoro
de
彼のところで

plain (not patterned) muji
(no)
無地（の）

plane hikōki
飛行機
by plane hikōki de
飛行機で

plant shokbuts
植物

plasters bansōkō
ばんそうこう

plastic purastik·k
プラスティック

(credit cards) kurejit·to-kādo
クレジットカード

plastic bag binīru-bukuro
ビニール袋

plate sara
さら

platform purat·to-hōm
プラットホーム

which platform is it for Nara?
Nara-iki wa dono purat·to-hōm des ka?
奈良行きはどのプラットホームですか？

play (verb: sports, game) shimas
します

(musical instrument) hikimas
ひきます

(music) kakemas
かけます

(noun: in theatre) shibai
芝居

playground asobiba
あそび場

pleasant kimochi no ī
気持ちのいい

please (requesting) onegai shimas
お願いします

(go ahead) dōzo
どうぞ

yes, please hai, onegai shimas
はい、お願いします

could you please ...? ... -te kuremasen ka?
…ーてくれませんか？

please don't dōka yamete kudasai
どうかやめてください

pleased: pleased to meet you hajimemashte
はじめまして

pleasure: my pleasure dō itashimashite
どういたしまして

plenty: plenty of ... taksan no ...
たくさんの…

there's plenty of time jikan wa jūbun arimas
時間は十分あります

that's plenty, thanks mō kek·kō des, dōmo
もうけっこうです、どうも

plug (electrical, for car) purag
プラグ

(in sink) sen
せん

plum (Western) sumomo
すもも

(Japanese) ume
うめ

plumber suidō-ya
水道屋

pm gogo
午後

poached egg otoshi-
tamago
おとしたまご

pocket poket·to
ポケット

point: two point five ni-ten-go
2.5

there's no point muda des
むだです

poisonous yūdok (na)
有毒（な）

police keisats
警察

call the police! keisats o
yonde kudasai!
警察を呼んで
ください

The number for the police is
110.

policeman keikan
警官

police station keisats-sho
警察署

policewoman fukei
婦警

polish (noun) tsuyadashi
つや出し

polite teinei (na)
ていねい（な）

polluted yogoreta
よごれた

pool (for swimming) pūru
プール

poor (not rich) bimbō (na)
びんぼう（な）

(quality) somats (na)
そまつ（な）

pop music pop·ps
ポップス

pop singer kashu
歌手

popular ninki no aru
人気のある

pork butanik
豚肉

port (for boats) minato
みなと

(drink) pōto-wain
ポートワイン

porter (in hotel) bōi
ボーイ

portrait shōzōga
肖像画

posh (restaurant) shareta
しゃれた

(people) jōhin (na)
上品（な）

possible kanō (na)
可能（な）

is it possible to …? … -koto
ga dekimas ka?
…ことができます
か？

as … as possible dekiru-
dake …
できるだけ…

post (noun: mail) yūbin
郵便
(verb) yūsō shimas
郵送します
could you post this for me?
kore o tōkan shite
kuremasen ka?
これを投函してくれ
ませんか？
postcard ehagaki
絵はがき
postcode yūbimban·gō
郵便番号
poster postā
ポスター
poste restante
kyok-dome-yūbin
局止め郵便
post office yūbinkyok
郵便局

Although there are numerous
local branches, it's best to use
main post offices where staff,
more often than not, speak English and are used to handling
foreign mail and parcels. The
standard opening hours of main
post offices are 8.30am–6pm,
Mon–Fri, and 8.30am–noon on
Saturday. The main post office
near Tokyo station is open
around the clock 365 days a
year. Stamps are also on sale in
a variety of shops.

potato chips (US: crisps)
poteto-chip·p
ポテトチップ
pottery (objects) tōki
陶器
pound (money) pondo
ポンド
(weight) paundo
パウンド
power cut teiden
停電
power point konsento
コンセント
practise: I want to practise my
Japanese Nihon-go o renshū
shitai des
日本語を練習したい
です
prawns ebi
えび
prefer: I prefer … … no hō ga
suki des
…のほうが好きです
pregnant ninshin-chū
(no)
妊娠中（の）
prescription (for medicine)
shohōsen
処方せん
present (gift) purezento
プレゼント
president (of country) daitōryō
大統領
(of company) shachō
社長

pretty kirei (na)
きれい（な）
it's pretty expensive kanari
takai des
かなり高いです
price nedan
値段
priest obō-san
お坊さん
(Shinto) kan·nushi-san
神主さん
prime minister sōridaijin
総理大臣
printed matter insatsbuts
印刷物
prison keimusho
刑務所
private shi-teki (na)
私的（な）
private bathroom sen·yō no
bas-toire
専用のバス・トイレ
probably osorak
おそらく
problem mondai
問題
no problem! daijōb!
大丈夫！
product seihin
製品
program(me) (TV, radio)
ban·gumi
番組
(theatre, computer) puroguram
プログラム

promise: I promise yaksok
shimas
約束します
pronounce: how is this
pronounced? kore wa dō
hats·on shimas ka?
これはどう発音
しますか？
properly (repaired, locked etc)
chanto
ちゃんと
protection factor faktā
ファクター
Protestant purotestanto
プロテスタント
public baths sentō
銭湯
public holiday saijits
祭日

Japan has the following public
holidays:

1 January
   New Year's Day
15 January
   Adult's Day
12 February
   National Foundation Day
21 or 22 March
   Vernal Equinox Day
29 April
   Green Day
3 May
   Constitution Memorial Day
                              →

5 May
Children's Day
20 July
Sea Day
15 September
Respect for the Aged Day
23 or 24 September
Autumnal Equinox Day
10 October
Health-Sports Day
3 November
Culture Day
23 November
Labour Thanksgiving Day
23 December
Emperor's Birthday

There are three holiday periods when people travel nation-wide: Golden Week (29 April–5 May), Obon Festival (13–16 August), which is a time of Buddist ceremonies, and over the New Year period (27 December–3 January). Try to avoid travelling in Japan around these times.

public toilets kōshūbenjo
公衆便所
pull hikimas
引きます
puncture (noun) pank
パンク
puppet nin·gyō
人形

puppet show nin·gyō-geki
人形劇
puppet theatre (Japanese traditional) bunrak
文楽
purple murasaki (no)
むらさき（の）
purse (for money) saif
さいふ
(US: handbag) handobag·g
ハンドバッグ
push oshimas
押します
pushchair kuruma-isu
車いす
put okimas
置きます
where can I put ...? ... o doko ni okimashō ka?
…をどこに置きましょうか？
could you put us up for the night? komban tomete itadakemasen deshō ka?
今晩泊めていただけませんでしょうか？
pyjamas pajama
パジャマ

Q

quality hinshits
品質
quarantine ken·eki
検疫

quarter (amount) yom-bun no
ichi
四分の一
(time) jū-go-fun
15分
quayside: on the quayside
hatoba de
波止場で
question shitsmon
質問
queue (noun) gyōrets
行列
quick hayai
速い
that was quick hayakat·ta
des
速かったです
what's the quickest way there?
soko ni iku niwa nani ga
ichiban hayai des ka?
そこに行くには何が
いちばん速いです
か？
fancy a quick drink? ip·pai
yat·te ikimasen ka?
一杯やっていき
ませんか？
quickly hayak
速く
quiet (place, hotel) shizka (na)
しずか（な）
quiet! shizka ni!
しずかに！
quite (fairly) kanari
かなり

(very) totemo
とても
that's quite right mat·tak
sono tōri des
まったくそのとおり
です
quite a lot kanari taksan
かなりたくさん

R

race (for horses) keiba
競馬
(for cars, runners) rēs
レース
racket (tennis, squash) raket·to
ラケット
radiator (of car) rajiētā
ラジエーター
(in room) dambōki
暖房器
radio rajio
ラジオ
on the radio rajio de
ラジオで
rail: by rail tetsdō de
鉄道で
rail pass teikiken
定期券
railway tetsdō
鉄道
rain (noun) ame
雨
in the rain ame no naka de
雨の中で

it's raining ame ga fut·te imas

雨が降っています

rainy season tsuyu

梅雨

raincoat reinkōto

レインコート

rape (noun) fujobōkō

婦女暴行

rare (uncommon) mezurashī

めずらしい

(steak) reya

レア

rash (on skin) fukidemono

ふきでもの

raspberry razberī

ラズベリー

rat nezumi

ねずみ

rate (for changing money) ryōgae-rēto

両替レート

rather: it's rather good nakanaka ī des

なかなかいいです

I'd rather ... ... hō ga ī des

…ほうがいいです

raw nama (no)

なま（の）

raw fish sashimi

さしみ

razor kamisori

かみそり

(electric) denki-kamisori

電気かみそり

read yomimas

読みます

ready yōi ga dekita

用意ができた

are you ready? mō ī des ka?

もういいですか？

I'm not ready yet mada yōi ga dekite imasen

まだ用意ができていません

•••••• DIALOGUE ••••••

when will it be ready? itsu dekimas ka?

it should be ready in a couple of days ni-san-nichi-chū ni dekimas

real hom·mono (no)

本物（の）

really hontō ni

ほんとう（の）

I'm really sorry hontō ni sumimasen

ほんとうにすみません

that's really great sore wa hontō ni sugoi des

それはほんとうにすごいです

really? (doubt) hontō?

ほんとう？

(polite interest) hontō des ka?

ほんとうですか？

rear lights tēru-ramp

テールランプ

reasonable (prices etc) tegoro (na)

手ごろ（な）

receipt reshīto

レシート

recently saikin

最近

reception (in hotel) fronto

フロント

(for guests) kan·geikai

歓迎会

at reception uketske de

受付で

reception desk uketske

受付

receptionist uketske-gakari

受付係

(in hotel) fronto-gakari

フロント係

recognize ki ga tskimas

気がつきます

recommend: could you
recommend ...? osusume no
... o oshiete kuremasen ka?

おすすめの…をおし
えてくれませんか？

record (music) rekōdo

レコード

red akai

赤い

red wine aka-wain

赤ワイン

refund (noun) harai-modoshi

払い戻し

can I have a refund? okane o
haraimodoshite kure-

masen ka?

お金を払い戻して
くれませんか？

region chihō

地方

registered: by registered mail
kakitome-yūbin de

書留郵便

registration number
tōrokban·gō

登録番号

religion shūkyō

宗教

Most Japanese are adherents of
both Shinto and Buddhism, and
go to their shrine and temple on
festival days only. There are no
sermons – only brief prayers
for good luck (after tossing a
coin into a receptacle at the entrance), clapping of hands and
bowing. A lot of families have a
house altar where the spirits of
family ancestors are venerated:
kamidana is a Shinto altar (also
used for worship of Shinto gods)
and **butsudan** is a Buddhist
altar.

remember: I don't remember
oboete imasen

おぼえていません

I remember oboete imas

おぼえています

do you remember? oboete
imas ka?

おぼえていますか？

rent (noun: for apartment) yachin

家賃

(verb: car etc) karimas

借ります

to rent rentaru (no)

レンタル

• • • • • • DIALOGUE • • • • • •

I'd like to rent a car kuruma o
karitai no des ga

for how long? kikan wa dono
kurai des ka?

two days futska des

this is our range kochira ga
shashu des

I'll take the ... ... ni shimas

is that with unlimited mileage?
sōkōkyori wa museigen des ka?

yes, it is hai, sō des

can I see your licence please?
menkyoshō o misete itadakemas
ka?

and your passport paspōto mo
onegai shimas

is insurance included? hoken wa
komi des ka?

yes, but you pay the first 3,600 yen
hai, tada saisho ni san-zen-
rop·pyaku-en o oshiharai
itadakimas

can you leave a deposit of 2,000
yen? hoshōkin o ni-sen-en
oshiharai itadakemas ka?

rental (for car, boat etc) ryōkin

料金

rented car renta-kā

レンタカー

repair (verb) shūri shimas

修理します

can you repair it? shūri
dekimas ka?

修理できますか？

repeat kurikaeshimas

繰り返します

could you repeat that? mō
ichido it·te kuremasen ka?

もう一度言ってくれ
ませんか？

representative (noun: of company)
daihyō

代表

reservation yoyak

予約

I'd like to make a reservation
yoyak o shitai no des ga

予約をしたいのです
が

• • • • • • DIALOGUE • • • • • •

I have a reservation yoyak o shite
arimas

yes sir, what name please?
kashikomarimashta,
dochira-sama des ka?

reserve (verb) yoyak shimas

予約します

• • • • • DIALOGUE • • • • •

can I reserve a table for tonight?
tēburu o komban yoyak dekimas
ka?

yes madam, for how many people?
hai, uketamawarimas,
nam·mei-sama des ka?

for two futari des

and for what time? ojikan wa?

for eight o'clock hachiji ni onegai
shimas

and could I have your name
please? onamae o itadakemas
ka?

rest: I need a rest hitoyasumi
sasete kudasai
ひと休みさせて
ください
the rest of the group hoka no
hitotachi
ほかのひとたち
restaurant restoran
レストラン

In big Japanese cities there are
many restaurants specializing
in food from various countries.
The most common ethnic restaurants are Chinese and Korean. If you want eat inexpen-
sively, you should go to noodle
bars and diners. Cafés and tea-
rooms also have snacks and
light meals on offer. Most places
→

have set menus, especially for
lunch, which are often good
value. Choosing food in a restaurant is rarely a problem because
wax models of almost all menu
items are displayed at the entrance and often the menu con-
tains pictures of the food. There
is no tipping required, but a
10– 15 per cent service charge is
added to the bill in more expensive places. Also, a 5 per cent
federal consumer tax will be
added to the price, and a further
3 per cent local tax if the bill
exceeds 7,500 yen. In traditional
restaurants, the price is sometimes written in Chinese characters rather than Arabic
numerals.
American fast food chains have
also influenced Japanese cuisine. Apart from Kentucky Fried
Chicken, and McDonalds, you
can now find Japanese lunch
box shops, called **hoka hoka
bentō.**
see **eating**

restaurant car shokdōsha
食堂車
rest room toire
トイレ
retired: I'm retired watashi wa

teinen-taishok shimashta

私は定年退職し
ました

return: a return to ... ... made
no ōfuk-kip·p o ichi-mai

…までの往復切符を
一枚

return ticket ōfuk-kip·p

往復切符

see ticket

reverse charge call
korekto-kōru

コレクトコール

reverse gear bak·k·giya

バックギア

revolting fuyukai (na)

ふゆかい（な）

rib abarabone

あばらぼね

rice (uncooked) kome

こめ

(boiled) gohan

ごはん

(fried) chāhan

チャーハン

rich (person) kanemochi (no)

金持ち（の）

(food) kot·teri shita

こってりした

ridiculous bakageta

ばかげた

right (correct) tadashī

正しい

(not left) migi (no)

右（の）

you were right anata no iu
tōri deshta

あなたの言うとおり
です

that's right sō des

そうです

this can't be right kon·na
hazu wa nai des

こんなはずはない
です

right here chōdo koko de

ちょうどここで

is this the right road for ...? ...e
iku niwa kono michi de ī des
ka?

…へ行くにはこの道
でいいですか？

on the right migi ni

右に

to the right migi e

右へ

turn right migi e magat·te
kudasai

右へ曲がって
ください

right-hand drive migi-handoru
(no)

右ハンドル

ring (on finger) yubiwa

ゆびわ

I'll ring you atode denwa
shimas

あとで電話します

ring back orikaeshi denwa

shimas

折り返し電話します

ripe (fruit) jukshita

熟した

rip-off: it's a rip-off! hōgai na nedan des!

法外な値段です！

rip-off prices hōgai na nedan

法外な値段

risky kiken (na)

危険な

river kawa

川

road michi

道

is this the road for …? kore wa … e iku michi des ka?

これは…へ行く道 ですか？

down the road konosaki

このさき

road map dōrochizu

道路地図

roadsign dōro-hyōshiki

道路標識

rob: I've been robbed gōtō ni osowaremashta

強盗におそわれ ました

rock iwa

岩

(music) rok·k

ロック

on the rocks (whisky)

on-za-rok·k de

オンザロック

roll (bread) rōrupan

ロールパン

roof (of house) yane

やね

(of car) rūf

ルーフ

room heya

部屋

in my room watashi no heya de

私の部屋で

•••••• DIALOGUE ••••••

do you have any rooms? heya wa arimas ka?

for how many people?

nam·mei-sama des ka?

for one/two hitori/futari des

yes, we have rooms free hai, oheya ga gozaimas

for how many nights will it be? nampak no goyotei des ka?

just for one night hitoban dake des

how much is it? ikura des ka?

… with bathroom, and … without bathroom ofuro-tski de …, nashi de …

can I see a room with bathroom? ofuro-tski no heya o misete kuremasen ka?

OK, I'll take it ki ni irimashta, yoroshik onegai shimas

room service rūm-sābis
ルームサービス

rope rōp
ロープ

rosé (wine) roze
ロゼ

roughly (approximately) daitai
だいたい

round: it's my round watashi
no ban des
私の番です

round-trip ticket ōfuk-kip·p
往復切符

a round-trip ticket to ...
... made no ōfuk-kip·p o
ichi-mai
…までの往復切符を
一枚

route ikikata
行き方

what's the best route? dore
ga ichiban ī ikikata des ka?
どれがいちばんいい
行き方ですか？

rubber (material) gom
ゴム

(eraser) keshigom
消しゴム

rubber band wagom
輪ゴム

rubbish (waste) gomi
ごみ

(poor quality goods) garakta
がらくた

rubbish! (nonsense)

bakabakashī!
ばかばかしい！

rucksack ryuk·k·sak·k
リュックサック

rude shitsurei (na)
失礼（な）

ruins iseki
遺跡

rum ram-shu
ラム酒

rum and Coke® ram-shu no
kōra-wari
ラム酒のコーラ割り

run (verb: person) hashirimas
走ります

I've run out of money
okane ga soko o
tskimashta
お金が底をつき
ました

rush hour ras-sh-awā
ラッシュアワー

S

sad kanashī
かなしい

saddle (for bike) sadoru
サドル

safe (adj) anzen (na)
安全（な）

safety pin anzen-pin
安全ピン

sailboard (noun) sāfbōdo
サーフボード

sailboarding uindosāfing
ウィンドサーフィ
ング

sailing sēring
セーリング

---

sake

Sake is the general term for alcoholic drinks, as well as being the word for Japanese rice wine. Sake is mostly served hot (except in summer) and is poured into very small containers (**sakazki**). The sake which is drunk to hail New Year's Day is a special kind of sweet sake flavoured with herbs and called **otoso**.

---

sake bottle tok·kuri
とっくり

sake cup sakazki
さかずき

salad sarada
サラダ

salad dressing dores·shing
ドレッシング

sale: for sale uridashi-chū
売り出し中

salesman sērusuman
セールスマン

salmon sake
さけ

salt shio
しお

same: the same onaji
同じ

the same as this kore to
onaji no
これと同じの

the same again, please onaji
no o mō hitots kudasai
同じのもうひとつ
ください

it's all the same to me dot·chi
demo onaji des
どっちでも同じです

sand suna
すな

sandals sandaru
サンダル

(wooden) geta
げた

sandwich sandoit·chi
サンドイッチ

sanitary napkins/towels seiri-yō
napkin
生理用ナプキン

sash obi
帯

Saturday Doyōbi
土曜日

sauce sōs
ソース

saucepan katatenabe
片手なべ

saucer ukezara
受け皿

sauna sauna
サウナ

sausage sōsēji
ソーセージ

say (verb) īmas
言います

how do you say ... in Japanese? Nihon-go de ... o nan te īmas ka?
日本語で…を何て言いますか？

what did he say? kare wa nan te īmashta ka?
彼は何て言いましたか？

she said ... kanojo wa ... to īmashta
彼女は…と言いました

could you say that again? mō ichido it·te kuremasen ka?
もういちど言ってくれませんか？

scarf skāf
スカーフ

scenery keshiki
けしき

schedule yotei
予定

(US: timetable) jikokhyō
時刻表

scheduled flight teikibin
定期便

school gak·kō
学校

scissors: a pair of scissors

hasami
はさみ

scooter skūtā
スクーター

scotch Skot·chi-uiskī
スコッチウィスキー

Scotch tape® serotēp
セロテープ

Scotland Skot·torando
スコットランド

Scottish (adj) Skot·torando (no)
スコットランド（の）

I'm Scottish watashi wa Skot·torando-jin des
私はスコットランド人です

scrambled eggs iri-tamago
いりたまご

screen (Japanese) byōb
びょうぶ

scroll (hanging) kakejik
かけじく

(rolled) makimono
まきもの

sea umi
海

by the sea umibe de
海辺で

seafood shīfūdo
シーフード

seafront kaigan-zoi
海岸沿い

on the seafront kaigan-zoi ni
海岸沿いに

seal: personal seal hanko
はんこ

search (verb) sagashimas
さがします

seasick: I feel seasick fune ni
yoimashta
船に酔いました

I get seasick funayoi suru
tachi des
船酔いするたちです

seaside: by the seaside kaigan
de
海岸で

seat seki
席

is this seat taken? kono seki
wa fusagat·te imas ka?
この席はふさがって
いますか？

seat belt shīto-beruto
シートベルト

seaweed kaisō
海草

secluded hempi (na)
へんぴ（な）

second (adj) ni-bam·me (no)
二番目（の）

(of time) byō
秒

just a second! chot·to mat·te
kudasai!
ちょっと待って
ください

second class (train etc)
futsūseki
普通席

second-hand chūko (no)
中古（の）

second floor san-kai
三階

(US) ni-kai
二階

secretary hisho
秘書

see mimas
見ます

can I see? mite mo ī des ka?
見てもいいですか？

have you seen …? … o
mimashta ka?
…を見ましたか？

I saw him this morning kesa
kare ni aimashta
けさ彼に会いました

see you! ja, mata!
じゃ、また！

I see (I understand)
naruhodo
なるほど

self-service seruf-sābis
セルフサービス

sell urimas
売ります

do you sell …? … wa arimas
ka?
…はありますか？

Sellotape® serotēp
セロテープ

send okurimas
送ります
I want to send this to England
kore o Igiris ni okuritai no
des ga
これをイギリスに
送りたいのですが

separate betsbets (no)
べつべつ（の）

separated: I'm separated
watashi wa bek·kyo-chū
des
私は別居中です

separately (pay, travel) betsbets
ni
べつべつに

September Kugats
九月

serious (problem) jūdai (na)
重大（な）
(illness) omoi
おもい
(person) majime (na)
まじめ（な）

service charge (in restaurant)
sābis-ryo
サービス料

service station gasorin-stando
ガソリンスタンド

serviette napkin
ナプキン

set menu teishok
定食

several ikutska (no)
いくつか（の）

sew nuimas
ぬいます
could you sew this back on?
kore o nuitskete kuremasen
ka?
これをぬいつけて
くれませんか？

sex sek·ks
セックス

sexy sekshī (na)
セクシー（な）

shade: in the shade
hikage ni
ひかげに

shallow (water) asai
浅い

shame: what a shame! (it's a pity)
zan·nen!
残念！

shampoo (noun) shampū
シャンプー
shampoo and set shampū to
set·to
シャンプーとセット

share (verb: room) aibeya ni
narimas
相部屋になります
(table) aiseki shimas
相席します

sharp (knife) yok kireru
よく切れる
(pain) surudoi
するどい

shaver denki-kamisori
電気かみそり

shaving foam shēbing-fōm
シェービングフォーム

shaving point
denki-kamisori-yō konsento
電気かみそり用
コンセント

she* kanojo
彼女

is she here? kanojo wa imas ka?
彼女はいますか？

sheet (for bed) shīts
シーツ

shelf tana
たな

shellfish kai
貝

sherry sherī
シェリー

Shinto (adj) Shintō (no)
神道（の）

Shintoism Shintō
神道

ship fune
船

by ship fune de
船で

shirt shats
シャツ

shit! kso!
くそ！

shock (noun) shok·k
ショック

I got an electric shock from the … … de kanden shimashta
…で感電しました

shocking hidoi
ひどい

shoe kuts
くつ

a pair of shoes kuts is·sok
くつ 一足

---

shoes

Take off your shoes before entering a Japanese house. All outside footwear is slipped off in the **genkan** (porch area) and slippers are worn to pad around the house. When you go to the toilet, you must also take care to change into the specially provided toilet slippers. Some Japanese restaurants, shrines and temples require you to remove your shoes before entering. There will sometimes be small lockers in which you can deposit your shoes.

---

shoelaces kuts·himo
くつひも

shoe polish kutszumi
くつずみ

shoe repairer kutsnaoshi
くつなおし

shop mise
店

In urban areas, shops are usually open Mon–Sat 10am–7pm and do not close for lunch. Some department stores are open later than 7pm. Department stores and other big stores usually open on Sundays and close one day during the week, but some are open seven days. A five per cent consumer tax is added to most purchases; usually the displayed price does not include this tax.

shopping: I'm going shopping kaimono ni ikimas
買物にいきます

shopping centre shop·ping-sentā
ショッピングセンター

shop window shōuindō
ショーウィンドー

shore (of sea) umibe
海辺
(of lake) kishibe
岸辺

short (person) se no hikui
背の低い
(time, journey) mijikai
みじかい

shortcut chikamichi
近道

shorts pants
パンツ

should: what should I do? do shitara ī desho?
どうしたらいいでしょう？

you should … … -ta hō ga ī des
…—たほうがいいです

you shouldn't … … -nai hō ga ī des
…—ないほうがいいです

he should be back soon kare wa sug modot·te kuru hazu des
彼はすぐ戻ってくるはずです

shoulder kata
かた

shout (verb) sakebimas
さけびます

show (in theatre) shō
ショー

could you show me? misete kuremasen ka?
見せてくれませんか？

(direction) oshiete kuremasen ka?
おしえてくれませんか？

shower (in bathroom) shawā
シャワー

(of rain) niwaka-ame
にわか雨

with shower shawā-tski (no)
シャワー付き（の）

shower gel bodī-sōp
ボディーソープ

shrine jinja
神社

shut (verb) shimemas
閉めます

when do you shut? koko wa
nanji ni shimarimas ka?
ここは何時に閉
まりますか？

when does it shut? itsu
shimarimas ka?
いつ閉まりますか？

they're shut shimat·te imas
閉まっています

I've shut myself out kagi o
naka ni wasuremashta
かぎを中に忘れ
ました

shut up! damare!
だまれ！

shutter (on camera) shat·tā
シャッター

(on window) amado
あまど

sick (ill) byōki (no)
病気（の）

I'm going to be sick (vomit)
hakisō des
吐きそうです

side yoko
よこ

the other side of the street

tōri no mukōgawa
通りの向こう側

side street wakimichi
わき道

sidewalk hodō
歩道

on the sidewalk hodō de
歩道で

sight: the sights of ... ... no
meisho
…の名所

sightseeing: we're going
sightseeing kankō ni
dekakeru tsmori des
観光にでかけるつも
りです

sightseeing tour kankōryokō
観光旅行

sign kamban
看板

(roadsign) hyōshiki
標識

signature shomei
署名

silk kinu
きぬ

silly baka (na)
ばか（な）

silver (noun) gin
銀

similar onaji yō (na)
同じような

simple (easy) kantan (na)
かんたん（な）

since: since last week senshū

kara
先週から

since I got here koko ni kite
irai
ここに来て以来

sing utaimas
歌います

Singapore Shin·gapōru
シンガポール

singer kashu
歌手

single: a single to ... ... made
katamichi-kip·p o ichi-mai
…まで片道切符を一
枚

I'm single watashi wa
dokshin des
私は独身です

single bed shin·guru-bed·do
シングルベッド

single room shin·guru
シングル

single ticket katamichi-kip·p
片道切符

sink (in kitchen) nagashi
ながし

sister (elder: one's own) ane
姉

(someone else's) onē-san
お姉さん

(younger: one's own) imōto
妹

(someone else's) imōto-san
妹さん

sister-in-law (elder: one's own) giri

no ane
義理の姉

(someone else's) giri no
onē-san
義理のお姉さん

(younger: one's own) giri no
imōto
義理の妹

(someone else's) giri no
imōto-san
義理の妹さん

sit: can I sit here? koko ni
suwat·te mo ī des ka?
ここに座ってもいい
ですか？

is anyone sitting here? koko ni
wa dare ka suwat·te imas ka?
ここにはだれか座っ
ていますか？

sit down suwarimas
座ります

sit down osuwari kudasai
お座りください

size saizu
サイズ

skin hif
ひふ

skinny yaseta
やせた

skirt skāto
スカート

sky sora
空

skyscraper kōsōbiru
高層ビル

sleep (verb) nemurimas
眠ります
  did you sleep well? yok
  nemuremashta ka?
  よく眠れましたか？

sleeper (on train) shindaisha
寝台車

sleeping bag nebukuro
寝袋

sleeping car shindaisha
寝台車

sleeping pill suimin·yak
睡眠薬

sleeve sode
そで

slide (photographic) suraido
スライド

slippers surip·pa
スリッパ
  see shoes

slippery suberiyasui
すべりやすい

slow osoi
おそい
  slow down! mot·to yuk·kuri!
  もっとゆっくり！

slowly yuk·kuri
ゆっくり
  very slowly unto yuk·kuri
  うんとゆっくり

small chīsai
ちいさい

smell: it smells (smells bad)
  nioimas ne
  においますね

smile (verb) hohoemimas
ほほえみます

smoke (noun) kemuri
けむり
  do you mind if I smoke?
  tabako o sut·te mo ī des ka?
  たばこを吸っても
  いいですか？
  I don't smoke tabako wa
  suimasen
  たばこは吸いません
  do you smoke? tabako o
  suimas ka?
  たばこを吸います
  か？

snack: just a snack chot·to
oyats
ちょっとおやつ

sneeze (noun) kushami o
shimas
くしゃみをします

snow yuki
雪
  it's snowing yuki ga fut·te
  imas
  雪が降っています

so: it's so good totemo ī des
とてもいいです
  it's so expensive totemo
  takai des
  とても高いです
  not so much son·na ni
  taksan ja nak
  そんなにたくさん
  じゃなく

not so bad son·na ni waruk nai
そんなに悪くない

so am I watashi mo sō des
私もそうです

so do I watashi mo sō des
私もそうです

so-so māmā des
まあまあです

soaking solution (for contact lenses) hozon·eki
保存液

soap sek·ken
せっけん

soap powder kona-sek·ken
粉せっけん

sober shiraf (no)
しらふ（の）

sock sok·ks
ソックス

socket (electrical) soket·to
ソケット

soda (water) sōda-sui
ソーダ水

sofa sofā
ソファー

soft (material etc) yawarakai
やわらかい

soft-boiled egg hanjuk-tamago
半熟たまご

soft drink softo-dorink
ソフトドリンク

soft lenses softo-kontakto
ソフトコンタクト

sole (of shoe) kuts no soko
くつの底

(of foot) ashi no ura
足の裏

could you put new soles on these? kuts no soko o harikaete kuremasen ka?
くつの底を張り替えてくれませんか？

some: can I have some water/apples? mizu/rin·go o skoshi moraemas ka?
水／りんごをすこしもらえますか？

can I have some? skoshi morat·te mo ī des ka?
すこしもらってもいいですか？

somebody, someone dare ka
だれか

something nani ka
何か

something to eat nani ka taberu mono
何か食べるもの

sometimes tokidoki
ときどき

somewhere doko ka
どこか

son (one's own) musko
息子

(someone else's) musko-san
息子さん

song uta
歌

son-in-law (one's own) giri no
musko
義理の息子
(someone else's) giri no
musko-san
義理の息子さん
soon sug
すぐ
I'll be back soon sug
modot·te kimas
すぐ戻ってきます
as soon as possible narubek
hayak
なるべくはやく
sore: it's sore itai des
痛いです
sore throat nodo no
itami
のどの痛み
I've got a sore throat nodo ga
itai des
のどが痛いです
sorry: (I'm) sorry dōmo
sumimasen
どうもすみません
sorry? (didn't understand) nante
īmashta ka?
何て言いましたか？
sort: what sort of ...? dono
yōna ...?
どのような…？
soup sūp
スープ
sour (taste) sup·pai
すっぱい

south minami
南
in the south minami ni
南に
South Africa Minami-Afrika
南アフリカ
South African (adj)
Minami-Afrika (no)
南アフリカ（の）
I'm South African watashi wa
Minami-Afrika-jin des
私は南アフリカ人
です
southeast nantō
南東
South Korea Kankok
韓国
southwest nansei
南西
souvenir omiyage
おみやげ
soya milk tōnyū
豆乳
Spain Spein
スペイン
Spanish (adj) Spein (no)
スペイン（の）
spare tyre yobi no taiya
予備のタイヤ
speak: do you speak English?
Eigo o hanasemas ka?
英語を話せますか？
I don't speak ... ... wa
hanasemasen
…は話せません

• • • • • DIALOGUE • • • • •

can I speak to Yoko? Yōko-san wa
iras·shaimas ka?

who's calling? dochira-sama des
ka?

it's Patricia Patricia des

I'm sorry, Yoko's not in, can I take a
message? mōshiwake arimasen
ga, Yōko wa ima rus ni shite
orimas, nani ka den·gon wa
arimas ka?

no thanks, I'll call back later īe,
kek·kō des, atode
kakenaoshimas

please tell her I called kanojo ni
Patricia kara denwa ga at·ta to
otsutae kudasai

spectacles megane
めがね

speed limit sokdoseigen
速度制限

spend okane o tskaimas
お金をつかいます

spider kumo
クモ

spin-dryer das·suiki
脱水機

spoon spūn
スプーン

sport spōts
スポーツ

sprain: I've sprained my ... ... o
kujiite shimaimashta
…をくじいてしまい
ました

spring (season) haru
春

(of car, seat) spuring
スプリング

in the spring haru ni
春に

square (in town) hiroba
広場

stairs kaidan
階段

stale furui
ふるい

stamp (noun) kit·te
切手

• • • • • DIALOGUE • • • • •

a stamp for England, please Igiris
made no kit·te o kudasai

what are you sending? nani o
yūso saremas ka?

this postcard kono hagaki des

standby kyanseru-machi
キャンセル待ち

star hoshi
ほし

(in film) stā
スター

start (noun) stāto
スタート

(verb) hajimemas
始めます

when does it start? itsu
hajimarimas ka?
いつ始まりますか？

the car won't start kuruma no

enjin ga kakarimasen
車のエンジンがかか
りません

starter (of car) shidōki
始動機

(food) zensai
前菜

station eki
駅

statue zō
像

stay: where are you staying?
doko ni tomat·te imas ka?
どこに泊まって
いますか？

I'm staying at ... ... ni
tomat·te imas
…に泊まっています

**I'd like to stay another two
nights** mō ni-hak shitai to
omoimas
もう二泊したいとお
もいます

steak stēki
ステーキ

steal nusumimas
盗みます

my bag has been stolen
bag·g o nusumaremashta
バッグを盗まれ
ました

steep (hill) kewashī
けわしい

step: on the steps kaidan de
階段で

sterling Igiris-pondo
イギリスポンド

steward (on plane) schuwādo
スチュワード

stewardess schūwādes
スチュワーデス

still: I'm still here mada koko ni
imas
まだここにいます

(on the phone) hai,
moshi-moshi
はい、もしもし

is he still there? kare wa
mada soko ni imas ka?
彼はまだそこにいま
すか？

keep still! ugokanaide
kudasai!
うごかないで
ください！

sting: I've been stung hachi ni
sasaremashta
ハチにさされました

stockings stok·king
ストッキング

stomach onaka
おなか

stomachache fuktsū
腹痛

stone (rock) ishi
石

stop (verb) tomarimas
止まります

please, stop here (to taxi driver
etc) koko de tomete

kudasai
ここで止めて
ください

do you stop near ...?
... no chikak de tomarimas
ka?
…の近くで止まり
ますか？

stop it! yamete kudasai!
やめてください！

stopover keiyu
経由

storm arashi
あらし

straight (whisky) storēto
ストレート

it's straight ahead mas·sug
it·ta tokoro des
まっすぐ行ったとこ
ろです

straightaway sug ni
すぐに

strange (odd) hen (na)
へん（な）

stranger shiranai hito
知らないひと

I'm a stranger here koko wa
hajimete des
ここは初めてです

strap (on watch) bando
バンド

(on dress, suitcase) storap·p
ストラップ

strawberry ichigo
いちご

straw mat tatami
たたみ

stream kawa
川

street tōri
通り

on the street tōri de
通りで

streetmap dōrochizu
道路地図

string himo
ひも

strong tsyoi
つよい

stuck tskaeta
つかえた

it's stuck tskaete
shimaimashta
つかえてしまい
ました

student gaksei
学生

stupid baka (na)
ばか（な）

suburb kōgai
郊外

subway (US: railway) chikatets
地下鉄

see underground

suddenly totszen ni
突然に

suede suēdo
スエード

sugar satō
さとう

suit (noun) sūts
スーツ
  it doesn't suit me (jacket etc)
  watashi niwa niaimasen
  私には似合いません
  it suits you yok niaimas
  よく似合います
suitcase sūtskēs
スーツケース
summer nats
夏
  in the summer nats ni
  夏に
sumo wrestling sumō
すもう
sun taiyō
太陽
  in the sun hinata de
  ひなたで
  out of the sun hikage de
  ひかげで
sunbathe nik·kōyok
日光浴
sunblock (cream) hiyake-dome
ひやけ止め
sunburn hiyake
ひやけ
sunburnt hiyake shita
ひやけした
Sunday Nichiyōbi
日曜日
sunglasses san·guras
サングラス
sunny: it's sunny harete imas
晴れています

sunset nichibots
日没
sunshade hiyoke
ひよけ
sunshine nik·kō
日光
sunstroke nis·shabyō
日射病
suntan hiyake
ひやけ
suntan lotion santan-
rōshon
サンタンローション
suntanned hi ni yaketa
日にやけた
suntan oil san-oiru
サンオイル
super sugoi
すごい
supermarket sūpā
スーパー
supper yūshok
夕食
supplement (extra charge)
tsuikaryōkin
追加料金
supply (noun) takwae
たくわえ
  (verb) chōtats shimas
  調達します
sure: are you sure? tashika des
ka?
たしかですか？
sure! mochiron!
もちろん！

surface mail sarubin
サル便

surname myōji
名字

---

swearwords

With their great emphasis on politeness, especially towards Westerners, Japanese rarely admit to the existence of swearwords in their language, apart from the rather tame: '**baka!**' (you fool!), '**kso!**' (shit!) and '**chiku-shō**' (damn!). Japanese insist that these and other **warui kotoba** (bad words) should not be divulged to outsiders.

---

sweater sētā
セーター

sweatshirt torēnā
トレーナー

Sweden Suēden
スウェーデン

Swedish (adj) Suēden (no)
スウェーデン (の)

sweet (adj: taste) amai
あまい

sweets kyandī
キャンディー

swelling hare
腫れ

swim (verb) oyogimas
泳ぎます

I'm going for a swim oyogi ni

ikimas
泳ぎにいきます

let's go for a swim oyogi ni
ikimashō
泳ぎにいきましょう

swimming costume mizugi
水着

swimming pool pūru
プール

swimming trunks mizugi
水着

switch (noun) suit·chi
スイッチ

switch off (engine) tomemas
止めます
(TV, lights) keshimas
消します

switch on (engine) kakemas
かけます
(TV, lights) tskemas
つけます

swollen hareta
腫れた

T

table tēburu
テーブル

a table for two futari-bun no
seki
二人分の席

tablecloth tēburu-kuros
テーブルクロス

table tennis tak·kyū
卓球

table wine tēburu-wain
テーブルワイン

tailor shinshifuku-ten
紳士服店

Taiwan Taiwan
台湾

take (verb: lead a peson) tsurete ikimas
連れていきます
(object) mot·te ikimas
持っていきます
(accept) torimas
取ります
can you take me to the ...? ... made tsurete it·te kuremasen ka?
…まで連れていって くれませんか？
do you take credit cards? kurejit·to-kādo wa tskaemas ka?
クレジットカードは つかえますか？
fine, I'll take it ja, sore ni shimas
じゃ、それにします
can I take this? (leaflet etc) kore o morat·te mo ī des ka?
これをもらっても いいですか？
how long does it take? jikan wa dono kurai kakarimas ka?
時間はどのくらいか かりますか？
it takes three hours san-jikan

kakarimas
三時間かかります

is this seat taken? kono seki wa fusagat·te imas ka?
この席はふさがって いますか？

hamburger to take away hanbāga o teik·auto de
ハンバーガーをティ クアウトで

can you take a little off here? (to hairdresser) koko o mō skoshi kit·te kuremasen ka?
ここをもうすこし切 ってくれませんか？

talcum powder tarukam-paudā
タルカムパウダー

talk (verb) hanashimas
話します

tall (person) se ga takai
背が高い
(building) takai
高い

tampons tampon
タンポン

tan (noun) hiyake
ひやけ
to get a tan hiyake shimas
ひやけします

tap jaguchi
じゃ口

tape (cassette) tēp
テープ

taste (noun) aji
味

can I taste it? ajimi shite mo ī
des ka?

味見してもいいです
か？

---

tax

Japan has an across-the-board
5 per cent federal consumer tax.
It's advisable to check before
purchasing goods whether the
tax is already included in the
price. In addition, a further local tax of 3 per cent is added to
hotel bills if they exceed 15,000
yen and to restaurant bills if
they exceed 7,500 yen.

---

taxi takshī

タクシー

will you get me a taxi? takshī
o yonde kuremasen ka?

タクシーを呼んでく
れませんか？

where can I find a taxi? doko
de takshī o tskamaeraremas
ka?

どこでタクシーをつ
かまえられますか？

•••••• DIALOGUE ••••••

to the airport/to the ... Hotel, please
kūkō/... hoteru made, onegai
shimas

how much will it be? ikura kurai
kakarimas ka?

about 2,500 yen daitai ni-sen-go-

hyak-en kurai des

that's fine right here, thanks
sumimasen, koko de oroshite
kudasai

Japanese taxis are expensive
and luxurious, with air-conditioning, white-gloved drivers,
and doors that open and shut
automatically. Late at night, you
may have to pay a 20 per cent
surcharge. Tipping is not necessary.

It's a good idea to enter the taxi
with your destination address
clearly written on a piece of paper. If you stay at a hotel, somebody at the reception desk
(**fronto**) will usually oblige.

---

taxi-driver takshī no untenshu

タクシーの運転手

taxi rank takshī-noriba

タクシー乗り場

tea (drink) kōcha

紅茶

green tea ocha

お茶

tea for one/two please kōcha
o hitots/futats kudasai

紅茶をひとつ／ふた
つください

Japanese make a strict distinction between Indian tea (**kōcha**) and Japanese tea (**ocha**). While the former is offered with the usual Western additions of milk and sugar, ocha is drunk from cups without handles, and without any additives. Recently other Chinese teas and herbal teas have become popular and they are also drunk without milk or sugar. You will also see these teas in cans.

The tea ceremony has made a very strict ritual of the serving of Japanese tea, emphasising the inherent simplicity of the act and the equality of all those who take part. It has turned into an art form and you never come across it in a domestic situation.

---

teabags tībag·g
ティーバッグ

teach: could you teach me?
oshiete kuremasen ka?
教えてくれません
か？

teacher sensei
先生

teahouse kis·sa·ten
喫茶店

team chīm
チーム

teaspoon tīspūn
ティースプーン

tea towel fukin
ふきん

teenager tīn·eijā
ティーンエイジャー

telephone denwa
電話
see **phone**

television terebi
テレビ

tell: could you tell him ...? kare ni
... to tstaete kuremasen ka?
彼に…と伝えてくれ
ませんか？

temperature (weather) kion
気温
(fever) nets
ねつ

temple (Buddhist) otera
お寺

tent tento
テント

term (at university, school) gak·ki
学期

terminus (rail) shūten
終点

terrible hidoi
ひどい

terrific subarashī
すばらしい

than ... yorimo
…よりも

ENGLISH ◆ JAPANESE | Th

smaller than ... ... yorimo chīsai

…よりもちいさい

thank: thank you, thanks arigatō

ありがとう

thank you very much hontō ni arigatō gozaimas

ほんとうにありがとうございます

thanks for the lift nosete kurete arigatō

乗せてくれてありがとう

no thanks īe kek·kō des

いいえ、けっこうです

• • • • • • DIALOGUE • • • • • •

thanks arigatō

that's OK, don't mention it īe, dō itashimashte

that (nearby) sore

それ

(further away) are

あれ

(adj: nearby) sono

その

(further away) ano

あの

that one (nearby) sore

それ

(further away) are

あれ

I hope that ... ... -tara ī

des ne

…— たらいいですね

that's nice steki des

すてきです

is that ...? sore wa ... des ka?

それは…ですか？

that's it (that's right) sono tōri des

そのとおりです

the* sono

その

theatre gekijō

劇場

their(s)* (male) karera no

彼らの

(female) kanojotachi no

彼女たちの

them* (things) sore

それ

(male) karera (o)

彼ら（を）

(female) kanojotachi (o)

彼女たち（を）

for them karera/kanojotachi no tame ni

彼ら／彼女たちのために

with them karera/kanojotachi to is·sho ni

彼ら／彼女たちと一緒に

to them karera/kanojotachi ni

彼ら／彼女たちに

who? – them dare des ka? –

karera/kanojotachi des
だれですか？ ―
彼ら／彼女たちです

then (at that time) sono toki
その時

(after that) sore kara
それから

there soko de
そこで

over there mukō ni
むこうに

up there asoko ni
あそこに

is there …? … ga arimas ka?
…がありますか？

are there …? … ga arimas
ka?
…がありますか？

there is … … ga arimas
…があります

there are … ga arimas
…があります

there you are (giving something)
hai, dōzo
はい、どうぞ

Thermos® flask mahōbin
魔法びん

these* korera
これら

(adj) kono
この

I'd like these kore ga ki ni
irimashta
これが気に入り
ました

they* (things) sorera
それら

(male) karera
彼ら

(female) kanojotachi
彼女たち

thick atsui
厚い

(stupid) nibui
にぶい

thief dorobō
どろぼう

thigh momo
もも

thin (person) yaseta
やせた

(object) usui
うすい

thing mono
もの

my things watashi no shibuts
私の私物

think kan·gaemas
考えます

I think so watashi wa sō
omoimas
私はそうおもいます

I don't think so watashi wa sō
wa omoimasen
私はそうはおもい
ません

I'll think about it sore ni
tsuite wa kan·gaete okimas
それについては考え
ておきます

third party insurance
daisansha-hoken
第三者保険

thirsty: I'm thirsty nodo ga
kawakimashta
のどがかわきました

this kore
これ

(adj) kono
この

this one kore
これ

this is my wife watashi no
tsma des
私の妻です

is this …? kore wa … des
ka?
これは…ですか？

those arera
あれら

(adj) ano
あの

which ones? – those dore
des ka? – are des
どれですか？ーあれ
です

thread (noun) ito
いと

throat nodo
のど

throat pastilles torōchi
トローチ

through tōt·te
通って

does it go through …? (train,

bus) … o tōrimas ka?
…を通りますか？

throw (verb) nagemas
投げます

throw away stemas
捨てます

thumb oya-yubi
おやゆび

thunderstorm rai-u
雷雨

Thursday Mok·yōbi

ticket ken
券

(for transport) kip·p
切符

• • • • • • DIALOGUE • • • • • •

a return to Sendai Sendai made
ōfuk-kip·p o ichi-mai

coming back when? kaeri wa itsu
des ka?

today/next Tuesday kyō/tsgi no
Kayōbi des

that will be 13,000 yen ichi-man-
san-zen-en ni narimas

see train

ticket office kip·p-uriba
切符売り場

tie (necktie) nektai
ネクタイ

tight (clothes etc) kitsui
きつい

it's too tight kits·sugimas
きつすぎます

tights pantī-stok·king
パンティーストッキ
ング

time* jikan
時間

what's the time? ima nanji
des ka?
いま何時ですか？

this time konkai
今回

last time zenkai
前回

next time kondo
今度

three times san-kai
三回

timetable jikokhyō
時刻表

tin (can) kan
缶

tin-opener kankiri
缶切り

tiny totemo chīsai
とてもちいさい

tip (to waiter etc) chip·p
チップ

Tipping is not expected in Japan. The only person that it's usual to tip is the maid at a **ryokan** (traditional hotel).

tired tskareta
つかれた

I'm tired tskaremashta
つかれました

tissues tis·sh
ティッシュ

to: to Tokyo/London Tōkyō/
Rondon e
東京／ロンドンへ

to Japan/Britain nip·pon/
Igiris e
日本／イギリスへ

to the post office yūbinkyok e
郵便局へ

toast (bread) tōsto
トースト

today kyō
きょう

toe tsmasaki
つまさき

together is·sho ni
一緒に

we're together (in shop etc)
is·sho des
一緒です

toilet toire
トイレ

where is the toilet? toire wa
doko des ka?
トイレはどこです
か？

I have to go to the toilet toire
ni ikitai no des ga
トイレにいきたいの
ですが

Public toilets can always be found at a train or subway station and in all department stores. Sometimes they will be the squatting variety, but more often these days you'll be confronted by a hi-tech model. Unusual things to be aware of are electronically-warmed seats and devices that play the sound of a flushing toilet so as to cover up any embarrassing noises you might make. Also, in public toilets, there is usually no toilet paper. Make sure you take the free packs of tissues, carrying advertising, offered outside most major train stations and the main shopping districts.

toilet paper toiret·to-pēpā
トイレットペーパー
Tokyo Bay Tōkyō-wan
東京湾
tomato tomato
トマト
tomato ketchup kechap·p
ケチャップ
tomorrow ashita
あした
tomorrow morning ashita no asa
あしたの朝

the day after tomorrow asat·te
あさって
tongue shita
舌
tonic (water) tonik·k·uōtā
トニックウォーター
tonight komban
今晩
too (excessively) ... sugimas
…すぎます
(also) mo
も
too hot atsu-sugimas
あつすぎます
too much ōsugimas
多すぎます
me too watashi mo
私も
tooth ha
歯
toothache haita
歯痛
toothbrush haburashi
歯ブラシ
toothpaste hamigakiko
歯みがき粉
top: on top of ... ... no ue ni
…の上に
at the top tep·pen ni
てっぺんに
top floor saijōkai
最上階
topless top·pures
トップレス

torch kaichūdentō
懐中電灯

total gōkei
合計

tour (noun) tsuā
ツアー

is there a tour of …? … no
tsuā ga arimas ka?
…のツアーがあり
ますか？

tour guide gaido
ガイド

tourist ryokōkyak
旅行客

tourist information office
kankō-an-naijo
観光案内所

towards … … no hō e
…のほうへ

towel taoru
タオル

town machi
町

in town machi de
町に

just out of town machihazure
町はずれに

town centre hankagai
繁華街

toy omocha
おもちゃ

track purat·to·hōm
プラットホーム

which track is it for Nara?
Nara-iki wa dono

purat·to·hōm des ka?
奈良行きはどのプラ
ットホームですか？

tracksuit suet·t·sūts
スエットスーツ

trade fair mihon·ichi
見本市

traditional dentō-teki (na)
伝統的（な）

traffic kōtsū
交通

traffic jam jūtai
渋滞

traffic lights shin·gō
信号

train densha
電車

by train densha de
電車で

For those planning to travel extensively in Japan by train, a Japan Rail Pass is great value for money. With a one-, two- or three-week pass, you get unlimited travel on the trains of Japan Rail (JR). You need to obtain a rail pass voucher prior to your departure to Japan and the pass is valid for three months from the date of purchase. The voucher can be exchanged at the JR desk in Narita Airport or at any major JR stations, and you can choose the starting date.
→

The pass can also be used on the long-distance bus services operated by JR.

JR has the most extensive network in Japan and operates the famous **shinkansen** (bullet train). Other inter-city services are classified as **tok·kyū** (super express) with an extremely limited number of stops, **kyūkō** (express) with slightly more but still limited stops, and a local services called **futsū**. Inter-city services have a first-class carriage called **gurīnsha** (green car). For the faster express services (shinkansen, tok·kyū, kyūkō), you should have two tickets for a journey: one for boarding and the other for the express service. You can reserve seats by paying extra at the **midori no madoguchi** (ticket counter), but reservations are not compulsory unless you are travelling on the **nozomi** (the fastest bullet train service). There is an English timetable available from the Japan National Tourist Organization.

Within local networks, services are **futsū** (standard) and **kaisok** (limited stops), but the prices are the same. Most tickets can →

be bought from machines. Before you go onto the platform you show your ticket at the ticket gate or put it though the ticket barrier; to board the shinkansen you need to go through another ticket control point. Unfortunately, there are no luggage carts at train stations, so be prepared and pack light.

• • • • • • DIALOGUE • • • • • •

is this the train for Otaru? kore wa Otaru-iki no densha des ka?

I am not sure sã, chot·to wakarimasen

no, you want that platform there īe, mukō no purat·to-hōm des

trainers (shoes) sunīkā
スニーカー
train station eki
駅
tram romendensha
路面電車
translate hon·yak shimas
翻訳します
could you translate that?
sore o yak shite kuremasen ka?
それを訳してくれませんか？
translation hon·yak
翻訳

translator hon·yaksha
翻訳者

trash (waste) gomi
ごみ

trashcan gomibako
ごみ箱

travel ryokō shimas
旅行します

we're travelling around
achikochi ryokō shite
imas
あちこち旅行して
います

travel agent's ryokōgaisha
旅行会社

traveller's cheque
traberāz-chek·k
トラベラーズチェッ
ク

do you take traveller's
cheques? traberāz-chek·k
wa tskaemas ka?
トラベラーズチェッ
クはつかえますか？

tray obon
おぼん

tree ki
木

tremendous sugoi
すごい

trendy oshare (na)
おしゃれ（な）

trim: just a trim, please (to
hairdresser) kesaki o
soroeru teido ni onegai

shimas
毛先をそろえる程度
にお願いします

trip (excursion) kankōryokō
観光旅行

I'd like to go on a trip to … …
o ryokō shite mitai des
…を旅行してみたい
です

trolley (for luggage) nimots-yō
kāto
荷物用カート

trouble (noun) yak·kaigoto
やっかいごと

I'm having trouble with … …
de komat·te imas
…で困っています

trousers zubon
ズボン

true hontō (no)
ほんとう（の）

that's not true sore wa hontō
ja arimasen
それはほんとうじゃ
ありません

trunk (US: of car) torank
トランク

trunks (swimming) mizugi
水着

try (verb) tameshimas
試します

can I try it? (food) ajimi shite
mo ī des ka?
味見してもいいです
か？

(at doing something) yat·te mite mo ī des ka?

やってみてもいい
ですか？

try on shichak shimas

試着します

can I try it on? shichak shite mo ī des ka?

試着してもいいです
か？

T-shirt tī-shats

Ｔシャツ

Tuesday Kayōbi

火曜日

tuna maguro

まぐろ

tunnel ton·neru

トンネル

turn: turn left/right
hidari/migi e magat·te kudasai

左／右へ曲がって
ください

turn off: where do I turn off?
doko de magarimas ka?

どこで曲がります
か？

can you turn the heating off?
dambō o kit·te kuremasen ka?

暖房を切ってくれ
ませんか？

turn on: can you turn the heating on? dambō o tskete

kuremasen ka?

暖房をつけてくれ
ませんか？

turning (in road) magarikado

曲り角

TV terebi

テレビ

tweezers kenuki

毛抜き

twice ni-kai

二回

twice as much ni-bai

二倍

twin beds tsuin-bed·do

ツインベッド

twin room tsuin

ツイン

twist: I've twisted my ankle
ashikubi o kujiite shimaimashta

足首をくじいてし
まいました

type (noun) shurui

種類

another type of ... bets no shurui no ...

別の種類の…

typhoon taifū

台風

typical (dish etc) daihyō-teki (na)

代表的（な）

tyre taiya

タイヤ

U

ugly minikui
みにくい

UK Igiris
イギリス

ulcer kaiyō
かいよう

umbrella kasa
かさ

uncle (one's own) oji
おじ

(someone else's) oji-san
おじさん

unconscious muishiki (no)
無意識（の）

under (in position) ... no shita ni
…のしたに

(less than) ... ika
…以下

underdone (meat) namayake
(no)
なまやけ（の）

underground (railway) chikatets
地下鉄

There are underground railways
in most of the major cities;
they're safe, clean, fast, air-
conditioned and not too expensive, but they can be very
crowded. All stations display
their names in Japanese and
romanized Japanese. In Tokyo,
there are two underground →

networks in operation; these
and other local train networks
are conveniently linked, but
you need to obtain a special
ticket for a linked service when
you buy a ticket from vending
machine.

underpants pants
パンツ

understand: I understand
wakarimas
わかります
I don't understand
wakarimasen
わかりません
do you understand?
wakarimas ka?
わかりますか？

unemployed shitsgyō-chū
失業中

unfashionable ryūkō-okure
(no)
流行おくれ（の）

United States Gas·shūkok
合衆国

university daigak
大学

unleaded petrol muen-gasorin
無鉛ガソリン

unlimited mileage
sōkōkyori-museigen
走行距離無制限

unlock kagi o akemas
かぎを開けます

unpack nihodoki shimas
荷ほどきします

until: until 6 o'clock rokji made
六時まで

until Saturday Doyōbi made
土曜日まで

unusual mezurashī
めずらしい

up ue ni
上に

up there asoko ni
あそこに

he's not up yet (not out of bed)
kare wa mada nete imas
彼はまだ寝ています

what's up? (what's wrong?) dō
ka shimashta ka?
どうかしましたか？

upmarket kōkyū (na)
高級（な）

upset stomach i no chōshi ga
yok nai
胃の調子がよくない

I have an upset stomach i no
chōshi ga yok arimasen
胃の調子がよく
ありません

upside down sakasama
さかさま

upstairs ue
上

up-to-date saishin (no)
最新（の）

urgent kinkyū (na)
緊急（な）

us* watashitachi (o)
私たち（を）

with us watashitachi to
私たちと

for us watashitachi no tame
ni
私たちのために

USA Amerika Gas·shūkok
アメリカ合衆国

use (verb) tskaimas
つかいます

may I use …? … o tskat·te mo
ī des ka?
…をつかってもいい
ですか？

useful yak ni tats
役にたつ

usual futsū (no)
ふつう（の）

the usual (drink etc)
itsmono
いつもの

V

vacancy: do you have any
vacancies? (hotel) akibeya ga
arimas ka?
空き部屋があります
か？
see room

vacation yasumi
休み

on vacation yasumi de
休みで

vaccination yobōchūsha
予防注射

vacuum cleaner sōjiki
そうじ機

valid (ticket etc) yūkō (na)
有効（な）

how long is it valid for?
yūkōkikan wa dono kurai
des ka?
有効期間はどの
くらいですか？

valley tani
たに

valuable (adj) kichō (na)
貴重（な）

can I leave my valuables here?
kichō-hin o koko ni
azkeraremas ka?
貴重品をここに
預られますか？

value (noun) kachi
価値

van ban
バン

vanilla banira
バニラ

a vanilla ice cream
banira-aiskurīm
バニラアイスクリー
ム

vary: it varies bāi ni
yorimas
場合によります

vase kabin
花びん

veal koushi no nik
仔牛の肉

vegetables yasai
野菜

vegetarian (noun)
saishok-shugisha
菜食主義者

vending machine
jidō-hambaiki
自動販売機

very totemo
とても

very little for me hon·no
skoshi dake
ほんのすこしだけ

I like it very much totemo
suki des
とても好きです

via keiyu de
経由で

video (noun: film) bideo-tēp
ビデオテープ

(recorder) bideo-kamera
ビデオカメラ

view nagame
ながめ

village mura
村

vinegar su
酢

visa biza
ビザ

visit (verb) tazunemas
訪ねます

I'd like to visit … … o

tazunetai des
…を訪ねたいです

vital: it's vital that … … wa
totemo taisets des
…はとてもたいせつ
です

vodka uok·ka
ウォッカ

voice koe
こえ

volcano kazan
火山

voltage den·ats
電圧

vomit hakimas
吐きます

W

waist uesto
ウェスト

waistcoat besto
ベスト

wait machimas
待ちます

wait for me mat·te kudasai
待ってください

don't wait for me matanaide
kudasai
待たないでください

**can I wait until my wife gets
here?** tsma ga kuru made
mat·te mo ī des ka?
妻が来るまで待って
もいいですか？

can you do it while I wait?
mat·te iru aida ni yat·te
kuremasen ka?
待っているあいだに
やってくれません
か？

could you wait here for me?
koko de chot·to mat·te ite
kuremasen ka?
ここでちょっと待っ
ていてくれません
か？

waiter uētā
ウェイター

waiter! chot·to sumimasen!
ちょっとすみ
ません！

waitress uētores
ウェートレス

waitress! chot·to
sumimasen!
ちょっとすみ
ません！

**wake: can you wake me up at
5.30?** goji-han ni okoshite
kuremasen ka?
5時半に起こして
くれませんか？

wake-up call mōning-kōru
モーニングコール

Wales Uēruz
ウェールズ

walk: is it a long walk? arukto
tōi des ka?
歩くととおいですか？

it's only a short walk aruite
sug des
歩いてすぐです
I'll walk aruite ikimas
歩いていきます
I'm going for a walk sampo ni
dekakemas
散歩にでかけます
wall kabe
かべ
wallet saif
さいふ
want: I want a ... ... ga hoshī des
…が欲しいです
I don't want any ... ... wa
irimasen
…はいりません
I want to go home uchi ni
kaeritai des
うちに帰りたいです
I don't want to sō shitak nai
des
そうしたくないです
he wants to ... kare wa ...-tai
des
彼は…ーたいです
what do you want? nani ga
hoshī des ka?
何が欲しいですか？
ward (in hospital) byōtō
病棟
warm atatakai
あたたかい
I'm so warm atsui des
あついです

was* ... deshta
…でした
wash (verb) araimas
洗います
can you wash these? kore o
arat·te kuremasen ka?
これを洗ってくれ
ませんか？
washhand basin sem·mendai
洗面台
washing (clothes) sentakmono
せんたくもの
washing machine sentak·ki
せんたく機
washing powder senzai
洗剤
washing-up: to do the washing-
up shok·ki o araimas
食器を洗います
washing-up liquid shok·ki·yō
senzai
食器用洗剤
wasp hachi
ハチ
watch (wristwatch) udedokei
腕時計
will you watch my things for
me? watashi no nimots o
mite ite kuremasen ka?
私の荷物を見ていて
くれませんか？
watch out! abunai!
あぶない！
watch strap tokei no bando
時計のバンド

water mizu

水

may I have some water? mizu
o moraemas ka?

水をもらえますか？

waterproof (adj) bōsui (no)

防水（の）

waterskiing suijō-skī

水上スキー

way: it's this way kot·chi no hō
des

こっちのほうです

it's that way at·chi no hō des

あっちのほうです

is it a long way to ...? ... made
tōi des ka?

…までとおいですか？

no way! dame des!

だめです！

•••••• DIALOGUE ••••••

could you tell me the way to ...? ...
ewa dō ikeba ī des ka?

go straight on until you reach the
traffic lights shin·go ni ikiataru
made mas·sug des

turn left hidari e magat·te
kudasai

take the first on the right saisho
no magarikado o migi ni
magat·te kudasai

we* watashitachi

私たち

weak yowai

よわい

(tea) usui

うすい

weather tenki

天気

•••••• DIALOGUE ••••••

what's the weather forecast?
tenkiyohō wa dō des ka?

it's going to be fine hareru yō des

it's going to rain ame ni naru yō
des

it'll brighten up later ato de hareru
yō des

wedding kek·kon-shiki

結婚式

wedding ring kek·kon-yubiwa

結婚指輪

Wednesday Suiyōbi

水曜日

week (one, two, three etc) shūkan

週間

(this, last, next etc) shū

週

a week (from) today raishū
no kyō

来週のきょう

a week (from) tomorrow
raishū no ashita

来週のあした

weekend shūmats

週末

at the weekend shūmats ni

週末に

The Western idea of weekends is becoming popular, though many schools and offices still function on Saturdays. Being a non-Christian country, Sunday is the great day for going out and shopping. Avoid public transport into the countryside on this day. Large shops, especially department stores, close on one of the weekdays; museums usually close on Mondays.

weight omosa
おもさ

weird hen (na)
へん（な）

weirdo henjin
変人

welcome: welcome to ... ... e yōkoso
…へようこそ

you're welcome (don't mention it) dō itashimashte
どういたしまして

well: I don't feel well kibun ga yok arimasen
気分がよく
ありません

she's not well kanojo wa byōki des
彼女は病気です

you speak English very well Eigo ga totemo jōz des ne
英語がとてもじょう

ずですね

well done! sugoi!
すごい！

this one as well kore mo des
これもです

well well! (surprise) oya oya!
おやおや！

•••••• DIALOGUE ••••••

how are you? gokigen ikaga des ka?

very well, thanks, and you? hai, okagesama des ga, sochira wa?

well-done (meat) uerudan
ウェルダン

Welsh (adj) Uēruz (no)
ウェールズ

I'm Welsh watashi wa Uēruz-jin des
私はウェールズ人
です

were* ... deshta
…でした

West: the West Ōbei
欧米

west nishi
西

in the west nishi ni
西に

Western Ōbei (no)
欧米（の）

Westerner Ōbei-jin
欧米人

Western-style yōfū (no)
洋風（の）

wet nureta
ぬれた

whale kujira
くじら

what? nan des ka?
なんですか？

what's that? sore wa nan des ka?
それは何ですか？

what's happening? nani ga arundes ka?
何があるんですか？

(what's on?) nani o yat·te imas ka?
何をやっていますか？

(what's wrong?) dō shitandes ka?
どうしたんですか？

what should I do? dō shitara ī deshō ka?
どうしたらいいでしょうか？

what a view! ī nagame des ne!
いいながめですね！

what bus do I take? dono bas ni noreba ī des ka?
どのバスに乗ればいいですか？

wheel sharin
車輪

wheelchair kuruma-isu
車いす

when? itsu?
いつ？

when we get back kaet·te kara
帰ってから

when's the train/ferry? res·sha/ferī wa nanji des ka?
列車／フェリーは何時ですか？

where? doko?
どこ？

I don't know where it is doko daka shirimasen
どこだか知りません

• • • • • • DIALOGUE • • • • • •

where is the railway station? eki wa doko des ka?

it's over there mukō des

could you show me where it is on the map? chizu de doko daka oshiete kuremasen ka?

it's just here koko des

see way

which: which bus? dono bas?
どのバス？

• • • • • • DIALOGUE • • • • • •

which one? dore?

that one sore des

this one? kore?

no, that one ie, sore des

while: while I'm here koko ni iru aida ni
ここにいるあいだに

whisky uiskī
ウィスキー

white shiroi
しろい

white wine shiro-wain
白ワイン

who? dare?
だれ？

who is it? donata des ka?
どなたですか？

the man who ... ... hito
…ひと

whole: the whole week maru
is·shūkan
まる一週間

the whole lot zembu
ぜんぶ

whose: whose is this? kore wa
dare no des ka?
これはだれの
ですか？

why? dōshite des ka?
どうしてですか？

why not? dōshite des ka?
どうしてですか？

wide hiroi
ひろい

wife (one's own) tsma
妻

(someone else's) ok-san
奥さん

my wife watashi no tsma
私の妻

will*: will you do it for me? sō
shite kuremasen ka?
そうしてくれません
か？

wind (noun) kaze
風

window mado
まど

near the window mado no
soba de
まどのそばで

in the window (of shop)
shōuindō ni
ショーウィンドーに

window seat madogawa no
seki
窓側の席

windscreen fronto-garas
フロントガラス

windscreen wiper waipā
ワイパー

windsurfing uindosāfin
ウィンドサーフィン

windy: it's so windy kaze ga
tsyoi des
風がつよいです

wine wain
ワイン

can we have some more wine?
wain o mō skoshi moraemas
ka?
ワインをもうすこし
もらえますか？

wine list wain no risto
ワインのリスト

winter fuyu
冬

in the winter fuyu ni
冬に

wire waiyā
ワイヤー
(electric) kōdo
コード
with ... to is·sho ni
…と一緒に
I'm staying with ... ... no
tokoro ni tomat·te imas
…のところに泊まっ
ています
without nashi de
なしで
witness shōnin
証人
will you be a witness for me?
watashi no shōnin ni nat·te
kuremasen ka?
私の証人になってく
れませんか？
woman josei
女性

women
Although it has become illegal
to discriminate against women
at work, the traditional idea of
the female role being domestic
remains surprisingly common,
especially in rural areas. The
practice of women leaving their
job for marriage or motherhood
is still considered to be the
ideal. As a result, Japanese men
have little idea how to deal
with women in business. If an →

awkward situation arises, you
should discreetly remind your
business counterpart that you
would like them to treat you as
they would treat a male business associate.

wonderful subarashī
すばらしい
won't*: it won't start dō shite
mo stāto shimasen
どうしてもスタート
しません
wood (material) zaimok
材木
woods (forest) mori
森
wool ūru
ウール
word kotoba
ことば
work (noun) shigoto
仕事
it's not working ugokimasen
動きません
I work in ... ... de hataraite
imas
…で働いています
world sekai
世界
worry: I'm worried shimpai des
心配です
worse: it's worse nao warui
des
なおわるいです

worst sai-ak (no)
最悪（の）

worth: is it worth a visit? it·te
miru kachi ga arimas ka?
行って見る価値が
ありますか？

would: would you give this to ...?
kore o ... ni watashite
kuremasen ka?
これを…にわたして
くれませんか？

wrap: could you wrap it up?
tsutsunde kuremasen
ka?
包んでくれません
か？

wrapping paper hōsōshi
包装紙

wrestler resurā
レスラー

sumo wrestler rikishi
力士

wrestling resuring
レスリング

sumo wrestling sumō
すもう

wrist tekubi
手首

write kakimas
書きます

could you write it down? kaite
kuremasen ka?
書いてくれません
か？

how do you write it? dō

kakimas ka?
どう書きますか？

writing paper binsen
びんせん

wrong: it's the wrong key kagi
ga aimasen
かぎが合いません

this is the wrong train kore
wa chigau densha des
これはちがう電車
です

the bill's wrong okanjō ga
machigat·te imas
お勘定がまちがって
います

sorry, wrong number
sumimasen, ban·gō o
machigaemashta
すみません、番号
をまちがえました

sorry, wrong room
sumimasen, heya o
machigaemashta
すみません、部屋を
まちがえました

there's something wrong with
... ... wa doko ka okashī des
…はどこかおかしい
です

what's wrong? dō ka
shimashta ka?
どうかしましたか？

X

X-ray rentogen
レントゲン

Y

yacht yot·to
ヨット
yard yādo
ヤード
year toshi
年
yellow kīroi
きいろい
yen en
円
yes hai
はい
yesterday kinō
きのう
yesterday morning kinō no asa
きのうの朝
the day before yesterday ototoi
おととい
yet mada
まだ

•••••• DIALOGUE ••••••

is it here yet? mō tskimashta ka?
no, not yet īe, mada des
you'll have to wait a little longer yet
mō shibarak kakarimas

yoghurt yōguruto
ヨーグルト
you* (sing) anata
あなた
(pl) anatatachi
あなたたち
this is for you kore wa anata ni agemas
これはあなたに
あげます
with you anata to is·sho ni
あなたと一緒に

'You' is generally translated as **anata** in grammar books but personal pronouns are used less often in Japanese than in English and the best way to say, for example, 'where are you going?' in Japanese is to use the person's name plus **-san** instead of the word for 'you'. Another acceptable way to say this is to omit both 'you' and the name in Japanese.
see **The Basics** pages 5–6

young wakai
わかい
your(s)* (sing) anata no
あなたの
(pl) anatatachi no
あなたたちの
youth hostel yūs-hosteru
ユースホステル

Z

Zen Buddhism Zen
禅

Zen garden Zentei
禅庭

Zen priest Zensō
禅僧

Zen temple Zendera
禅寺

Zen sect Zenshū
禅宗

zero zero
ゼロ

zip fasnā
ファスナー

could you put a new zip on?
atarashī fasnā ni kaete
kuremasen ka?
あたらしいファス
ナーに替えてくれま
せんか？

zip code yūbimban·gō
郵便番号

zoo dōbutsu·en
動物園

Japanese-English

COLLOQUIALISMS

The following are words you may well hear. You shouldn't be tempted to use any of the stronger ones unless you are sure of your audience.

aho! fool!

baka! you fool!

bakamitai stupid

bakayarō! damn fool!

bijin beautiful woman

charinko bicycle

chikshō! damn!, hell! (literally: beast)

chot·to! hey!

damare! shut up!

dōmo thanks; hi

gaijin foreigner

ja nē bye, cheerio

kak·ko ī trendy; cool; handsome

konoyarō! damn fool!

kso! shit!

mansats ten-thousand yen note

naruhodo I see; indeed

shinjiran·nai unbelievable

subarashī! fantastic!

sugoi! great!, super!; well done!

sumimasen that's fine?; thanks; sorry; may I?

tondemo nai! no way!

urusai! shut up!

uso! that's a lie!

usotski! liar!

yada! no!; yuk!

yokat·ta! good!

A

abek·ku lovers, a couple
abunai dangerous
at·chi e it·te! go away!
agemas to give
ago chin; jaw
aibeya ni narimas to share
  (room)
aimas to meet
aiseki shimas to share (table)
aji taste; flavour
Ajia Asia
Ajia (no) Asian
akachan baby
akai red
akemas to open
akemashte omedetō gōzaimas!
  Happy New Year!
aki autumn, (US) fall
akiraka (na) clear, obvious
akseru accelerator
amai sweet (taste)
amari not very much
  amari ōk nai not many
ame candies, sweets; rain
Amerika Gas·shūkok USA
ana hole
anata (ga) you (sing)
anata no your; yours
anata o you (sing)
anata wa you (sing)
  anata wa … des you are
anatatachi (ga) you (pl)
anatatachi no your; yours (pl)
anatatachi o you (pl)
anatatachi wa you (pl)
ane sister (one's own: older)
ani brother (one's own: older)

an·naisho information desk
ano that; those (further away)
anzen (na) safe
aoi blue
apāto apartment, flat
araimas to wash
arashi storm
aratamat·ta formal
are that; that one; those (further
  away)
arigatō thank you, thanks
arimasen: sore ja arimasen not
  that one
  … ga arimasen no …
aruite walk; on foot
arukōru alcohol
arukōru-nuki (no) non-alcoholic
asa morning
asat·te the day after tomorrow
asayū-nishok-tski half board
ashi leg; foot
ashikubi ankle
ashita tomorrow
ashita no asa tomorrow
  morning
ashita no gogo tomorrow
  afternoon
asobiba playground
asoko ni up there; over there
as·sat·te the day after
  tomorrow
atama head
atama ga ī intelligent
atamakin deposit (as part
  payment)
atarashī new
atatakai warm; mild
at·chi: at·chi e it·te! go away!
  at·chi no hō des it's that way

ato de after; afterwards, later,
  later on
atsmemas to collect
atsui thick; hot
azayaka (na) bright

B

baka (na) silly; stupid
  baka! you fool!
bakageta ridiculous
bak·kin fine (punishment)
ban van
ban·gō number
ban·gō o machigaemashta
  wrong number
ban·gumi programme
bansōkō plasters, Bandaid®
bas·ryokō coach trip
bas·tāminaru coach station,
  bus station
bas·tei bus stop
bas·tski no heya with a private
  bathroom
bed·do bed (Western-style)
ben·goshi lawyer
benri (na) convenient
beruto belt
besto waistcoat
betsbets (no) separate
bets no another, different
bijines·hoteru business hotel
bijuts art
bijuts·kan art gallery
bimbō poor
bim·mei flight number
bin jar; bottle
binīru·bukuro carrier bag,
  plastic bag

binsen writing pad
biru building
bīru beer
biyōin hairdresser's (women's)
biza visa
bochi cemetery
bōi porter (in hotel)
bok (ga) I (fam, m)
bok no my; mine (fam, m)
bok o me (fam, m)
bokshi priest (Christian)
bok wa I (fam, m)
bon·net·to bonnet, (US) hood
bōru ball
bōrupen ballpoint pen
bōshi cap, hat
bōto boat
brajā bra
bubun part, bit
  ōkī bubun a big bit
buchō director, head of
  department
budō martial arts
Buk·kyō Buddhism
Buk·kyō (no) Buddhist
Buk·kyōto Buddhist
bunrak traditional puppet
  theatre
butsdan house altar
byō second (of time)
byōb screen
byōin hospital
byōki illness; disease
byōki (no) sick, ill
byōtō ward

C

cha-iro (no) brown

-chan diminutive suffix added to child's name or familiar suffix used between friends and family

chanto properly

chawan bowl (porcelain)

chek·k-in shimas to check in

chibusa breast

chichi father (one's own)

chigai difference

chigau different

chihō region, district

chikai near, nearby

chikatets underground, (US) subway

chīki area

chīm team

chip·p tip

chirashi leaflet

chīsai small

chizu map

chō area

chōdo koko de right here

chōka-tenimots excess baggage

choksets (no) direct

choktsū direct

chōkyori-bas coach, bus

chōkyori-denwa long-distance call

chōme area of a few square blocks

chōshi ga okashī faulty

chōshok breakfast

chōshok-tski yado bed and breakfast

chot·to! hey!

chot·to mat·te kudasai! just a minute!

chot·to sumimasen! excuse me!

Chūgok China

Chūgok (no) Chinese

chūibukai careful

chūko (no) second-hand

chū kurai (no) medium, medium-sized

chūmon order

chūmon shimas to order

chūsha injection

chūshajō car park, parking lot

chūshin centre

chūshok lunch

chūshok-go after lunch

D

daburu double; double room; double whisky

-dai classifier for machines, cars, bikes and stereos

daidokoro kitchen

daigak college; university

daihyō representative

daihyō-teki (na) typical

daijōb all right, OK; no problem

daisuki des to love

daitai roughly, approximately

daitōryō president (of country)

daiyaru shimas to dial

dake only, just

dambō heater, heating

dame! don't!

dame des! certainly not!

sore wa dame des it's no good

dandan gradually

dansei men

dansei-yō toire gents' toilet, men's room

dantai party, group

dare? who?

dare ka anybody; somebody, someone

dare mo ...-masen nobody, no-one; none

das-shimen cotton wool, absorbent cotton

de by, by means of; with; at; on; in

deguchi exit, way out

dekakemas to go away

dekimas can

dekimasen cannot

dekireba hopefully

dekirudake ... as ... as possible

dekirudake hayak as soon as possible

demo but; even the

... demo ... demo nai neither ... nor ...

den·ats voltage

denchi battery

den·gon message

denki electricity; light

denki (no) electric

denki-kamisori shaver

denki-kamisori-yō konsento shaving point

denki-seihin electrical appliances

denki-ya electrician; electrical goods shop

denkyū light bulb

densensei (no) infectious

densha train

denshi-renji microwave (oven)

dentō-teki (na) traditional

denwa telephone, phone

denwaban·gō phone number

denwaban·gō-an·nai directory enquiries

denwachō phone book

denwa shimas to call, to phone

depāto department store

des be; am; is; are; it is

anata wa ... des you are ...

watashi wa ... des I am ...

... des ka? is it ...?

deshta were; was; it was

dewa mata see you again

dīzeru-sha diesel

do degree

dō? how?

dō shimashta ka? what's the matter?

dō itashimashte don't mention it, you're welcome

doa door

doabōi doorman

dōbuts animal

dōbuts-en zoo

dochira which; who

dochira demo nai neither (one) of them

dochiraka either of them

dochira-sama des ka? who's calling?

Doits Germany

Doits (no) German

dōkan des I agree; all right

dōka yamete kudasai please
don't
doko? where?
  doko des ka? where is it?
doko demo everywhere;
  anywhere
doko ka somewhere
dokshin single, not married
dōmo thanks; hi
  dōmo arigatō thanks
  dōmo sumimasen sorry
dono? which?
dore? which one?
dore mo ...-masen none
doro mud
dorobō thief
dōrochizu road map;
  streetmap
dōshite des ka? why?; why not?
Doyōbi Saturday
dōzo I don't mind, please go
  ahead; here you are
  dōzo osaki ni after you
  dōzo yoroshik pleased to
  meet you

E

e to; towards; until; painting,
  picture; drawing
ē yes
ehagaki postcard
eiga film, movie
eigakan cinema, movie theater
Eigo English (language)
  Eigo de in English
eigyō-chū open
eigyōjikan opening times
Eikok Britain

Eikok (no) British
eizu AIDS
eki train station
empits pencil
em-saiz medium
en circle; yen
erabimas to choose
erebētā lift, elevator
eri collar
eru-saiz large
eya-kon air-conditioning

F

fak·ks fax
fak·ks o okurimas to fax
fasnā zip
Frans (no) French
Frans-go French (language)
fronto reception desk (in hotel)
fronto-gakari receptionist (in
  hotel)
fronto-garas windscreen
fu city
fuben (na) inconvenient
fūf married couple
fujinfuk-uriba ladies' wear
fukai deep
fukanō (na) impossible
fukin tea towel
Fuk·kats·sai Easter
fukmimas to include
fuktsū stomachache
fukuro bag, paper bag
fūmi flavour
fumoto bottom
fun minute
fune boat, ship
funsui fountain (ornamental)

furui old; stale
fusma sliding door (patterned)
futa cap; lid
futats two; a couple
fūtō envelope
futon mattress; bedding
futot·ta fat
futska two days
futskayoi hangover
futsū local intercity train
futsū (no) ordinary, usual
fuyu winter
fuyukai (na) unpleasant

G

ga subject particle that
  emphasizes the subject
  ... ga arimas there is ...; there
  are ...
  ... ga arimasen no ...; there's
  no ...; there are no ...
gaido guide
gaijin foreigner
gaikok abroad
gaikok (no) foreign
gaikok-go foreign language
gaikok-jin foreigner
gaishuts shimas to go out
gak amount
gake cliff
gak·kari shita disappointed
gak·ki term (at university, school)
gak·kō school
gaksei student
Gantan New Year's Day
garakta rubbish
garas glass
gasorin petrol, (US) gas

gasorin-stando petrol station,
  (US) gas station
geijuts-ka artist
gekijō theatre
genkan doorway, entrance,
  porch
genki? how are you?
  genki de ne take care, bye,
  see you
genkin cash
genkin-jidō-shiharaiki cash
  dispenser, ATM
genkin ni kaemas to cash
genzō film processing
genzo shimas to develop
geta wooden sandals
gēto gate (at airport)
gets month (this, last, next etc)
Getsyōbi Monday
gezai laxative
gin silver
ginkō bank (money)
giri no imōto sister-in-law (one's
  own: younger)
giri no musko son-in-law (one's
  own)
giri no musume daughter-in-
  law (one's own)
giri no okā-san mother-in-law
  (someone else's)
giri no onē-san sister-in-law
  (someone else's: older)
giri no onī-san brother-in-law
  (someone else's: older)
giri no otō-san father-in-law
  (someone else's)
giri no otōto brother-in-law
  (one's own: younger)
go five

go- polite prefix

-go after

gochisō-sama deshita it was delicious (literally: it was a feast)

gogak-kōs language course

Gogats May

gogo afternoon, pm
kyō no gogo ni this afternoon

go-hyak five hundred

go-jū fifty

gojūsho address
gojūsho wa? what's your address?

gōkei total

gokigen: gokigen ikaga des ka? how are you?
gokigen-yō! have a nice day!

gom rubber (material)

gomen·nasai excuse me, sorry

gomi rubbish, trash; waste

gomibako bin; dustbin, trashcan

goro about, approximately

goryōshin parents (someone else's)

goshujin husband (someone else's)

gozen am
gozen shichiji ni at 7am

gun county

gurīnsha first-class carriage

gurīnsha-jōshaken first-class train ticket

gyōrets queue

H

ha tooth

haburashi toothbrush

hachi eight; wasp

Hachigats August

hachi-jū eighty

hae fly

haguki gum (in mouth)

haha mother (one's own)

hai yes; lungs

-hai classifier meaning glassful or cupful

hai-iro (no) grey

hai-ok unleaded petrol

hairimas to come in

haisha dentist

haita toothache

haitats delivery

haitats shimas to deliver

haizara ashtray

hajimarimas to begin

hajime beginning

hajimemas to start

hajimemashte how do you do?, pleased to meet you

hajimete the first time

hakbutskan museum

hakike nausea

hako box

hamabe beach

hamaki cigar

hambun half

hamigakiko toothpaste

hana nose; flower

hanabi fireworks

hanashi-chū engaged, (US) occupied

hanashimas to speak; to talk

hana-ya florist's

han-dās (no) half a dozen

handobag·g bag, handbag, (US) purse

hanemas to knock over

hangak half fare

hangak (no) half-price

hanjikan half an hour

hankagai city centre, downtown

hanko personal seal

han·nama (na) not cooked

han·rit·toru half a litre

hantai opposite

   to hantai (no) against, opposed to

hap·pyak eight hundred

harai-modoshi refund

hareta fine (weather); swollen

harete imas it's sunny; it's swollen

hari needle

haru spring

hasami scissors

hashi bridge (over river); chopsticks

hashirimas to run

hata flag

hatake field

hayai fast, quick; early

hayak quickly

hei fence

heikin-teki average (not good)

hempi (na) secluded

hen (na) weird, strange, odd

heya accommodation; room

hi fire; day

hidari left

   hidari e to the left

   hidari ni on the left

hidari-kiki (no) left-handed

hidoi bad; dreadful; nasty

hidok badly

hif skin

higaeri-ryokō day trip

higashi east

hiji elbow

hijōguchi fire escape; emergency exit

hikage shade

hikari light

-hiki classifier for animals

hikidashi drawer

hikimas to pull; to play (instrument)

hikinobashi enlargement

hik·kuri kaeshimas to knock over

hikō flight

hikōki plane, airplane

hikui low

himo string

hinata sun

hi ni yaketa suntanned

hinshits quality

hiraita open

hiroba square

hiroi wide

hīru heel (of shoe)

hisho secretary

hitai forehead

hito person; people

hito-ban ni tski per night

hitogomi crowd

hito-hako packet

hito-kire piece

hito-kumi pair

hito-pak·k pack

hitori alone

hitots piece; one

   hitots mo ...-masen no

   mō hitots another, one more

hitots (no) a, an

hitsyō (na) necessary, essential

hiyake tan, suntan; sunburn

hiyake-dome sunblock

hiyake shimas to get a tan

hiyo ga kakarimas to cost

hiza knee

hō cheek (on face)

hodō pavement, sidewalk

hodo ... nai less ...than

hohoemimas to smile

hoka the rest

hoka hoka bentō lunch box
   shop

hoka ni nani ka something
   else, anything else

hoka niwa nai des nothing else

hoka no other

hoken insurance

hōki brush

hōkō direction

hokori dust

hoksei northwest

hoktō northeast

hom·mono (no) real, genuine

homo (no) gay

hon book

-hon classfier for pens,
   cigarettes and other
   cylindrical objects

hone bone

hone ga oreta broken

hon no skoshi just a little

hontō (ni) really
   hontō des ka? really?

hontō (no) true

hon·ya bookshop, bookstore

hon·yak translation

hon·yak shimas to translate

honyūbin baby's bottle

hōrits law

hōseki jewellery

hōseki-ten jeweller's

hoshi star

hoshī des to want

hoshō guarantee

hoshōkin deposit

hōsōshi wrapping paper

hos·sa fit, attack

hōtai bandage; dressing

hoteru hotel

hoteru no heya hotel room

hotoke-sama Buddha

hotondo almost, nearly

hotondo ...-masen hardly

hyak hundred

hyak man million

hyōshiki sign

I

ī good
   ī des that's good; that's fine

ichi one

ichiba market

ichiban suki (na) favourite

ichi-dās (no) dozen

Ichigats January

ichinichi-jū all day

ichiryū (no) excellent

ie house

īe no

igai dewa apart from

igai wa except

Igiris Britain

Igiris (no) British

Igiris-jin British person

Igiris-pondo sterling

ijō over, more than

sore ijō more than that
ika less than, under
ikebana flower arrangement
iki-iki shita lively
ikikata route
ikimas to go
ikimashō! let's go!
ikitai des I'd like to
ik-kai ground floor, (US) first
    floor; once
ik-kaibun dose
ikura des ka? how much is it?
ikuts? how many?; how old?
ikutska (no) several
ima now; just, only just
    ima wa dame des not just
    now
    ima nanji des ka? what time is
    it?
imamade ni ever
īmas to say; to call
ī-meiru email
imōto sister (one's own: younger)
inaka country; countryside
Indo (no) Indian
inryōsui drinking water
intāchenji interchange (on
    motorway)
inu dog
ip-pai full; a glass of
ip-pai ni shimas to fill up
ip-pak (no) overnight
ip-pan-teki (na) general
iraira suru annoying
iras-shaimase may I help you
ireba dentures
iriguchi entrance, way in
iro colour
iseki ruins

isha doctor
ishi stone, rock
isogashi busy
isogimas to hurry
is-sho ni together
    ... to is-sho ni with ...
is-sok pair; pair of shoes/socks
isu chair
Isuramkyo (no) Muslim
itadakimas! enjoy your meal!,
    bon appetit!
itai hurt; painful
itai des it's sore
itami pain, ache
itamidome painkillers
itamimas to hurt
Itaria Italy
Itaria (no) Italian
ito thread
itoko cousin
itska fifth
itsmo always
itsu? when?
itsuts five
it-tan ...-tara once, as soon as
iwa rock
iya (na) disgusting, nasty
izaka-ya pub

J

ja well
jaguchi tap, faucet
jama shimas to disturb
ja mata see you later
jā ne bye, cheerio
ji o'clock
jibun de myself; by myself
jidō automatic

jidō-hambaiki vending machine

jidōsha-hoken green card (car insurance)

jikan time; hour

jiko accident

jikokhyō timetable, (US) schedule

jimen ground

jimoto no local

jimusho office

jinja shrine

jishin earthquake

jitensha bicycle, bike

jitensha-okiba bicycle park

jōdan joke

jōhin (na) posh

jōhō information

jōkyak passenger

josei woman; lady

jū ten; gun; rifle

jūbun enough

jūdai (na) serious

jūgats October

jū-go fifteen

jugyō lesson

jū-hachi eighteen

jū-ichi eleven

jūichigats November

jūjiro crossroads, intersection

jukshita ripe

jū-kyū nineteen

jū-ni twelve

jūnigats December

jū-rok sixteen

jū-san thirteen

jū-shichi seventeen

jūsho address

jūshorok address book

jūtai traffic jam

jūtan carpet

jū-yon fourteen

K

ka mosquito

... ka ... ka either ... or ...

ka? question particle

kaban bag

kabe wall

kabin vase

kachō section chief

kādo card

kādo-denwa cardphone

kaerimas to go back, to return

kaeshimas to give back

kag furniture

kagami mirror

kagets month (one, two, three etc)

kagi key; lock

kagi o akemas to unlock

kago basket

kai floor, storey

kaichūdentō torch

kaidan steps, stairs

kaigan coast

kaigi meeting (business); conference

kaigishits conference room

kaikaishiki opening ceremony

kaikei cash desk

kaimas to buy

kaisha company, business

kaisok local train with limited stops

kaji fire (blaze)

kakebuton duvet

kakejik scroll (hanging)

kakemas to switch on (engine);
to play (music)

kakimas to write

kakitome-yūbin de by
registered mail

kaknin shimas to confirm

kamban sign

kamera-ya camera shop

kami paper; hair

kami-omuts disposable
nappies/diapers

kami-sama God

kamisori razor

kampai! cheers!

kampeki (na) perfect

kanari fairly, pretty, quite; a
bit

kanari taksan quite a lot

kanari (no) fair (amount)

kanashī sad

kanemochi (no) rich (person)

kan·gae idea

kan·gaemas to think

kan·geikai reception (for guests)

kan·gof nurse (woman)

kan·goshi nurse (man)

kanji character (written);
Chinese character

kanjimas to feel

kankiri can-opener, tin-opener

kankō-an·naijo tourist
information office

Kankok South Korea

Kankok (no) Korean

kankōryokō trip, excursion,
sightseeing tour

kan·nushi Shinto priest

kanō (na) possible

kanojo (ga) she

kanojo no her; hers

kanojo o her

kanojo wa she

kanojotachi (ga) they (f)

kanojotachi no their; theirs (f)

kanojotachi o them (f)

kanojotachi wa they (f)

kanpai! cheers!

kanrishok executive

kansen infection

kansha (no) grateful

kantan (na) simple, easy

kanzen ni completely

kanzō liver (in body)

kanzume can

kao face

kap·p cup

kap·pru couple

kara from; since

kara (no) empty

karada body

karada ni ī healthy

karai hot, spicy

kare he

kare ga he

kare no his

kare o him

kare wa he

karera (ga) they (m)

karera no their; theirs (m)

karera o them (m)

karera wa they (m)

karimas to rent, to hire; to
borrow

karui light (not heavy)

kasa umbrella

kashimas to lend

kashikoi clever

kashu singer; pop singer

kata shoulder
katahō one end; one side
katai hard
katamichi-kip·p single ticket,
  one-way ticket
kat·to cut
kawa leather; river
kawaita dry
kawari ni instead
kawase-tegata banker's draft
kawat·ta odd, strange, peculiar
Kayōbi Tuesday
kazan volcano
kaze wind
kazok family
kazu number, figure
kega o shita injured
keiba race (for horses)
keieisha manager (in business)
keikan policeman
keisats police
keisats·sho police station
keitai-denwa mobile phone
keiyak contract
keiyu stopover
keiyu de via
kek·kō des all right, fine
  īe kek·kō des no thanks
kek·kon marriage
  kek·kon shita married
  kek·kon shite imas I'm
  married
  kek·kon shite imas ka? are you
  married?
kek·kon-kinen-bi wedding
  anniversary
kek·kon-shiki wedding
kek·kon-yubiwa wedding ring
kek·kyok after all

kemuri smoke
ken ticket; prefecture
kendō Japanese fencing
ken·eki quarantine
kenka fight
kenkō (na) healthy
keredomo although
kesa this morning
keshiki scenery
keshimas to switch off
keshō make-up
keshōhin cosmetics
keshōshits ladies' toilets,
  ladies' room
kes·shite ...-masen never
kets·eki blood
kewashī steep
ki tree; mind; heart
kibako wooden box
kibō hope
kibun feeling
kichō (na) valuable
kiete iru off (lights)
kigaemas to get changed
kiji material (fabric)
kikai machine
kikan period (of time)
kiken (na) risky
kikimas to listen
kikoemas to hear
kimas to come
kimemas to decide
kimi (ga) you (sing, fam)
kimi no your; yours (sing, fam)
kimi o you (sing, fam)
kimi wa you (sing, fam)
kimochi no ī pleasant
kimono kimono; Japanese
  clothes

kimpats (no) blond

kin gold

kinen-hi monument

kin-en-koshits nonsmoking
compartment

kin-gyo goldfish

kinkyū emergency

kinkyū (na) urgent

kinō yesterday

kinō no asa yesterday
morning

kinu silk

Kin-yōbi Friday

kinyū shimas to fill in

kinzok metal

kion temperature (weather)

ki o tskete! look out!

kip-p ticket

kip-p-uriba box office; ticket
office

kirai des hate

kirei (na) beautiful; pretty;
nice; clean

kirei ni shimas to clean up

kiri mist, fog

kirimas to cut

kīroi yellow

kis kiss

kishibe shore (of lake)

kis-sa-ten teahouse; café

kis shimas to kiss

kita north

Kita-Chōsen North Korea

kitai hazure (no) disappointing

kitai shimas to look forward
to

kitanai dirty

kitsui tight

kit-te stamp

-ko classifer for fruit, cakes,
eggs and small chunky
objects

kōban police box

kōcha tea (drink)

kōdo wire; lead

kodomo child; children

kodomo-yō (no) children's

koe voice

kōen park

kogai open air

kōgai suburb

Kōgō-Heika Empress of Japan

kohei (na) fair, impartial

kōhī coffee

koi carp

koin-randorī launderette,
laundromat

kōjo factory

kōka coin

kōkan-rēto exchange rate

kok-kyō border (of country)

koknaisen domestic flight

koko here

koko des right here, just
here

... wa koko des here is/are ...

masa ni koko de just here

koko ni over here

koko no kore des this one
here

kokonoka ninth

kokonots nine

kokrits (no) national

koksai-teki (na) international

kokseki nationality

kōkūbin de by airmail

kōkūbin-yō fūtō airmail
envelope

kōkyū (na) upmarket
komban tonight, this evening
komban wa good evening
kome rice (uncooked)
komichi path
komori child minder
kona-sek·ken soap powder
konda crowded
konde iru busy
kondo next time
kon-iro (no) navy (blue)
konkai this time
konkūru contest
kon·nichi wa hello
kono this; these
konoha leaf
konosaki down the road
kono shita des down here
konsento power point
kop·p glass
kore this; this one; these
　kore des ka this one here
　kore kara in future
　kore wa ... des this is ...
korekto-kōru reverse charge
　call, collect call
kōri ice
korobimas to fall
koruk-nuki corkscrew
kōs course
kōsaten junction
koshō breakdown
kōshūbenjo public toilets
kōshūdenwa phone box,
　payphone
kōsōbiru skyscraper
kōsokdōro motorway, freeway,
　highway
kos·sets fracture

kōsui perfume
kotats footwarmer
kot·chi this; this way; here
kōto coat
kotoba word, language
kōtsū traffic
kōtsūjiko road accident
kot·tōhin antique
kot·tōhin-ten antique shop
kowareta damaged; broken
kowarete imas out of order
kowashimas to break, to
　damage
kōza bank account, account
kozeni change, money
kōzui flood
kozutsmi parcel, package
ksa grass
ksuri drug, medicine
ksuri-ya pharmacy
ku ward, area of a city
kubi neck
kuchi mouth
kuchibeni lipstick
kuchibiru lips
kudaketa informal
kudamono fruit
Kugats September
kuishimbō (no) greedy
kujira whale
kujō complaint
kujō o īmas to complain
kūki air
kūkō airport
kumo spider
kumori (no) cloudy, dull
-kun suffix used when
　addressing a young person
kuni country, nation

kurabemas to compare
kurai about, approximately
kuremas to give
   ... o kuremasen ka? could I
   have ...?
   ...-te kuremasen ka? could
   you ...?
kurikaeshimas to repeat
Kurismas-Ibu Christmas Eve
kuro black
kuroi dark
kurōk cloakroom
kuruma car
kushami o shimas to sneeze
kushi comb
kuts shoe
kuts-himo shoelaces
kutsnaoshi shoe repairer
kuts no soko sole (of shoe)
kutszumi shoe polish
kuzushimas to change (money)
kyak customer
kyaksha coach, carriage
kyakshits compartment
kyakshits-gakari maid
kyanseru-machi standby
kyō today
kyōdai brother
kyōdo-keiei-sha partner (in
   business)
kyoka permit
kyōkai church
kyok-dome-yūbin poste
   restante
kyori distance
kyōryok help
kyū nine
kyūden palace
kyūgyō closed

kyū-hyak nine hundred
kyū-jū ninety
kyūka holiday, vacation
kyūkei-jikan interval
kyūkō express train
kyūkyūbako first-aid kit
kyūkyūbyōtō casualty
   department
kyūkyūsha ambulance
kyūreki lunar calendar
kyūsuiki fountain (for drinking)

M

mabushī bright
machi town; area
machi-awase-basho meeting
   place
machigai error, mistake
machigat·ta false, not true
machimas to wait
mada still; only; yet
   īe, mada des not yet
made to; up to; until; as far as
   Mok·yōbi made ni by
   Thursday
mado window
madogawa no seki window
   seat
mae ago; front
   ichijikan mae an hour ago
   sono mae no hi the day
   before
mae mot·te in advance
mae ni in front, at the front;
   formerly, in the past; before
magarikado turning (in road)
magomusko grandson (one's
   own)

magomusme granddaughter
(one's own)

mahōbin Thermos® flask

-mai classifier for pieces of
paper, tickets and other
thin, flat objects

mainichi (no) daily

majime (na) serious

makura pillow

makura-kabā pillow case

mama mum

māmā des not bad, so-so

man·ga comic book

manikyua nail varnish

man·naka middle

manshon apartment block

Marē-hantō (no) Malay

maroyaka (na) mild

masaka! oh no!

-masen not
-masen deshta didn't

mata again

mata wa or

mats pine

mat·tak chigaimas definitely not

mat·tak sono tōri des definitely

mawari-michi diversion, detour

mayak drugs (narcotics)

mayonaka midnight
mayonaka ni in the middle of
the night; at midnight

me eye

megane spectacles, eyeglasses

mei niece (one's own)

meishi business card

meisho the sights

menkyo licence

menrui noodles

menzei(hin) duty-free (goods)

menzeihin-ten duty-free shop

met·ta ni not often
met·ta ni ...-masen hardly ever

mezurashī rare, uncommon,
unusual

miatarimasen missing

michi road

midori (no) green

midori no madoguchi ticket
counter

migi right
migi e to the right
migi ni on the right

mihon-ichi fair; trade fair

mijikai brief, short

mik·ka third

mimas to look at; to see

mimi ear

mimi ga kikoenai deaf

minami south
o minami in the south

minato harbour, port

min·geihin-ten craft shop

minikui ugly

min·na everyone; all
... wa min·na all the ...

minshuk guesthouse

miryok-teki (na) attractive

mise shop

mitskemas to find

mit·ts three

mizu water

mizugi swimming trunks;
swimming costume

mizūmi lake

mizusashi jug

mo also, too; even; both ...
and; neither ... nor

mō already

mō hitots another, one more

mochimas to have; to carry; to hold

mochinushi owner

mochiron of course

mochiron chigaimas of course not

mochite handle

modorimas to get back, to return

modot·te ikimas to go back

modot·te kimas to come back

mōf blanket

moktekichi destination

Mok·yōbi Thursday

momen cotton

momo thigh

mon gate

mondai problem

mono thing

more leak

mori woods, forest

moshi if

    moshi ... demo even if ...

moshi-moshi hello; I'm still here

mō skoshi some more, a little bit more

mot·te kimas to bring; to fetch

mot·to more

mot·to ī better

mot·to skunak less

mot·to taksan a lot more

mot·to tōk further

moyō pattern

muchū (na) crazy

muen-gasorin unleaded petrol

muika sixth

muishiki (no) unconscious

muji (no) plain

mukai no opposite

mukashi-fū (no) old-fashioned

mukō there; over there

    mukō des, mukō ni over there

mukōgawa across

mune chest, breast

mura village

murasaki (no) purple, violet

muryō free of charge

mushi insect

mushi-atsui humid

mushi-sasare insect bite

musko son (one's own)

musume daughter (one's own)

mut·ts six

muzkashī hard, difficult

myōji surname

N

nadare avalanche

nagai long

    nagai aida a long time

nagame view

nagashi sink

nagemas to throw

naisen telephone extension

naka inside

naka e hairimas to go in

nakai-san maid

naka ni inside

-nakereba narimasen I must ...

nakimas to cry

naknarimas to disappear

nakshimas to lose

nama (no) raw

namae name; first name, given name

namake-mono lazy
nana seven
nana-hyak seven hundred
nana-jū seventy
nanats seven
nani? what?
  nani des ka? what?
  sore wa nani des ka? what's
  that?
  nani demo ī des it doesn't
  matter
nani ka something, anything
  nani ka ... ka? would you like
  anything ...?
nani mo ...-masen nothing
nani mo nai des nothing else
nanoka seventh
nansei southwest
nante īmashta? pardon (me)?,
  sorry?
nantō southeast
naorimas to cure
naoshimas to mend
nao warui des it's worse; much
  worse
naraimas to learn
narubek hayak as soon as
  possible
naruhodo I see; indeed
nashi de without
nats summer
nazenara because
ne? isn't it?, haven't we?,
  haven't you? etc
nedan cost, price
nedoko bed (Japanese-style)
nega negative (film)
neko cat
nemurimas to sleep

nen·gajō New Year's Card
nenkin-seikats·sha pensioner
nets fever; temperature
netsup·poi feverish
nezumi mouse; rat
ni two; to; in; at; into; on;
  indirect object particle
ni-bai (no) double; twice as much
ni-bam·me (no) second
nibui stupid
nichibots sunset
Nichiyōbi Sunday
nigai bitter
Nigats February
nihodoki shimas to unpack
Nihon Japan
Nihon (no) Japanese
Nihon·go Japanese (language)
  Nihon·go de in Japanese
Nihon·jin Japanese (person)
ni-hyak two hundred
ni-jū twenty
nik meat
ni-kai first floor, (US) second
  floor; twice
nik·ki diary (for personal
  experiences)
nik·kō sunshine
nik·ya butcher's
nimots luggage, baggage
nimots o tsmemas to pack
-nin classifier for people
nin·gyō doll
nin·gyō-geki puppet show
ninki no aru popular
ninshin-chū (no) pregnant
Nip·pon Japan
nise (no) fake
nishi west

nishūkan fortnight

ni-tō second class (train etc)

niwa garden

niwaka-ame shower (of rain)

no of; possessive particle

no aida ni between; during

nodo throat

nodo no itami sore throat

no hō e towards

nōjō farm

nok-k shimas to knock

nomi flea

nomimas to drink

nomimono drink

no mukō ni beyond

norikaemas to change (trains etc)

norimas to get on (train etc)

no shita ni under (in position)

no soba near; by
  umi no soba by the sea
  no soba ni beside

no soko ni at the bottom of

no soto ni outside

no tame ni because of; for

no tonari next to

no ue on

no ushiro ni behind

nuimas to sew

nunoji cloth, fabric

nureta wet

nusumimas to steal

nyūjōryō admission charge

O

o object particle

o- polite prefix

o-ai-dekite ureshīdes nice to meet you

ōbā overcoat

oba-san aunt

obā-san grandmother (someone else's)

Ōbei the West

Ōbei (no) Western

Ōbei-jin Westerner

obi sash

oboete imas to remember

obon tray

ocha green tea

ōdōri main road; avenue

odorimas to dance

odorok-hodo (no) astonishing

ōfuk-kip-p return ticket, round-trip ticket

ofuro bath

ofuro-ba bathroom

ofuro-tski de ... ... with bathroom

ogenki des ka? how are you?

ohayō gozaimas good morning

oi nephew (one's own)

oishī delicious

oji-san uncle

oji-san grandfather

ojō-san daughter (someone else's)

ōk much
  ōk nai not a lot

oka hill

okagesama de fine; well

okane money

okane o tskaimas to spend

okanjō bill, (US) check

okā-san mother

okashī funny, strange

ōkī big, large

okimas to get up; to leave; to

keep; to put
okiwasuremas to leave behind
okorimas to happen
okot·ta angry
ok-san wife (someone else's)
okugai outdoor
okunai indoor
okure delay
okurimas to send
okurimono gift
okyak-sama guest
ōkyū-teate first aid
omago-san grandchild (someone else's)
omatase sorry to keep you waiting
omatsuri festival
omawari-san policeman
omedetō! congratulations!
Ōmisoka New Year's Eve
omiyage souvenir
omo (na) main
omocha toy
omoi serious, grave; heavy
omoimas to think
omosa weight
omoshiroi exciting; interesting; funny, amusing
omuts nappy, diaper
onaji the same
onaji yō (na) similar
onaka stomach
onaka ga suita hungry
onegai shimas please; thank you
    hai, onegai shimas yes, please
onē-san sister
on·gak music
on·gak-ka musician

onī-san brother
on·na no ko girl
onsen hot spring
Oranda Holland
Oranda (no) Dutch
orenji-iro (no) orange
origami paper folding
orikaeshi denwa shimas to ring back
orimas to get out; to get off
oroshimas to let off
osake alcoholic drink
osaki ni good night; goodbye; see you
osenkō joss stick
oshare (na) trendy, fashionable
oshibori moistened hand towel
oshikomi-gōtō burglary
oshimas to push
oshīre cupboard, closet
oshiri hip; bottom
Oshōgats New Year
osoi slow; late
osok slowly
osorak probably
osoroshī horrible, awful
osōshiki funeral
ōsugi too many, too much
ōsugimas that is too much
osuwari kudasai sit down
otanjōbi omedetō gozaimas! happy birthday!
otera Buddhist temple
otoko no hito man
otoko no ko boy
otona adult
otō-san father; dad
otoshiyori old person
otōto brother (one's own: younger)

ototoi the day before
  yesterday
owan bowl
owari end
owarimas to finish
owarimashta it's finished
oyasuminasai good night
oya-yubi thumb
oyogimas to swim

P

pachinko pinball
pak·k·ryokō package holiday
pan bread
panfret·to brochure
pank puncture
pantī-stok·king tights,
  pantyhose
pants underpants; shorts
pan-ya baker's
piru contraceptive pill
pop·pus pop music
posto letterbox, mailbox
purastik·k plastic
purat·to-hōm platform; track
pūru swimming pool

R

raishū next week
  raishū no ashita a week
  tomorrow
  raishū no kyō a week today
rai-u thunderstorm
regyurā regular unleaded
  petrol
rei example
reitō shita frozen

reizōko fridge
rek·kāsha breakdown service
renji cooker
renta-kā rented car; car rental
rentaru (no) to rent, for hire
renzu lens; camera lens;
  contact lens
reshīto receipt
rimujin-bas airport bus
rins conditioner (for hair)
roji lane
rok six
rōka corridor
Rokgats June
rok-jū sixty
romendensha tram
rop·pyak six hundred
rosenzu network map
rōsok candle
ryō amount (quantity)
ryōgae-jo bureau de change
ryōgae-rēto exchange rate
ryōhō both
ryōjikan consulate
ryokan Japanese traditional
  inn
ryōkin charge; fare; rental
ryōkinbako fare box
ryokō journey
  sore dewa tanoshī ryokō o!
  have a good journey!
ryokōgaisha travel agent's
ryokōkyak tourist
ryokō shimas to travel
ryōri food; dish (meal)
ryōri shimas to cook
ryōshin parents (one's own)
ryūkōokure (no) unfashionable

S

sābis-ryō service charge
sagashimas to search, to look for
sai-ak (no) worst
saif purse; wallet
saigai disaster
saigo (no) final, last
saijits public holiday
saijōkai top floor
saikin recently
saikō (no) best
saishin (no) latest, most recent, up-to-date
saisho (no) first
  saisho ni at first
saishok-shugisha vegetarian
saizu size
sakana fish
sakana-ya fishmonger's
sakasama upside down
sakazki sake cup
saki first
sakihodo earlier
sakura cherry blossom
sakura no ki cherry tree
-sama Mr; Mrs; Ms; Miss
sambashi jetty
sam-byak three hundred
samonaito otherwise
sampats haircut (man's)
samui cold
san three
-san Mr; Mrs; Ms; Miss
San-gats March
san-jū thirty
san-kai second floor, (US) third floor; three times

san-shok-tski full board
sara plate
sararī-man businessman; salaried worker
sarubin surface mail, overland mail
satō sugar
-sats classifier for books
sawagashī loud
sayōnara goodbye
se ga takai tall
seif government
seihin product
seijō (na) normal
seika net price
seikak (na) accurate
seikyūsho bill, (US) check; invoice
seiri period (menstruation)
seiri-yō napkin sanitary napkins/towels
seishiki (na) formal
seiyō (no) Occidental
sekai world
seki seat; cough
sek-ken soap
semai narrow (street)
-semas to let, to allow
sem-mendai washhand basin
sempūki fan (electrical)
sen thousand; line; plug (in sink)
senaka back (of body)
senaka no itami backache
senchi centimetre
sen-nuki bottle-opener
se no hikui short
sensei teacher; polite form of

address for teachers, doctors, dentists etc
senshits cabin
senshū last week
senshū kara since last week
senshū no Kin·yōbi last Friday
sensu fan
sentak-ki washing machine
sentak-mono washing, laundry
sentak-ya laundry (place)
sentō public baths
sen·yō no bas-toire private bathroom
senzai washing powder
serotēp Sellotape®, Scotch tape®
ses·shi centigrade
sētā pullover, sweater
setomono china
setsbi equipment
setsmei shimas to explain
setszok connection (in travelling)
setszokbin connecting flight
sewa o shimas to look after
shachō managing director, president (of company)
shako garage (for parking)
shareta posh
sharin wheel
shasen lane (on motorway)
shashin photo; picture
shats shirt
shawā-tski (no) with shower
shi death; city; four
shiai game, match
shibaf lawn
shibai play (in theatre)
shibuts belongings
shichak shimas to try on

shichak-shits fitting room
shichi seven
Shichigats July
shigai-kyokban dialling code, area code
Shigats April
shigoto business; job, work
shihainin manager
shiharai payment
shiharaimas to pay
shihei banknote, (US) bill
shijō market (in business)
shiken exam
shiki-buton mattress
shikiten ceremony
shik·ki lacquerware
shima island
shimarimas to close
shimas to do; to play; to give; to make; to work (as); to taste; to smell; to feel; to sound; to cost
shimat·ta closed
shimbun newspaper, paper
shimbun·ya newsagent's
shimemas to shut
shimet·ta damp
shimo frost
shimpai worried
shinai: ... shinai hō ga ī des you shouldn't ...
shincho height
shinda dead
shindaisha sleeper, sleeping car
shin·gō traffic lights
shin·gu bedding (Western-style)
shin·guru single room
shin·guru-bed·do single bed

shinimas to die

shinjiran·nai unbelievable

shinkansen bullet train

shinsen (na) fresh

shinsets (na) friendly, nice; kind; generous

shinshifuk-uriba menswear

shinshits bedroom

shintai-shōgai-sha disabled person; the disabled

shinzō heart

shirabemas to find out; to check

shiraf (no) sober

shirimasen I don't know

shiro castle

shiroi white

shita downstairs; tongue

shita (ni) below

shita e ikimas to go down

shite: ... shite kuremasen ka? could you please ...?

shi-teki (na) private

shitsgyō-chū unemployed

shitsmon question

shitsrei (na) rude

shitsrei shimas excuse me

shit·te imas to know

shiyō-chū engaged, occupied

shizen (na) natural; peaceful, quiet

shizka ni! quiet!

shōbōsho fire brigade

shōdok-zai antiseptic

shōgi Japanese chess

shōgo midday, noon

shohōsen prescription

shōji sliding door (wooden lattice and paper)

shōka-furyō indigestion

shōkai shimas to introduce

shōkaki fire extinguisher

shokbuts plant

shokdōsha restaurant car, buffet car

shokji meal

shokji o shimas to have dinner

shok·ki o araimas to do the washing-up

shok·ki-yō senzai washing-up liquid

shokryōhin food (in shop)

shokryōhin-ten food shop/store

shomei signature

shōmeisho certificate

shōnin witness

shōrai future

shorui document

shōtai invitation

shōtai shimas to invite

shōts pants, panties

shū week (this, last, next etc)

shujin husband (one's own)

shūkai meeting

shūkan custom; week (one, two, three etc)

shūkyō religion

shūmats weekend

shumi hobby

shup·pats departure

shup·pats-raunji departure lounge

shup·pats shimas to leave, to depart

shūri shimas to repair

shurui type, make, brand name

shut·chō business trip

shūten terminus

skoshi a little bit, not much; little; some

skoshi no a few

skunak-tomo at least

sō so
  sō des that's right

sōbi equipment

sōin monastery

sōjiki vacuum cleaner

soko (de) there

sōkō-kyori-museigen unlimited mileage

soktats express (mail)

somats (na) poor (quality)

son·na such; so; like that
  son·na ni taksan ja nak not so much
  son·na ni waruk nai not so bad

sono the; that (nearby)
  sono tōri des that's it

sono toki then, at that time

sō-on noise

sora sky

sore it; that (nearby); that one (nearby); those; them (objects)
  sore dake des that's all
  sore de ī des ka? is that OK?
  sore des that one
  sore wa ... des it is ...
  sore zembu all of it

sorekara and then

sorera (ga) they (inanimate objects)

sorera no their; theirs (inanimate objects)

sorera o them (inanimate objects)

sorera wa they (inanimate objects)

sorezore (no) each, every

sōridaijin prime minister

sōryo Buddhist priest

soshite and

soto ni outside

sōzai-ya delicatessen

stando lamp

steki (na) lovely

stemas to throw away

subarashī beautiful; excellent, great, wonderful

subete everything

subete no every

sug at once, immediately; soon
  sug ni straightaway; in a minute

-sugimas too

sugoi super, great
  sugoi! well done!

suichū-yoksen hydrofoil

suidō-ya plumber

suijō-skī waterskiing

suit·chi switch

Suiyōbi Wednesday

sūjits mae the other day

suki: ... ga suki des ka? do you like ...?
  suki des I like it
  suki ja arimasen I don't like it

sumi corner
  sumi ni in the corner

sumimasen that's fine; thanks; sorry; may I?

suna sand

sunde imas to live

sunikā trainers

sūpā supermarket

sup-pai sour
suwarimas to sit down
suzushī cool

T

tabako cigarette
tabemas to eat
tabemono food
tabitabi (no) frequent
tabun perhaps, maybe
  tabun chigau deshō perhaps
  not
tada free of charge
tadashī correct, right
taifū typhoon
Taiheiyō Pacific Ocean
taikuts bored
taikuts (na) boring
taira (na) flat
taisets (na) important
taishikan embassy
taitei most; mostly, most of
  the time
  taitei no most
taiyō sun
takai high; expensive; tall
takasa height
take bamboo
tak-kyū table tennis
tako kite
tako-age kite-flying
taksan a lot, lots
taksan (no) much; many; a lot,
  lots
  taksan no ... plenty of ..., a
  lot of ...
takshī-noriba taxi rank
takshī no unten-shu taxi-driver

takwae supply
tambo paddy field
tameshimas to try
tana shelf
tani valley
tanjōbi birthday
tanomimas to ask
tanoshimimas to enjoy oneself
tansha moped
taoru flannel; towel
tarimasen there's not enough
tashika certain, sure
  tashika des ka? are you sure?
  tashika ni certainly
tasukete! help!
tatami straw mat
tatoeba for example
tatoe ...-temo even if
taznemas to visit
te hand
tebukuro gloves
techō notebook; diary
tegami letter
tegoro (na) reasonable;
  inexpensive
tehai shimas to arrange
teiki-bin scheduled flight
teikiken rail pass
teinei (na) polite
tekubi wrist
tenchō manager (in shop)
te ni iremas to get, to fetch
tenimots baggage; hand
  luggage
tenimots-azkari-jo left luggage
  (office), baggage
  checkroom
tenimots-uketori-jo baggage
  claim

tenjikan pavilion
tenki weather
Ten·nō-Heika Emperor of
  Japan
tenrankai exhibition
tenso-saki forwarding address
tento tent
tep·pen ni at the top
terebi television
tēru-ramp rear lights
tetsdaimas to help
tetsdō railway
tis·sh (pēpā) tissues, Kleenex®
to with, accompanying; and;
  door (of house: Japanese-style)
-to metropolis
tō pagoda; ten
tobimas to fly
tōchak arrival
tōchak shimas to arrive, to get
  in
todana cupboard
tōi far
toire toilet, rest room
tōjiki crockery
tojikomemas to lock in
tōjōken boarding pass
tōk (no) distant
tōka tenth
tokei clock, watch
tōki pottery
tokidoki sometimes
tok·kyū super express train
tok ni especially
tokonoma alcove
tokoro place; someone's house
toko-ya barber's
Tōkyō wan Tokyo Bay
tomarimas to stop; to stay

tōmei (no) clear
tomemas to switch off (engine)
tomodachi friend
ton·neru tunnel
torank boot (of car), (US) trunk
torēnā sweatshirt
tori bird
tōri street
toridashimas to get out, to take
  out
torihiki deal (business)
torikaemas to change, to
  replace
torikeshimas to cancel
torimas to take, to accept
tōrokban·gō registration
  number, license number
toshi age; city; year
toshi o tot·ta old (person)
totemo quite; very, extremely;
  so; a lot
totemo oishī delicious,
  excellent
totszen ni suddenly
tot·te handle
tōt·te through
tot·te okimas to keep
tōyō (no) Oriental, Eastern
tozan mountaineering
tsgi (no) next
  sono tsgi no hi the day after
tsgō no ī convenient (time)
tskaeta stuck
tskaimas to use
tskamaemas to fetch; to catch
tskaremashta I'm tired
tskareta tired
tskemas to switch on (TV, lights)
tski moon

tskiatari end of a road

tskimas to arrive

tskurimas to make

tsma wife (one's own)

tsmaranai dull, uninteresting

tsmasaki toe

tsme nail (finger)

tsmetai cold

-tsū classifier for letters

tsuā tour

tsuika-ryōkin supplement, extra charge

tsuin twin room

tsui ni eventually

tsuitach first

tsuite no about, concerning

tsūjite imas to lead

tsurete ikimas to take, to lead

tsūrogawa no seki aisle seat

tsuyadashi polish

tsūyak interpreter

tsuyu rainy season

tsyoi strong

U

ubaguruma buggy

uchi home

uchimashō deal

  sore de te o uchimashō it's a deal

ude arm

udedokei wristwatch

ue upstairs; above

  ... no ue ni on top of ...

  ue ni up

ugokashimas to move

uketorimas to accept

uketske reception desk

uketske de at reception

uketske-gakari receptionist

uketskemas to accept

ukezara saucer

uma horse

umi sea

umibe shore

un luck

untem-menkyoshō driving licence

unten shimas to drive

untenshu driver

un-yok fortunately

ura back

ureshī happy, glad

uridashi-chū for sale

urimas to sell

ūru wool

urusai noisy

  urusai! shut up!

ushiro ni at the back

uso o tskimas to lie, to tell untruth

usu-... pale (colour)

usui weak; thin; light, pale

uta song

utaimas to sing

utskushī beautiful

W

wa subject particle

wafū Japanese-style

wakai young

wakarimas to understand

  wakarimas ka? do you understand?

  wakarimasen I don't understand

wakimichi side street
wan bay
waraimas to laugh
waribiki discount
warikan going Dutch
warui bad; ill
waruk badly
washi paper
wasuremas to forget
watakshi (ga) I (pol)
watakshi no my; mine (pol)
watakshi o me (pol)
watakshi wa I (pol)
watashi (ga) I
  watashi mo me too
  watashi mo sō des so am I,
  so do I
watashi no my; mine
  watashi no des it's mine
watashi o me
watashi wa I
  watashi wa ... des I am
watashitachi (ga) we
watashitachi no our; ours
watashitachi o us
watashitachi wa we
waza to deliberately
winkā indicator

Y

yakan kettle
yakedo burn
yakedo shimas to burn
yak·kai-goto trouble
yak·kyok pharmacy
yak ni tats helpful; useful
yaksō herbs (medicinal)
yakyū baseball

yama mountain
yamagoya cabin (in mountains)
yamete kudasai! stop it!
yane roof
yao-ya greengrocer's
yasai vegetables
yasashī easy
yaseta thin, skinny
yasui cheap, inexpensive; low
yasumi holiday, vacation
yat·ts eight
yawarakai soft
yoake dawn
yōfū (no) Western-style
yōfuk clothes (Western)
yogore dirt
yogoreta polluted
yōi ga dekita ready
yok often
yōka eighth
yokat·ta! good!
yokbari (na) greedy
yok·ka fourth
yok kireru sharp
yoko side
yoko ni narimas to lie down
yoksō bath, bathtub
yom-bun no ichi quarter
yomimas to read
yōmok foreign cigarettes
yon four
yon-hyak four hundred
yon-jū forty
yop·parat·ta drunk
yorimas: bāi ni yorimas it
  depends
yorimo than
yoru night
yōshi form, document

yoshinasai! don't do that!

yotei schedule

yot·ts four

yowai weak

yoyak reservation; appointment

yoyak shimas to book, to reserve

yūbe last night

yubi finger

yūbimban·gō postcode, zip code

yūbin post, mail

yubi-nin·gyō puppet

yūbinkyok post office

yūbinkyok no honkyok main post office

yubiwa ring (on finger)

yūdok (na) poisonous

yūen four-star petrol

yūenchi fair, funfair

yūgata evening

yuka floor (of room)

yukata cotton dressing gown

yuki snow

yuk·kuri slowly

yūkō (na) valid (ticket etc)

yūmei (na) famous

yurui loose

yūshok evening meal

yūsō shimas to post, to mail

yut·tari shita comfortable

Z

zabuton floor cushion

zan·nen (des)! what a shame!, it's a pity!

zas·shi magazine

zeikan Customs

zeitak (na) luxurious

zembu the whole lot, all of them

sore zembu all of it

zembu de altogether

Zen-dera Zen temple

zenkai last time

zensai starter, appetizer

Zen-sō Zen priest

Zen-tei Zen garden

zenzen not in the least

zet·tai chigaimas! certainly not!

zō statue

zubon trousers, (US) pants

zutsū headache

zut·to much, a lot more

Japanese-English:

Signs and Notices

Contents

GENERAL SIGNS

大人 otona adult
子供 kodomo child
危険 kiken danger
飲み水 nomimizu drinking water
・・・お断り ... okotowari ... forbidden
案内 an·nai information
芝生に入らないでください shibaf ni hairanaide kudasai keep off the grass
立ち入り禁止 tachiiri-kinshi keep out
禁漁区 kinryōk no fishing
禁煙 kin·en no smoking
故障 koshō out of order
ゴミ gomi litter
ゴミ捨てるな gomi steruna no litter
横断歩道 ōdanhodō pedestrian crossing
静かに shizkani quiet, please

AIRPORT, PLANES

空港 kūkō airport
空港バス kūkō-bas airport bus
航空便 kōkūbin flight
便名 bim·mei flight number
到着 tōchak arrival(s)
出発 shup·pats departure(s)
行き先 ikisaki destination

・・・行き ... iki bound for ...
経由 keiyu via
搭乗口 tōjōguchi boarding gate
搭乗券 tōjōken boarding pass
ゲート gēto gate
東口 higashi-guchi east exit (or entrance)
北口 kita-guchi north exit (or entrance)
南口 minami-guchi south exit (or entrance)
西口 nishi-guchi west exit (or entrance)
航空 kōkū airline
航空券 kōkūken airline ticket
全日空 Zen-Nik·kū All Nippon Airways
国内線 koknai-sen domestic airlines
国際線 koksai-sen international airlines
日本航空 Nihon-Kōkū Japan Airlines
予約 yoyak reservations
案内 an·nai information
案内係 an·nai-gakari information desk
手荷物受取所 tenimots-uketori-jo baggage claim
チェックイン chek·k-in

check-in

免税店 menzei-ten duty-free shop

BANKS, MONEY

銀行 ginkō bank

外国為替公認銀行 gaikok-kawase-kōnin-ginkō authorized foreign exchange bank

両替所 ryōgaejo bureau de change, foreign exchange

外国為替 gaikok-kawase foreign exchange

窓口 madoguchi counter

為替レート kawase-rēto exchange rate

振替 furikae transfer

為替手形 kawase-tegata banker's draft

トラベラーズチェック traberāz-chek-k travellers' cheque

クレジットカード kurejit-to-kādo credit card

カード可 kādo-ka credit cards accepted

口座番号 kōzaban-gō account number

口座 kōza bank account

料金 ryōkin fee

有料 yūryō fee charged

無料 muryō no charge

消費税 shōhi-zei VAT, (US) consumption tax

円 en yen

¥ yen

ドル doru dollar

ポンド pondo pound sterling

BUS TRAVEL

バス bas bus

バスセンター bas-sentā bus station

バス停 bas-tei bus stop

バス乗り場 bas-noriba bus boarding point

バスターミナル bas-tāminaru bus terminal

・・・行き … iki bound for …

市バス shi-bas municipal bus

都営バス toei-bas municipal bus (in Tokyo)

切符売り場 kip-p-uriba ticket office

切符 kip-p ticket

回数券 kaisūken book of tickets

運賃表 unchin-hyō table of fares

有効 yūkō valid

乗車は前扉から jōsha wa mae tobira kara enter at front door

降車は後扉から kōsha wa ushiro tobira kara exit at rear door

運賃箱 unchim-bako fare box

料金箱 ryōkin-bako fare box

回送 kaisō out of service

次は停車 tsugi-wa-te-sha stopping at the next stop

精算所 seisanjo excess fare office

COUNTRIES, NATIONALITIES

アメリカ Amerika America; American

オーストラリア Ōstoraria Australia; Australian

英 Ei Britain; British; England; English

英国 Eikok Britain; British; England; English

カナダ Kanada Canada; Canadian

中国 Chūgok China; Chinese

デンマーク Dem·māk Denmark; Danish

オランダ Oranda Holland; Dutch

イギリス Igiris England; English; Britain; British

ヨーロッパ Yōrop·pa Europe; European

フランス Frans France; French

仏 Futs France; French

ドイツ Doits Germany; German

独 Dok Germany; German

インド Indo India; Indian

イタリア Itaria Italy; Italian

日 Nichi Japan; Japanese

日本 Nihon Japan; Japanese

マレーシア Marēshia Malaysia; Malay

ニュージーランド Nyū-Jirando New Zealand

北朝鮮 Kita-Chōsen North Korea; North Korean

ノルウェー Noruē Norway; Norwegian

・・・人 ...-jin person

フィリピン Firipin Philippines; Filipina

ロシア Roshia Russia; Russian

韓国 Kankok South Korea; South Korean

スペイン Spein Spain; Spanish

スウェーデン Suēden Sweden; Swedish

米 Bei USA

米国 Beikok USA

CUSTOMS

税関 zeikan Customs

税関審査 zeikan-shinsa Customs check

税関告知書 zeikan-kokchi-sho Customs declaration form

税関申告用紙 zeikan-shinkok-yōshi Customs declaration form

出国 shuk·kok departure from a country

入国 nyūkok entry into a country

入国カード nyūkok-kādo entry card, landing card

入国審査 nyūkok-shinsa entry examination

外国人 gaikok-jin foreigners

出入国管理 shutsnyūkok-kanri immigration

日本人 Nihon-jin Japanese nationals

検疫 ken·eki quarantine

DAYS

月曜日 Getsyōbi Monday

火曜日 Kayōbi Tuesday

水曜日 Suiyōbi Wednesday

木曜日 Mok·yōbi Thursday

金曜日 Kin·yōbi Friday

土曜日 Doyōbi Saturday

日曜日 Nichiyōbi Sunday

EMERGENCIES

救急車 kyūkyū-sha ambulance

119番 hyak-jū-kyū-ban ambulance, fire brigade

病院 byōin hospital

救急病院 kyūkyū-byōin emergency hospital

応急手当て ōkyū-teate first aid

救急箱 kyūkyū-bako first-aid box

救急セット kyūkyū-set·to first-aid kit, emergency kit

110番 hyak-tō-ban police

警察 keisats police

火災報知器 kasai-hōchiki fire alarm

消防署 shōbōsho fire brigade

消火器 shōkaki fire extinguisher

避難口 hinan·guchi emergency exit

非常口 hijōguchi emergency exit

故障 koshō breakdown

非常呼び出し hijō-yobidashi emergency call

非常電話 hijō-denwa emergency telephone

ENTERTAINMENT

映画館 eigakan cinema, movie theater

映画 eiga film, movie

成人映画 seijin-eiga adult film

アニメーション animēshon cartoon

洋画 yōga Western film

字幕 jimak subtitles

ロードショー rōdoshō
special release

上映中 jōei-chū now
showing

会場時間 kaijō-jikan
opening time

前売券 maeuri-ken advance
booking

劇場 gekijō theatre

切符 kip·p ticket

切符売場 kip·p-uriba ticket
office, box office

席 seki seat

座席 zaseki seat

座席番号 zaseki-ban·gō seat
number

指定席 shiteiseki reserved
seat

指定券 shitei-ken reserved
seat ticket

満席 manseki all seats taken

満員 man·in full

劇 geki play, drama

時代劇 jidai-geki historical
play or film

帝国劇場 Teikok-Gekijō
Imperial Theatre

歌舞伎座 Kabuki-za kabuki
theatre

国立劇場 Kokurits-Gekijō
National Theatre

文楽 Bunrak traditional
puppet theatre

能 Nō Noh play

狂言 Kyōgen traditional

comic drama

歌舞伎 Kabuki traditional
drama from the Edo period

ディスコ disko disco

ナイトクラブ naito-kurab
nightclub

ホステスバー hostes-bā
hostess bar

カラオケ karaoke karaoke
bar

未成年お断り
miseinen-okotowari minors
not admitted

未成年者入場無効
miseinensha-nyūjō-mukō
minors not admitted

パチンコ pachinko pinball

ゲームセンター gēm-sentā
amusement arcade

ターキッシュ・バス
takis·sh bas Turkish bath

FERRY, BOAT SERVICES

救命ボート kyūmei-bōto
lifeboat

フェリー ferī ferry; ferry
service

ホバークラフト hobā-
kurafto hovercraft

水中翼船 suichū-yoksen
hydrofoil

FORMS

用紙 yōshi form

アンケート ankēto questionnaire

ボールペンで御記入ください bōrupen de gokinyū kudasai write in ink

氏名 shimei full name

お名前 onamae name

住所 jūsho address

滞在住所 taizaijūsho address during stay

連絡先 renraksaki contact address

年齢 nenrei age

生年月日 seinen-gap·pi date of birth

国籍 kokseki nationality

職業 shokgyō occupation

パスポート番号 paspōto-ban·gō passport number

旅券番号 ryoken-ban·gō passport number

外国人登録証明書 gaikok-jin-tōrok-shōmeisho foreign resident's ID card, alien registration card

身分証明書 mibun-shōmeisho ID card

出発予定日 shup·pats-yoteibi intended date of departure

滞在日数 taizai-nis·sū length of stay

泊数 haksū length of visit

訪日目的 hōnichi-mokteki purpose of visit

御署名 go-shomē signature

サイン sain signature

GARAGES

ガソリンスタンド gasorin-stando petrol station, (US) gas station

ガソリン gasorin petrol, (US) gas

石油 sekiyu petrol, (US) gas

軽油 keiyu diesel

ハイオク hai-ok high octane

スーパー sūpā super, premium

レギュラー regyurā regular unleaded

オイル oiru oil

灯油 tōyu paraffin, kerosene

自動車整備工場 jidōsha-seibi-kōjō auto repairs

洗車 sensha car wash

料金 ryōkin fee, charge

有料 yūryō fee, charge

無料点検 muryōtenken free inspection

無料 muryō no charge

点検サービス tenken-sābis service

タイヤチェック taiya-chek·k tyre check,

(US) tire check
水 mizu water
エア eya air

GEOGRAPHICAL TERMS

岬 misaki cape, promontory
国 kuni country
森 mori forest
温泉 onsen hot spring
島 shima island
湖 mizūmi lake
地図 chizu map
山 yama mountain
山脈 sam·myak mountain range
半島 hantō peninsula
川 kawa river
海 umi sea
頂上 chōjō summit
谷 tani valley
火山 kazan volcano
滝 taki waterfall
市 shi town, city
村 mura village
県 ken prefecture
東 higashi east
北 kita north
地方 chihō region, area
南 minami south
西 nishi west
関西 Kansai Kansai Region
　(Osaka etc)
関東 Kantō Kanto Region
　(Tokyo etc)

HAIRDRESSER'S, BEAUTY SALON

美容院 biyōin hairdresser's, beauty salon
床屋 tokoya barber's shop
理髪店 rihats·ten barber's shop
ビューティーサロン byūtī-saron beauty salon
ブロードライ burō-dorai blow dry
カット kat·to cut
調髪 chōhats cut
ヘアスタイル heya-stairu hairstyle
ヘアセット heya-set·to set
シャンプーセット shampū-set·to shampoo and set
洗髪 sempats wash
マニキュア manikyua manicure
マッサージ mas·sāji massage

HEALTH

医者 isha doctor
歯医者 haisha dentist
医院 īn (small) hospital
病院 byōin hospital
診療所 shinryōjo clinic
保健所 hokenjo public health centre
診療 shinryō consultation

診療時間 shinryō-jikan consultation hours

HIRING, RENTING

貸し・・・ kashi-... ... hire, ... rental

貸し自転車 kashi-jitensha bicycle hire

貸しボート kashi-bōto boat hire

貸し自動車 kashi-jidōsha car rental

レンタカー rentakā car rental

貸し部屋 kashibeya room to let

時間貸し jikan-gashi hourly rental

頭金 atama-kin deposit

手付金 tetskekin deposit

距離払い kyori-barai payment by distance

時間払い jikan-barai payment by the hour

レンタルサービス rentaru-sābis rental service

2 DK ni-dī-kē two rooms and dining kitchen

HOTELS

ホテル hoteru hotel

民宿 minshuk guesthouse

ビジネスホテル bijines-hoteru business hotel

カプセルホテル kapseru-hoteru capsule hotel

旅館 ryokan traditional inn

会計係 kaikei-gakari cashier

フロント fronto reception

受付 uketske reception

ロビー robī lobby

日本交通公社（JTB） Nihon-Kōtsū-Kōsha Japan Travel Bureau

団体 dantai group

予約 yoyak reservations

部屋 heya room

和室 washits Japanese-style room

洋室 yōshits Western-style room

冷房 reibō air-conditioning

お風呂 ofuro bath

ダイニングルーム daining-rūm dining room

食堂 shokdō dining room

飲料水 inryōsui drinking water

飲み水 nomimizu drinking water

クリーニング kurīning dry-cleaning

暖房 dambō heating

温泉 onsen hot spring

ラウンジ raunji lounge

ルームサービス rūm-sābis room service

電話 denwa telephone

自動販売機 jidō-hambaiki vending machine

JAPANESE CULTURE AND FESTIVALS (see also Public Holidays)

寺院 jīn temple
寺 tera temple
神社 jinja shrine
相撲 sumō traditional Japanese wrestling
正月 Shōgats New Year
節分 Setsubun Bean-Throwing Festival (3 February)
雛祭 Hina-matsuri Girl's Festival, Doll's Festival (3 March)
花見 Hanami Cherry Blossom Viewing
花祭 Hana-matsuri Buddha's Birthday (8 April)
七夕 Tanabata Star Festival (7 July)
お盆 obon Bon Festival, Buddhist festival celebrated in summer
七五三 Shichigosan Festival for 3-, 5- and 7- year olds' (15 November)
クリスマス Kurismas Christmas
美術館 bijutskan art gallery
博物館 hakbutskan museum
温泉 onsen hot spring
お風呂 ofuro public bath

LIFTS (ELEVATORS)

エレベーター erebētā lift, elevator
階 ...-kai floor, storey
地階 chikai basement
一階 ik-kai ground floor, (US) first floor
二階 ni-kai first floor, (US) second floor
定員 tē-in capacity
満員 man-in full
閉 hei close
開 kai open
上 ue up
下 shita down
非常停止 hijōteishi emergency stop
非常電話 hijōdenwa emergency telephone
故障 koshō out of order

MEDICINES

1日・・・錠 ichinichi ...-jō ... tablets a day
1日・・・回 ichinichi ...-kai ... times a day
食後 shokgo after meals
就寝前 shūshinzen before going to bed
食前 shokzen before meals
食間 shok-kan between meals
服用方法 fūk-yōhōhō directions for oral use

適量 tekiryō dosage

匙 saji spoonful(s)

錠剤 jōzai tablets

アスピリン aspirin aspirin

鎮痛剤 chintsū-zai painkiller

非ピリン系鎮痛剤 hi-pirin-kei-chintsū-zai paracetamol

咳止めドロップ sekidome-dorop-p throat lozenges

MONTHS

一月 Ichigats January

二月 Nigats February

三月 San-gats March

四月 Shigats April

五月 Gogats May

六月 Rokgats June

七月 Shichigats July

八月 Hachigats August

九月 Kugats September

十月 Jūgats October

十一月 Jūichigats November

十二月 Jūnigats December

NOTICES ON DOORS

入口 iriguchi entrance, way in

出口 deguchi exit, way out

自動ドア jidō-doa automatic door

引く hik pull

押す osu push

営業中 eigyōchū open

開く hirak to open

開 kai open

閉 hei closed

閉じる tojiru to close, to shut

休日 kyūjits closed

営業中 eigyōchū open for business

年中無休 nenjū-mukyū open all year round

月曜定休日 Gets-yō-teikyūbi closed Mondays

日祭日休み nichi-saijits-yasumi closed on Sundays and National Holidays

本日休業 honjits-kyūgyō closed today

定休日 teikyūbi closed for holidays

非常出口 hijōdeguchi emergency exit

非常口 hijōguchi emergency exit

避難口 hinan-guchi emergency exit

開放厳禁 kaihō-genkin keep closed

入場お断り nyūjō okotowari no admittance

関係者以外の立ち入り禁止 kankeisha igai no tachiiri kinshi no admittance for unauthorized personnel

立ち入り禁止 tachiiri-kinshi no entry

PHONES

電話 denwa phone

公衆電話 kōshūdenwa public phone

電話ボックス denwa-bok·ks phone booth

国際電信電話 Kokusai-Denshin-Denwa Overseas Telecommunications Service

テレホンカード terehōn-kādo phonecard

電話代 denwadai call charge

通話料 tsūwaryō call charge

交換手 kōkanshu operator

電話帳 denwachō directory

内線 naisen extension

電話番号 denwaban·gō phone number

国際電話 koksai-denwa international call

市内電話 shinai-denwa local call

長距離電話 chōkyori-denwa long-distance call

市外電話 shigai-denwa out-of-town call

ファックス fak·ks fax; fax machine

PLACE NAMES

箱根 Hakone

広島 Hiroshima

北海道 Hok·kaidō

本州 Honshū

伊勢 Ise

鎌倉 Kamakura

神戸 Kōbe

京都 Kyōto

九州 Kyūshū

長崎 Nagasaki

名古屋 Nagoya

奈良 Nara

日光 Nik·kō

大阪 Ōsaka

四国 Shikoku

東京 Tōkyō

横浜 Yokohama

POST OFFICE

郵便局 yūbinkyok post office

〒 yūbinkyok no māk symbol for Japanese post office

窓口 madoguchi counter

切手 kit·te stamp

手紙 tegami letter

小包 kozutsmi parcel, package

航空書簡 kōkū-shokan aerogramme

航空便 kōkūbin airmail

速達 soktats express mail

書留 kakitome registered mail

船便 funabin sea mail

サル便 sarubin surface mail, overland mail

住所 jūsho address

宛名 atena addressee

印刷物 insatsbuts printed matter

留置 tomeoki poste restante, general delivery

為替 kawase money order

地方 chihō out of town

外国向け gaikok-muke overseas mail

都区内 toknai to other parts of Toyko

他府県 tafuken to other prefectures

PUBLIC HOLIDAYS

祝日 shukjits public holiday

元日 Ganjits New Year's Day

成人の日 Sējin-no-hi Coming-of-Age Day (15 January)

建国記念日 kenkok-kinem-bi National Foundation Day (11 February)

春分の日 shum-bun-no-hi Vernal Equinox

みどりの日 midori-no-hi The Greenery Day (29 April)

憲法記念日 kempōkinem-bi Constitution Day (3 May)

子供の日 kodomo-no-hi Boy's Festival, Children's Day (5 May)

海の日 Sea Day (20 July)

敬老の日 keirō-no-hi Respect the Aged Day (15 September)

秋分の日 shūbun-no-hi Autumnal Equinox

体育の日 tai-ik-no-hi Sport's Day (10 October)

文化の日 bunka-no-hi Culture Day (3 November)

勤労感謝の日 kinrōkansha-no-hi Labour Thanksgiving Day (23 November)

天皇誕生日 Ten-nō-tanjōbi The Emperor's Birthday (23 December)

RESTAURANTS, CAFÉS, BARS

食堂 shokdō restaurant

料理屋 ryōri-ya restaurant

レストラン restoran restaurant

割烹 kap-pō upmarket restaurant

料亭 ryōtei upmarket restaurant

和食 washok Japanese restaurant

中華料理 chūka-ryōri Chinese restaurant

天ぷら tempura restaurant

specializing in deep-fried
food

小料理屋 koryōri-ya small
restaurant usually serving
local dishes

飯屋 meshi-ya small local
restaurant

寿司処 sushi-dokoro sushi
restaurant

精進料理屋 shōjin-ryōri-ya
vegetarian restaurant

食事処 shokji-dokoro very
small local restaurant

営業中 eigyō-chū meals
being served

定食 teishok set meal

蕎麦 soba noodles

ラーメン rāmen Chinese
noodles

お会計 okaikei cashier

喫茶店 kis·saten coffee shop

軽食喫茶 keishok-kis·sa
coffee shop serving light
meals

軽食 keishok snackbar

スナック snak·k snackbar

スナックバー snak·kbā
snackbar

バー bā bar

居酒屋 izaka-ya bar, serving
local cuisine

飲み屋 nomi-ya bar, serving
food, often from a mobile
stall

ROAD SIGNS

左折禁止 sasets-kinshi no
left turn

右折禁止 usets-kinshi no
right turn

停車禁止 teisha-kinshi no
stopping

通行禁止 tsūkō-kinshi no
through traffic

通行止め tsūkō-dome no
through traffic

スピードを落とせ spīdo o
otose reduce speed

最高速度 saikō-sokdo
maximum speed

道路工事 dōrokōji road
under construction

工事中 kōji-chū road works

急カーブ kyūkāb sharp
bend

徐行 jokō slow

一旦停止 it·tan-teishi stop

一旦停車 it·tan-teisha stop

止まれ tomare stop

この先百メートル kono
saki hyak-mētoru 100 metres
ahead

事故 jiko accident

注意 chūi caution

危険 kiken danger

回り道 mawari-michi
diversion, detour

高速道路 kōsokdōro
expressway

国道 kokdō national motorway/highway

有料道路 yūryōdōro toll road

料金 ryōkin fee

有料 yūryō fee charged

無料 muryō no charge

交差点 kōsaten junction, intersection

本線 honsen lane for through traffic

踏切 fumikiri level crossing, railroad crossing

駐車場 chūshajō car park, parking lot

非常駐車帯 hijō-chūsha-tai emergency parking area

一時預かり ichiji-azkari short-term parking

駐車禁止 chūsha-kinshi no parking

満車 mansha car park/ parking lot full

SHOPPING

・・・屋 ...-ya ... shop/ store

・・・店 ...-ten ... shop/ store

レジ reji cash desk, cashier

会計 kaikei cashier

お勘定 okanjō pay here

骨董品店 kot·tōhin-ten antique shop, curiosity shop

オーディオ製品 ōdio-seihin audio and hi-fi equipment

パン屋 pan-ya baker's

本屋 hon-ya bookshop, bookstore

書店 shoten bookshop, bookstore

肉屋 nik-ya butcher's

ケーキ屋 kēki-ya cake shop

カメラ屋 kamera-ya camera shop

子供服（ 売場 ） kodomofuk(-uriba) children's wear

陶器 tōki china

瀬戸物屋 setomono-ya china shop

喫茶店 kis·saten coffee shop

お菓子屋 okashi-ya confectioner's, candy store

化粧品 keshōhin cosmetics

デパート depāto depart- ment store

クリーニング店 kuriñing-ten dry cleaner's

電気製品 denki-seihin electrical goods

電気屋 denki-ya electrical goods shop

魚屋 sakana-ya fishmonger

花屋 hana-ya florist

食品 shokhin food

果物屋 kudamono-ya fruit shop

八百屋 yao-ya greengrocer's

食料品店 shokryōhin-ten
grocer's

金物屋 kanamono-ya
hardware store

着物 kimono kimonos

売店 baiten kiosk

台所用品 daidokoro-yōhin
kitchen goods

婦人服（売場）fujin-
fuk(-uriba) ladies' wear

コインランドリー
koin-randorī launderette,
laundromat

市場 ichiba market

紳士服（売場）
shinshifuku(-uriba) menswear
department

酒屋 saka-ya off-licence,
liquor store

メガネ（店）megane(-ten)
optician

香水 kōsui perfumery

薬屋 ksuri-ya pharmacy

薬局 yak·kyok pharmacy

写真屋 shashin-ya photogra-
phy shop

レコード店 rekōdo-ten
record shop, music store

古本屋 furuhon-ya second-
hand bookshop/bookstore

靴屋 kuts-ya shoe shop

土産店 miyage-ten souvenir
shop

スポーツ用品店
spōts-yōhin-ten sports shop

文房具屋 bumbōg-ya
stationery shop

スーパー sūpā supermarket

おもちゃ売場 omocha-uriba
toy department

おもちゃ屋 omocha-ya toy
shop

旅行代理店 ryokōdairi-ten
travel agency

旅行会社 ryokōgaisha travel
agency

下着売場 shitagi-uriba
underwear department

お手を触れないでください
ote o furenaide kudasai
please do not touch

バーゲン bāgen bargains

大売り出し ōuridashi
bargains, sale

セール sēru sale

セール実施中
sēru-jis·shi-chū sale now on

特別価格 tokbets-kakak
special price

お歳暮 oseibo year-end gifts

歳末売り出し
saimats-uridashi year-end
sale

お中元 ochūgen mid-
summer presents

エスカレーター eskarētā
escalator

・・・階 …-kai floor

屋上 okjō roof

STREETS AND ROADS

路線 rosen lane
道路 dōro road
幹線道路 kansen-dōro
arterial road, trunk road
高速道路 kōsok-dōro
motorway, highway
追い越し線 oikoshi-sen
lane for overtaking
広場 hiroba square

TAXIS

タクシー takshī taxi
個人タクシー kojin-takshī
mini-cab
タクシー乗場 takshī-noriba
taxi rank
空車 kūsha for hire, free
料金メーター ryōkin-mētā
fare meter
夜間割り増し料金 yakan-
warimashi-ryōkin late-night
fare
回送 kaisō out of service
自動ドア jidō-doa auto-
matic door

TIMETABLES

時刻表 jikokhyō timetable,
schedule
到着 tōchak arrival
出発 shup·pats departure
発車 has·sha departure
方面 hōmen direction

行き先 ikisaki destination
乗場 noriba boarding
platform/track
・・・行き … iki bound
for …
経由 keiyu via
・・・線 … sen … line

TOILETS

公衆便所 kōshū benjo
public toilet
化粧室 keshōshits toilet, rest
room
お手洗い otearai toilet(s),
rest room(s)
トイレ toire toilet, rest
room
便所 benjo toilet, rest room
男子用 danshi-yō gents'
toilet, men's room
女子用 joshi-yō ladies'
toilet, ladies' room
紳士用 shinshi-yō gents'
toilet, men's room
婦人用 fujin-yō ladies' toilet,
ladies' room
男 otoko men
女 onna women
使用中 shiyō-chū occupied,
engaged
空 aki vacant

TRAIN TYPES

電車 densha train

列車 res·sha train

新幹線 shinkansen bullet train

急行 kyūkō express

ひかり hikari fastest bullet train

普通 futsū local slow train stopping at all stations

準急 junkyū semi-express

こだま kodama slower bullet train

特別急行 tokbets-kyūkō super express with limited stops only

特急 tok·kyū super express with limited stops only

グリーン車 gurīn-sha green car (first class)

TRAIN AND UNDERGROUND TRAVEL

鉄道 tetsdō railway, railroad

私鉄 shitets private railway

駅 eki station

・・・券 ...-ken ... ticket

切符 kip·p ticket

回数券 kaisūken book of tickets

定期券 teiki-ken season ticket

前売券 maeuri-ken advance sale tickets

予約 yoyak reservations

指定席(券) shiteiseki (-ken) reserved seat (ticket)

自由席 jiyūseki unreserved seat

切符売場 kip·p-uriba ticket office; ticket vending machine

窓口 madoguchi ticket window

出札口 shus·sats-guchi ticket window

みどりの窓口 midori no madoguchi first-class ticket window

料金表 ryōkinhyō table of charges

運賃表 unchinhyō table of fares

大人 otona adult

子供 kodomo child

団体 dantai group

個人 kojin individual

改札口 kaisats-guchi ticket barrier

入場券 nyūjōken platform ticket

ホーム hōm platform, (US) track

・・・番線 ...-bansen platform ..., (US) track ...

座席 zaseki seat

席 seki seat

有効 yūkō valid

無効 mukō not valid

・・・円区間行き ...-en-kukan-yuki for destinations within the ...-yen zone (eg 200-yen zone)

下車前途無効 gesha-zento-mukō after alighting, not valid for further travel

発売当日限り有効 hatsbai-tōjits-kagiri-yūkō valid only on day of purchase

精算所 seisanjo excess fare office

到着 tōchak arrival(s)

発車 has·sha departure(s)

出発 shup·pats departure(s)

乗り換え口 norikae-guchi this way for changing trains

車掌 shashō conductor

・・・号車 ...-gō-sha carriage ...

食堂車 shokdō-sha dining car

満員 man·in full

回送 kaisō out of service

荷物 nimots luggage, baggage

コインロッカー koin-rok·kā coin-operated locker

一時預かり所 ichiji-azkari-jo left luggage office, baggage checkroom

遺失物取扱所 ishitsbuts-toriatskai-jo lost property office, lost and found

お忘れ物 owasure-mono lost property, lost and found

待合室 machiai-shits waiting room

地図 chizu map

左側通行 hidarigawa-tsūkō keep to the left

右側通行 migigawa-tsūkō keep to the right

東口 higashi-guchi east exit (or entrance)

北口 kita-guchi north exit (or entrance)

南口 minami-guchi south exit (or entrance)

西口 nishi-guchi west exit (or entrance)

地下鉄 chikatets underground, (US) subway

YOUTH HOSTELS

ユースホステル yūs-hosteru youth hostel

台所 daidokoro kitchen

キッチン kit·chin kitchen

コインランドリー koin-randorī launderette, laundromat

売店 baiten shop

シャワー shawā shower

Menu Reader:

Food

ESSENTIAL TERMS

bowl chawan
茶碗

chopsticks hashi
はし

cup kap·p
カップ

dessert dezāto
デザート

fork fōk
フォーク

fried rice chāhan
チャーハン

glass kop·p
コップ

knife naif
ナイフ

menu menyū
メニュー

noodles menrui
めん類

plate sara
さら

rice (boiled) gohan
ごはん

soup sūp
スープ

soy sauce shōyu
しょうゆ

spoon spūn
スプーン

table tēburu
テーブル

excuse me!

chot·to sumimasen!
ちょっとすみませ
ん！

could I have the bill, please?

okanjō o onegai shimas
お勘定をお願いし
ます

BASIC FOODS

パン pan bread

バター batā butter

みそ miso fermented soybean paste

ケチャップ kechap-p ketchup

油 abura oil

こしょう koshō pepper

しお shio salt

しょうゆ shōyu soy sauce

さとう satō sugar

BASIC PREPARATION AND COOKING METHODS

バーベキューした bābekyū shita barbecued

ゆでた yudeta boiled

土鍋で煮た donabe de nita casseroled

煮た nita cooked

揚げた ageta deep-fried

干した hoshita dried

焼いた yaita grilled

漬けた tsketa pickled

ローストした rōsto shita roast

蒸した mushita steamed

煮込んだ nikonda stewed

炒めた itameta stir-fried

詰めものした tsmemono shita stuffed

BASIC SET MEALS

定食 teishok set meal with rice, soup, pickles and main dish of meat or fish

日替り定食 higawari-teishok set meal of the day

てんぷら定食 tempura-teishok set meal with deep-fried prawns

うなぎ定食 unagi-teishok set meal with eel

焼魚定食 yakizakana-teishok set meal with fried fish

焼肉定食 yakinik-teishok set meal with grilled meat

とんかつ定食 tonkats-teishok set meal with pork

刺身定食 sashimi-teishok set meal with raw fish

BEAN CURD DISHES

豆腐 tōf bean curd

油揚げ abura-age deep-fried bean curd

田楽 dengak grilled bean curd on a wooden skewer

BEEF AND BEEF DISHES

牛肉 gyūnik beef

ビーフ bīf beef

すきやき sukiyaki beef and vegetables cooked with soy sauce in a pot at the table

鉄板焼き tep-pan-yaki beef

and vegetables grilled at the table

牛しょうが焼き gyūshōgayaki beef cooked in soy sauce with ginger

牛照り焼き gyūteriyaki beef cooked in soy sauce and sake

ビフテキ bifuteki beef steak

焼肉 yakinik fried beef marinated in soy sauce

ローストビーフ rōsto-bīf roast beef

サーロイン sāroin sirloin

しゃぶしゃぶ shabshab sliced beef with vegetables boiled at the table

ステーキ stēki steak

BISCUITS, CAKES, CRACKERS AND SWEETS

ビスケット bisket-to biscuits, cookies

クッキー kuk-kī biscuits, cookies

ケーキ kēki cake

わたあめ wata-ame candy floss, cotton candy

チーズケーキ chīz-kēki cheesecake

チョコレート chokorēto chocolate

お菓子 okashi confection-ery

シュークリーム shūkurīm cream puff

ドーナッツ dōnat-ts doughnut

エクレア ekurea éclair

和菓子 wagashi Japanese-style confectionery

おこし okoshi popped rice confectionery

ぜんざい zenzai rice cake with sweet bean sauce

もち mochi rice cakes

塩せんべい shio-sembei rice crackers flavoured with salt

せんべい sembei rice crackers flavoured with soy sauce

まんじゅう manjū rice-flour cakes with sweet bean paste

ようかん yōkan soft, sweet bean paste

ショートケーキ shōto-kēki sponge cake with fresh cream and strawberries

カステラ kastera sponge cake

おしるこ oshiruko sweet bean soup with rice cake

くずもち kuzumochi triangles of arrowroot jelly in brown sugar syrup

もなか monaka wafers filled with sweet bean paste

CHICKEN, POULTRY etc

鶏肉 torinik chicken

鶏料理 tori-ryōri poultry dishes

やきとり yakitori barbecued chicken on a skewer

ささみ sasami breast

がちょう gachō goose

きじ kiji pheasant

うずら uzura quail

ローストチキン rōsto-chikin roast chicken

七面鳥 shchimenchō turkey

CHINESE FOOD

中華料理 Chūka-ryōri Chinese-style cuisine

麻婆豆腐 mābōdōf bean curd in spicy sauce

かに卵 kanitama crab omelette

からあげ kara-age deep-fried pieces of pork or chicken

はるまき harumaki deep-fried spring rolls

ぎょうざ gyōza fried dumplings stuffed with minced pork

八宝菜 hap-pōsai fried pork with vegetables

チャーハン chāhan fried rice

野菜炒め yasai-itame fried vegetables

肉団子 nikdango meatballs

やきそば yakisoba noodles fried in a wok

ラーメン rāmen noodles in bouillon

チャーシューメン chāshūmen noodles in bouillon with slices of pork

みそラーメン miso-rāmen noodles in bouillon with fermented soybean paste

タンメン tam·men noodles in bouillon with vegetables

ワンタンメン wantam·men pork dumplings, served in bouillon with noodles

シューマイ shūmai steamed pork meatballs in thin pastry

すぶた subuta sweet and sour pork

CONDIMENTS, HERBS, SPICES AND PICKLES

梅干し umeboshi dried, pickled sour Japanese plums

納豆 nat·tō fermented soybeans

しょうが shōga ginger

みつば mitsba Japanese coriander

しそ shiso Japanese basil

マヨネーズ mayonēz mayonnaise

からし karashi mustard
パセリ paseri parsley
こしょう koshō pepper
ドレッシング dores·shing salad dressing
しお shio salt
しょうゆ shōyu soy sauce
とんかつソース tonkatsu-sōs thick sweet fruity sauce
酢 su vinegar
たくあん tak·an yellow radish pickles

DESSERTS

デザート dezāto desserts
アップルパイ ap·puru-pai apple pie
チョコレートアイスクリーム chokorēto-ais-kurīm chocolate ice cream
チョコレートムース chokorēto-mūs chocolate mousse
チョコレートサンデー chokorēto-sandē chocolate sundae
コーヒーゼリー kohī-zerī coffee-flavoured jelly
クレープ kurēp crepe
宇治氷 uji-gōri crushed ice with green tea syrup
宇治金時 uji-kintoki crushed ice with green tea syrup and sweet bean paste
氷レモン kōri-remon crushed ice with lemon syrup
氷メロン kōri-meron crushed ice with melon syrup
氷いちご kōri-ichigo crushed ice with strawberry syrup
氷あずき kōri-azki crushed ice with sweet bean paste
フルーツサラダ frūts-sarada fruit cocktail, fruit salad
フルーツゼリー frūts-zerī fruit jelly
みつまめ mitsmame gelatin cubes and sweet bean paste with pieces of fruit
あんみつ am·mits gelatin cubes with sweet bean paste and pieces of fruit
アイスクリーム ais-kurīm ice cream
ゼリー zerī jelly
レモンパイ remon-pai lemon pie
レモンスフレ remon-sufre lemon soufflé
ムース mūs mousse
シャーベット shābet·to sorbet
ストロベリーアイスクリーム storoberī-ais-kurīm strawberry ice cream

ストロベリーサンデー
storoberī-sandē strawberry
sundae
プリン purin caramel
custard
バニラアイスクリー
ム banira-ais-kurīm vanilla
ice cream
ヨーグルト yōguruto
yoghurt

EGGS AND EGG DISHES

卵 tamago egg
かに卵 kanitama crab
omelette
めだまやき medama-yaki
fried egg
ゆでたまご yude-tamago
hard-boiled egg
オムレツ omurets omelette
たまごやき tamago-yaki
Japanese-style omelette
オムライス omurais
omelette with rice
おとしたまご otoshi-
tamago poached egg
茶碗蒸し chawam-mushi
savoury custard with egg
and fish
半熟たまご hanjuk-tamago
soft-boiled egg
たまごスープ tamago-sūp
soup with egg
たまご豆腐 tamago-dōf
steamed egg

FISH

あわび awabi abalone
赤貝 akagai ark shell
ふぐ fug blowfish
みる貝 mirugai boiled
round clams
かつお katsuo bonito,
tunny
こい koi carp
はまぐり hamaguri clams
たら tara cod
たらこ tarako cod roe
あなご anago conger eel
しじみ shijimi corbicula
かに kani crab
からすみ karasumi dried
mullet roe
うなぎ unagi eel
ひらめ hirame flatfish
とびうお tobi-uo flying
fish
きんめだい kim-me-dai
gold-eyed bream
にしん nishin herring
かずのこ kazunoko herring
roe
あじ aji horse mackerel
くらげ kurage jellyfish
たらばがに taraba-gani
king crab
どじょう dojō loach
いせえび ise-ebi lobster
さば saba mackerel
中トロ chū-toro medium
fatty tuna

あんこう ankō monkfish

ムール貝 mūru-gai mussels

たこ tako octopus

かき kaki oyster

さんま sam·ma Pacific saury

かます kamas pike, barracuda

くるまえび kuruma-ebi prawns

にじます nijimas rainbow trout

刺身 sashimi raw fish

たいらぎ tairagi razor shell ligament

さけ sake salmon

イクラ ikura salmon roe

いわし iwashi sardines

たちうお tachi-uo scabbard fish

ほたて貝 hotategai scallops

貝柱 kai-bashira scallops

すずき suzki sea bass

たい tai sea bream

はも hamo sea eel

きす kis sea smelt

うに uni sea urchin

さめ same shark

あさり asari short-necked clam

えび ebi shrimps, prawns

ししゃも shishamo smelt

スモークサーモン sumōk-sāmon smoked salmon

トロ toro soft, fatty pink belly of tuna

したびらめ shita-birame sole

いか ika squid

あゆ ayu sweet smelt

かじき kajiki swordfish

さざえ sazae top-shell

なまこ namako trepang

ます mas trout

まぐろ maguro tuna

かれい karei turbot

すっぽん sup·pon turtle

ふか fuka type of shark

くじら kujira whale

しらす shiras whitebait

ぶり buri yellowtail

FISH DISHES

ふぐ料理 fug-ryōri blowfish cuisine

かばやき kabayaki broiled eel

うな重 unajū broiled eel on rice

うな丼 unadon broiled eel on rice in a bowl

炉ばた焼き robata-yaki charcoal-grilled fish and vegetables

あじのたたき aji no tataki chopped raw horse mackerel, mild ginger and herbs

てんぷら tempura deep-fried seafood and vegetables

たこやき takoyaki dumplings with small pieces of octopus

鍋物 nabemono fish and vegetables cooked in a pot at the table

寄せ鍋 yosenabe fish and vegetables cooked in a pot at the table

刺身 sashimi raw fish

すし sushi raw fish on rice balls

ふぐ刺し fug-sashi raw sliced blowfish

鉄火丼 tek·kadon rice in a bowl topped with slices of raw tuna

ふぐちり fug-chiri shredded blowfish in vegetable chowder

おでん oden vegetables and fish dumplings stewed in a thin soy soup, served hot

FRUIT, NUTS AND SEEDS

くだもの kudamono fruit

フルーツ frūts fruit

アーモンド āmondo almonds

りんご rin·go apple

バナナ banana banana

さくらんぼ sakurambo cherries

くり kuri chestnuts

ココナッツ kokonat·ts coconut

いちじく ichijik figs

ぎんなん gin·nan gingko nuts

グレープフルーツ grēp-frūts grapefruit

ぶどう budō grapes

うめ ume Japanese plum

レモン remon lemon

メロン meron melon

オレンジ orenji orange

もも momo peach

ピーナッツ pīnat·ts peanuts

なし nashi pear

かき kaki persimmon, sharon fruit

パイナップル painap·puru pineapple

すもも sumomo plum

ざくろ zakuro pomegranate

ごま goma sesame seeds

いちご ichigo strawberries

みかん mikan tangerine

くるみ kurumi walnuts

すいか suika watermelon

LUNCH BOXES

弁当 bentō boxed lunch

幕の内弁当 makunouchi-bentō boxed lunch with rice, meat and vegetables

MEAT AND MEAT DISHES (see also beef, chicken, poultry etc and pork)

肉 nik meat

ベーコン bēkon bacon

バーベキュー bābekyū barbecue

ロールキャベツ rōru-kyabets cabbage rolls filled with minced meat

あばら肉 abaranik chops

コロッケ korok·ke croquettes

カツレツ katsrets cutlets

串揚げ kushi-age deep-fried meat on skewers

ヒレ肉 hirenik fillet

ハム ham ham

ハンバーグ hambāg hamburger

腎臓 jinzō kidney

ラム ram lamb

レバー rebā liver

肉団子 nikdango meat-filled dumplings

ひき肉 hikinik minced beef, pork or chicken

マトン maton mutton

骨付き honetski on the bone

ソーセージ sōsēji sausage

仔羊肉の串焼き ram-no-kushiyaki skewered lamb

スペアリブ speyarib spare ribs

ちゃんこ鍋 chanko-nabe thick meat and vegetable stew

タン tan tongue

モツ mots tripe

仔牛肉 koushi-nik veal

MENU TERMS

メニュー menyū menu

並 nami cheaper selection

本日のおすすめ品 honjits no osusume-hin chef's speciality of the day

中華料理 Chūka-ryōri Chinese-style cuisine

デザート dezāto desserts

上 jō expensive selection

フランス料理 Frans-ryōri French-style cuisine

くだもの kudamono fruit

イタリア料理 Itaria-ryōri Italian-style cuisine

日本料理 Nihon-ryōri Japanese-style cuisine

壊石料理 kaiseki-ryōri Japanese haute cuisine

メインコース mein-kōs main course

肉 nik meat

郷土料理 kyōdo-ryōri regional specialities

定食 teishok set meal

スープ sūp soups

オードブル ōdoburu starters, appetizers

野菜 yasai vegetables

精進料理 shōjin-ryōri vegetarian cuisine

西洋料理 seiyō-ryōri Western-style cuisine

NOODLES

そば soba buckwheat noodles

うどん udon thick noodles made from wheatflour

しらたき shirataki translucent, thin noodles made from potato flour

そうめん sōmen very thin wheatflour vermicelli served cold with soy-sauce dipping sauce

やきそば yakisoba Chinese noodles fried in a wok

ラーメン rāmen Chinese noodles in bouillon

チャーシューメン chāshūmen Chinese noodles in bouillon with slices of pork

みそラーメン miso-rāmen Chinese noodles in bouillon with fermented soybean paste

チャンポン champon Chinese noodles in salted bouillon with vegetables

天ざる ten-zaru cold noodles served with deep-fried shrimps

冷し中華 hiyashi-chūka cold noodles with slices of meat and vegetables in vinegary sauce

ざるそば／うどん zaru-soba/udon cold noodles with sweet soy sauce for dipping

かきたま kakitama noodles and egg in fish soup

五目そば gomok-soba noodles in bouillon with vegetables and meat

カレー南蛮 karē-namban noodles in curry-flavoured soup with pork or beef

とろろそば tororo-soba noodles in fish bouillon garnished with grated yam

月見そば／うどん tskimi-soba/udon noodles in fish bouillon with a raw egg

鴨南蛮 kamo-namban noodles in fish bouillon with chicken

きつねそば／うどん kitsne-soba/udon noodles in fish bouillon with deep-fried bean curd

てんぷらそば tempura-soba noodles in fish bouillon with deep-fried shrimps

おかめそば／うどん

okame-soba/udon noodles in fish bouillon with fish dumplings

なめこそば／うどん nameko-soba/udon noodles in fish bouillon with Japanese small mushrooms

肉南蛮 nik-namban noodles in fish bouillon with pork or beef

たぬきそば／うどん tanuki-soba/udon noodles in fish bouillon with small pieces of deep-fried batter

あんかけそば／うどん ankake-soba/udon noodles in thick bouillon with fish dumplings and vegetables

PORK AND PORK DISHES

豚肉 butanik pork

ポーク pōk pork

とんかつ tonkats deep-fried pork cutlets

かつ丼 katsdon deep-fried pork on rice

骨付き豚肉 honetski-butanik pork chop

豚しょうが焼き buta-shōgayaki pork cooked in soy sauce with ginger

カツカレー katskarē pork cutlets with curry

豚照り焼き buta-teriyaki pork cooked in soy sauce and sake

ローストポーク rōsto-pōk roast pork

バター焼き batāyaki sliced pork (or beef) fried in butter

RICE AND RICE DISHES

ごはん gohan rice

ライス rais rice

うな重 unajū broiled eel on rice

丼物 dom-mono bowl of rice with something on top

親子丼 oyakodon domburi with chicken and egg

かつ丼 katsdon domburi with deep-fried breaded pork cutlet

天丼 tendon domburi with deep-fried shrimps

卵丼 tamagodon domburi with soft scrambled eggs and onions

うな丼 unadon domburi with broiled eel

中華丼 chūkadon domburi with pork and vegetables

牛丼 gyūdon domburi with sliced beef

チャーハン chāhan fried rice

おにぎり onigiri riceballs

もち mochi rice cakes

お茶づけ ochazke rice in tea or fish bouillon

釜飯 kamameshi rice steamed in fish bouillon with pieces of meat, fish and vegetables

チキンライス chikin-rais rice with chicken, cooked in tomato sauce

カレーライス karērais rice with curry-flavoured stew

オムライス omurais rice wrapped in a plain omelette

ハヤシライス hayashi-rais diced beef in gravy on rice

SALADS

サラダ sarada salad

生野菜 nama-yasai salad

ミックスサラダ mik·ks-sarada mixed salad

ポテトサラダ poteto-sarada potato salad

ドレッシング dores·shing salad dressing

SNACKS

チーズバーガー chīz-bāga cheeseburger

ポテトフライ poteto-frai chips, French fries

ポテトチップ poteto-chip crisps, (US) potato chips

ハンバーガー hambāga hamburger

ハムサンド hamusando ham sandwich

ホットドッグ hot·todog·g hotdog

とうもろこし tōmorokoshi roasted corn on the cob

サンドイッチ sandoit·chi sandwich

スパゲッティ spaget·ti spaghetti

トースト tōsto toast

ツナサンド tsnasando tuna sandwich

SOUPS

スープ sūp soups (usually Western-style)

汁物 shirumono soups (Japanese-style)

吸物 suimono clear fish bouillon with meat, fish or vegetable

すまし汁 sumashi-jiru clear fish bouillon with meat, fish or vegetable

コンソメスープ konsome-sūp consommé

野菜のクリームスープ yasai no kurīm-sūp cream of vegetable soup

オニオングラタンスープ onion-guratan-sūp onion soup au gratin

味噌汁 misoshiru soup with

bean paste

ポタージュ potāju thick soup

トマトスープ tomato-sūp tomato soup

そば soba buckwheat noodles in bouillon

うどん udon thick noodles made from wheatflour in bouillon

ラーメン rāmen Chinese noodles in bouillon

STARTERS, APPETIZERS

オードブル ōdoburu starters, appetizers

おつまみ otsmami Japanese-style starter/appetizer

アスパラガス asparagas asparagus

キャビア kyabia caviar

セロリ serori celery

はまぐり hamaguri clams

かに kani crab

フルーツジュース frūts-jūs fruit juice

ハム ham ham

にしん nishin herring

いせえび ise-ebi lobster

メロン meron melon

マッシュルーム mashrūm mushrooms

かき kaki oysters

くるまえび kuruma-ebi prawns

魚の卵 sakana no tamago roe

サラダ sarada salad

サラミ sarami salami

さけ sake salmon

ソーセージ sōsēji sausage

小えび ko-ebi shrimps

まぐろ maguro tuna

SUSHI DISHES

すし sushi raw fish on riceballs

握りずし nigiri-zushi raw fish on seasoned riceballs

五目ずし gomok-zushi mixed fish and vegetables on rice

ちらしずし chirashi-zushi mixed raw fish on rice

押しずし oshi-zushi sushi cut in squares

さばずし saba-zushi sushi with vinegared mackerel

かっぱ巻き kap-pa-maki cucumber and seasoned rice wrapped in seaweed

お新香巻き oshinko-maki pickles and seasoned rice wrapped in seaweed

茶巾ずし chakin-zushi seasoned rice wrapped in egg crepe

いなりずし inari-zushi seasoned rice wrapped in deep-fried bean curd

のり巻き norimaki sliced roll of rice, vegetables or cooked gourd wrapped in seaweed

鉄火巻き tek·ka·maki tuna and seasoned rice wrapped in seaweed

わさび wasabi very spicy horseradish served with sushi

VEGETABLES

野菜 yasai vegetables

あずき azki adzuki beans

アスパラガス asparagas asparagus

なす nas aubergine, eggplant

アボカド abokado avocado

やきいも yaki-imo baked yam

たけのこ takenoko bamboo shoots

しなちく shinachik bamboo shoots cooked in soy sauce, sugar and sesame oil

まめ mame beans

もやし moyashi bean sprouts

ビーツ bīts beet

てんさい tensai beetroot

えだまめ edamame boiled green soybeans

おひたし ohitashi boiled spinach with seasoning

そらまめ soramame broad beans

ブロッコリ burok·kori broccoli

しめじ shimeji brown button mushrooms

芽キャベツ mekyabets Brussels sprouts

ごぼう gobō burdock root

キャベツ kyabets cabbage

にんじん ninjin carrot

カリフラワー karifrawā cauliflower

セロリ serori celery

プチトマト puchi-tomato cherry tomatoes

チコリ chikori chicory

白菜 haksai Chinese cabbage

春菊 shun·gik chrysanthemum greens

とうもろこし tōmorokoshi corn on the cob

ズッキーニ zuk·kīni courgette, zucchini

きゅうり kyūri cucumber

かんぴょう kampyō dried gourd shavings

しいたけ shītake dried mushrooms

のり nori dried seaweed

なめこ nameko edible fungus

きくらげ kikurage edible

tree fungus

エンディーブ endīb
endive

きんぴら kimpira fried
burdock root and carrot

にんにく nin-nik garlic

ししとう shishitō green
chilli pepper

ピーマン pīman green
pepper

さやいんげん saya-ingen
haricot beans

わさび wasabi Japanese
green horseradish

まつたけ matstake
Japanese mushrooms, with
a distinctive aromatic
flavour

いんげんまめ
ingem-mame kidney beans

小松菜 komatsna leafy
cabbage

ねぎ negi leeks

レタス retas lettuce

れんこん renkon lotus root

かぼちゃ kabocha pump-
kin, squash

マッシュルーム mash-
rūm mushrooms (Western)

きのこ kinoko mushrooms
(general term)

からし菜 karashina
mustard greens

おくら okura okra

たまねぎ tamanegi onion

えんどうまめ endōmame
peas

ポテト poteto potato

じゃがいも jagaimo
potato

はつかだいこん hatska-
daikon radish

ひじき hijiki seaweed
cooked in soy sauce and
sugar

ごま goma sesame seeds

だいず daizu soybeans

ほうれんそう hōrensō
spinach

にら nira spring onions

わけぎ wakegi spring
onions

コーン kōn sweetcorn

さつまいも satsmaimo
sweet potato

さといも satoimo taro
potato

トマト tomato tomato

かぶ kabu turnip

わかめ wakame type of
seaweed

こんぶ kombu type of
seaweed

クレソン kureson water-
cress

ふき fuki wild butterbur
(green vegetable stalk)

やまいも yamaimo yam

えのきだけ enokidake
yellow button mushrooms

Menu Reader:

Drink

ESSENTIAL TERMS

beer bīru
ビール

bottle bin
びん

coffee kōhī
コーヒー

cup kap·p
カップ

glass kop·p
コップ

milk miruk
ミルク

mineral water mineraru-uōtā
ミネラルウォーター

orange juice orenji-jūs
オレンジジュース

red wine aka-wain
赤ワイン

rice wine sake
酒

soft drink softo-dorink
ソフトドリンク

sugar satō
さとう

tea kōcha
紅茶

(green) ocha
お茶

water mizu
水

white wine shiro-wain
白ワイン

wine wain
ワイン

whisky uiskī
ウィスキー

a cup of ..., please ... o hitots
kudasai
…をひとつください

another beer, please bīru o mō
hitots onegai shimas
ビールをもうひとつ
お願いします

a glass of sake sake o ip·pai
酒を一杯

BEER, SPIRITS, WINE etc

ビール bīru beer

ブランディー brandī brandy

シャンペン shampen champagne

日本酒冷や Nihonshu hiya chilled rice wine

生ビール nama-bīru draught beer

辛口 karakuchi dry

ジン jin gin

ジントニック jin-tonik gin and tonic

ジンフィズ jin-fiz gin fizz

日本酒熱燗 Nihonshu atskan heated rice wine

リキュール rikyūru liqueur

マティーニ matīni martini

ポートワイン pōto-wain port

赤ワイン aka-wain red wine

酒 sake rice wine

地酒 jizake rice wine (local variety)

升酒 maszake rice wine served in wooden box cup

ラム ram rum

オンザロック onza-rok·k scotch on the rocks

スパークリング spākuring sparkling

甘口 amakuchi sweet

トニックウォーター tonik-uōtā tonic

ベルモット berumot·to vermouth

焼酎 shōchū very strong, transparent, colourless spirit

ウォッカ uok·ka vodka

ウィスキー uiskī whisky

水割り mizuwari whisky with water

白ワイン shiro-wain white wine

ワイン wain wine

COFFEE, TEA etc

お飲物 o-nomimono beverages

玄米茶 gem·mai-cha ban-cha tea with roasted rice

抹茶 mat·cha bitter green tea made of fine tea powder

ブラックコーヒー burak-kōhī black coffee

紅茶 kōcha black tea, similar to English tea

ウーロン茶 ūron-cha Chinese tea

コーヒー kōhī coffee

お茶 ocha green tea

ココア kokoa hot chocolate

アイスティー ais-tī iced tea

アイスコーヒー ais-kōhī

iced coffee

番茶 ban-cha inexpensive tea with large leaves

レモンティー remon-tī lemon tea

煎茶 sencha medium-grade green tea

ミルク miruk milk

お砂糖 osatō sugar

ほうじ茶 hōjicha tea made with roasted ban-cha leaves

ミルクティー miruk-tī tea with milk

ミルクコーヒー miruk-kōhī white coffee, coffee with milk

SOFT DRINKS

りんごジュース rin-go-jūs apple juice

コーヒー牛乳 kōhī-gyūnyū coffee-flavoured milk

コカコーラ kōka-kōra Coke®

コーラ kōrā cola

ファンタ fanta Fanta®

グレープフルーツジュース gurēp-frūts-jūs grapefruit juice

グレープジュース gurēp-jūs grape juice

ソーダ水 sōdā-sui green, sweet soda pop

お冷や ohiya iced water

レモネード remonēdo lemonade

レモンスカッシュ remon-skash lemon squash

メロンジュース meron-jūs melon juice

ミルク miruk milk

ミネラルウォーター mineraru-uōtā mineral water

オレンジジュース orenji-jūs orange juice

オレンジスカッシュ orenji-skash orange squash

ペプシ Pepusi Pepsi®

パインジュース pain-jūs pineapple juice

サイダー saidā soda pop

いちご牛乳 ichigo-gyūnyū strawberry milk

トマトジュース tomato-jūs tomato juice

みず mizu water

氷水 kōrimizu water with ice